first certificate

Gold

exam maximiser

Sally Burgess

with Richard Acklam

Contents

Introduction to the *Exam Maximiser*

What is the *First Certificate Gold Exam Maximiser*?

The *First Certificate Gold Exam Maximiser* is specially designed to maximise students' chances of success in the First Certificate in English examination.

The Exam Maximiser offers:

- *further practice* with all the important vocabulary, grammar and skills that you study in the *First Certificate Gold Coursebook*.

- *the facts* on the papers and questions in the First Certificate exam. The *Exam overview* on page 6 gives you information on each of the five papers.

- *step-by-step guidance* with the strategies and techniques you need to get a good grade in the exam. There are also lots of **Hot tips!** to help you get extra marks.

- *exam-style exercises* so that you can practise using the techniques.

- *sample answers* to exam questions, showing you things you should try to do and things you should avoid doing in the exam. There are also typical teacher's corrections and examiner's comments as well as sample answers for you to grade.

- *practice with transferring rough work to answer sheets* used in the exam. This means that you know exactly what to expect in each paper and that there are no unpleasant surprises.

- *help with using time effectively* in the exam so that you can avoid the problem of losing marks because you run out of time.

- *a complete sample exam* which covers what you have learnt while using the *First Certificate Gold Coursebook* and the *Exam Maximiser*. This means that you know what it actually feels like to do the First Certificate exam. You can then get further practice in this by working through the *First Certificate Gold Practice Exams*.

Who is the *First Certificate Gold Exam Maximiser* for and how can it be used?

The *Exam Maximiser* is extremely flexible and can be used by students in a variety of situations and in a variety of ways. Here are some typical situations:

1

> You are doing a First Certificate course with other students probably over an academic year. You are all planning to take the exam at the same time.

You are using the *First Certificate Gold Coursebook* in class. Sometimes you will also do the related exercises or even a whole unit from the *Exam Maximiser* in class, though your teacher will ask you to do exercises from it at home as well. You will use the entire *Exam Maximiser* or you and your teacher will use it selectively, depending on your needs and the time available.

2

> You have already done a First Certificate course and you are now doing an intensive course to prepare for the exam.

Since you have already worked through the *First Certificate Gold Coursebook* or perhaps another First Certificate coursebook, you will use the *Exam Maximiser* in class. This, together with the *First Certificate Gold Practice Exams*, will give you a concentrated and highly focused short exam course.

3

> You have a very short period in which to take the First Certificate exam.

The level of your English is already nearing First Certificate exam standard, though you have not been following a First Certificate coursebook. You now need examination skills. You will use the *Exam Maximiser* independently, that is to say without a coursebook, because you need practice in the exam tasks and how to approach them.

4

> You are re-taking the First Certificate exam as unfortunately you were not successful in your first attempt.

You may be having to re-take the exam because you were not sufficiently familiar with the exam requirements. You will not need to follow a coursebook, but you will use the *Exam Maximiser* to develop your exam techniques and build up your confidence.

5

> You are preparing for the exam on your own.

- Perhaps you are in a class where the teacher is using the *First Certificate Gold Coursebook* as a general English course. This means there are probably students in your class who are not actually taking the exam. Your teacher will recommend use of the *Exam Maximiser* for homework, so that everyone can revise and practise what they have learnt. However, you can also use it on your own to prepare for the exam. You can give yourself additional practice by using the *First Certificate Gold Practice Exams* just before you take the exam.

- You are not attending a First Certificate class, but wish to take the exam and prepare for it independently. You will get the practice and preparation by using the *Exam Maximiser* by itself. Near the exam time you may wish to use the *First Certificate Gold Practice Exams* as well.

Exam overview

Paper	Name	Timing	Content	Test focus
Paper 1	Reading	1 hour 15 minutes	4 long texts, or 3 long and 2 or more short texts; 35 reading comprehension questions.	Questions test your understanding of the general idea, the main points, specific details, the structure of the text and specific information.
Paper 2	Writing	1 hour 30 minutes	Part 1: compulsory letter Part 2: a choice of writing tasks	Questions test your ability to write letters, reports, articles and compositions for specific audiences.
Paper 3	Use of English	1 hour 15 minutes	5 sections with 65 questions altogether focusing on grammar and vocabulary.	Questions test your knowledge of grammar and vocabulary.
Paper 4	Listening	40 minutes (approximately)	2 longer recorded texts and 2 series of short extracts; 30 listening comprehension questions.	Questions test your ability to understand the main idea, the main points, detail or specific information.
Paper 5	Speaking	15 minutes (approximately)	A conversation divided into four parts between two candidates and an interlocutor. Another examiner will be in the room with you to assess your performance.	The four parts test your ability to exchange personal and factual information, to express your own opinions and attitudes and to find out about other people's opinions and attitudes.

1 A sense of adventure

Vocabulary: travel

Paper 3, Part 2

About the exam
In Paper 3, Part 2 you fill in the gaps in a text.

Strategy
Always read the whole text all the way through **before** you begin to fill in the gaps.

1 Fill in the gaps in the following text with an appropriate word or phrase from the box. You do not need to use all of the words.

canoe	travelling	liner	missing	trip
destination	taking off	visit	checking in	sail
hire	maps	fly	catching	departure	travel

Welcome aboard the First Certificate Gold Exam Maximiser!

Imagine that you are about to set out on a rather complicated but exciting journey. Perhaps you are going to drive a jeep across the Sahara desert, (1)........................ across the Pacific Ocean or travel down the Amazon in a (2) ....

Naturally you will prepare for a journey like this very thoroughly. It is not just a question of (3)........................ at an airport and getting on a plane or (4)........................ a train or bus. You will need to consult (5)........................ and atlases, talk to people who have already been to the places you will (6)........................ and decide what to take with you.

Preparing to take First Certificate is very like going on a journey. You have to know what the examination will be like and what kinds of questions you will be asked. You need to learn how to answer the various kinds of questions well and what dangers to avoid.

Like (7)........................ alone through the desert or in the mountains, across an ocean or down a river, preparing for FCE on your own would be very difficult. But with a guide it is much easier. When you are travelling, a guide can help you make the most of your money and time so that you enjoy your journey and get to wherever you are going. In other words a guide can help you **maximise** your chances of travelling safely and arriving at your (8)........................ on time.

The *First Certificate Gold Exam Maximiser* is like a guide. It is designed to help you learn everything you need to know to pass FCE, in other words it **maximises** your chances of exam success. So welcome aboard the *First Certificate Gold Exam Maximiser*. We hope you have an enjoyable and safe (9)........................ and that you reach your final destination, FCE, with absolutely everything you need to do really well in the exam.

2 The following groups of words relate to *ships, trains, planes, cars* or *buses*, but there is one word or phrase in each group that does not belong. Circle this word or phrase and then write which type of transport the other words relate to.

EXAMPLE: a steering wheel   brakes   a boot

(a deck)   ...*cars*...

1 a dual carriageway   a platform
the fast lane   a lay-by   ....

2 a cruise   a liner   a flight   a lifeboat   ....

3 a guard   a port   a platform   a track   ....

4 to check in   a single
a departure lounge   to take off   ....

5 a parking meter   a driving test
a seatbelt   an inspector   ....

6 an inspector   a stop   a fare
a steward   ....

7 a cabin   a seatbelt   a cruise   a deck   ....

> **Learner training**
> When you learn new words, put them into categories, for example *Transport: ships; cars; planes.* Later, think of a category and write down all the words you can remember.

Reading: multiple matching

> **Paper 1, Part 4**

> **About the exam**
> In Paper 1, Part 4 you match statements or questions to paragraphs. The texts usually give information about something.

> **Strategy**
> Read the text through quickly to get a general idea. Then study the questions. Read the text again and underline the relevant information in each paragraph.

1 Read the text opposite through once quickly. Which of the games would you like to play on a long journey?

from *Travel Games* by Lynn Guest

Travel Games

1 Long car journeys can be pretty boring – especially if you are using motorways. Before too long everyone is fighting over what cassette to put on or what radio station to listen to – Dad wants the football, Mum wants the classical music station, someone else wants heavy
10 metal and nobody can agree. One way to get over this problem is to play some kind of game as you are driving along. The following travel games might be just the thing when tempers are getting frayed or when you simply want to have some fun.

A OBSERVATION
20 With your partners, make a list of ten items you are likely to see out of the window on your journey such as a woman with a pram, a boy on a bicycle, somebody hitchhiking, a bank, a statue, etc. Each player has to try and spot the ten items first. When a player sees one of the objects, he or she shouts out
30 and claims it; it cannot be used by other players. The one to spot all the items first is the winner.

B CRAZY STORIES
Each player takes it in turn to be the story-teller. During the story he or she will make the occasional deliberate mistake which the other players will
40 have to try and spot. When they do, they must shout out and the first one to shout gets a point. An example of a mistake would be: 'I went to the football pitch and had a game of golf. While I was there I met a little girl who was my nephew.' There are two mistakes here as you do not play golf on a football pitch and
50 she was his niece, not his nephew. Now you have a go.

C ADDING UP
Each player picks a number between 10 and 20. The object of the game is to find car number plates which add up to your chosen number. For example, if you chose the number 17 then a number plate
60 of F458 GHU would be a success. However a number plate of D981 SYT would be of no use to you. The first player to spot his or her number wins the round. Everyone chooses another number and the game begins again. Continue until one player has won three rounds.

D ANIMAL,
70 VEGETABLE OR MINERAL?
One player has to think of an object, but all he or she tells the others is whether it is animal, vegetable, or mineral. Mineral can be used for all objects which are not animal or vegetable. For example, a horse or an egg would be animal. A
80 tomato or a loaf of bread would be vegetable. A diamond ring would be mineral. The other players have to try and find out what the object is by asking questions which the player is only allowed to answer with a 'Yes' or 'No'. If you think you know what the object is, you can ask a question like: 'Is it a
90 horse?'. If the answer is 'Yes', you win. If no one has guessed the object after 20 questions, the person who thought of the object wins.

E I WENT ON A TRIP
One player begins, 'I went on a trip and took a fishing net'. The next player says, 'I went on a trip and took a fishing net and
100 my bowler hat'. The next in turn says, 'I went on a trip and I took a fishing net, my bowler hat and a bucket and spade.' The game continues until one of the players forgets something on the list. Start again with a new list.

'The salesman said that this was the ideal car for life in the fast lane'

2 Now read the following questions and write the appropriate letter for each game in the gaps. Some games are used more than once. The first two questions have been answered for you. Look at the notes before you answer the other questions.

Which game:

would be best for people who enjoy guessing games?

1 ...*D*...

Notes: *the relevant information for this question is in line 84. It says the purpose of the game is to 'find out what the object is'. 'Find out' means almost the same thing as 'guess'.*

could only be played if you were travelling by car?

2 ...*C*...

Notes: *the important information here is 'find car number plates' in line 55.*

involves listening very carefully?

3 ....

could be played on a plane as well?

4 ....   5 ....   6 ....

must be played by more than two players to be effective?

7 ....

Word formation

> **Paper 3, Part 5**

About the exam
In Paper 3, Part 5 you read a text with gaps. At the end of each line of the text there is a word in capital letters. You use this word to form a new word for each gap.

Strategy
Before you try to fill in the gaps, decide whether the missing word is an adjective (e.g. *beautiful*), an adverb (e.g. *carefully*), a noun (e.g. *information*) or a verb (e.g. *believe*).

1 The following sentences all come from the listening exercise on page 14 in the *First Certificate Gold Coursebook*. Look at the underlined words in each sentence and decide whether they are adjectives, adverbs, nouns or verbs.

1 And so began two hours and forty minutes of disbelief (......*noun*......), fear and finally horror for the 2,300 passengers of the 'unsinkable' (...*adjective*...) Titanic.

2 For that was all the time that it took for the biggest and supposedly (....................) safest liner in the world to sink beneath the icy waters of the North Atlantic.

3 The myth of the *Titanic's* unsinkability was only one of an incredible (....................) combination (....................) of human errors.

4 Although the *Titanic* struck the iceberg at 11.40 p.m., it was not until five minutes after midnight that the order was given, 'Uncover (....................) the lifeboats!'

5 In one of the last overcrowded (....................) lifeboats to leave the *Titanic* stood Mrs Emily Richards, then twenty-four, and going off to join her husband in the USA.

6 The sea was full of wreckage (....................) and bodies.

7 One of the strangest aspects of this disaster was that it had been foreseen in extraordinary (....................) detail in a novel published fourteen years earlier.

8 The book, written by Morgan Robertson, told the story of the biggest and most luxurious (....................) liner ever built.

> **Hot tip!** ←
> Always read the whole sentence to decide if you need a **positive** or a **negative** word to fill each gap. For example, do you need the positive or the negative form of the word in this sentence?
>
> .... we arrived late and missed the first ten minutes of the film. (FORTUNATE)

2 Now fill in the gaps in the following sentences with the correct form of the word in capitals. Decide what part of speech to use and whether you need a positive or a negative word.

1 The local people are sometimes rather ..*unfriendly*.. and often seem to want to avoid the tourists. (FRIEND)
Notes: *the missing word is an adjective. You know this because 'are' and 'rather' come before it. The idea of the sentence is negative.*

2 It's no use getting .... just because there's a long queue to check in. (PATIENT)

3 The man in the tourist information office was very .... and gave us lots of free maps and brochures. (HELP)

4 They decided to close the hotel because it had never been very .... (PROFIT)

5 We had lovely .... weather the whole time we were there. (SUN)

6 Don't .... the cost of hotel accommodation when you plan your next holiday. (ESTIMATE)

7 A dishonest waiter tried to .... us for our meal. (CHARGE)

8 Take an umbrella if you go in autumn as it is very .... to rain. (LIKE)

9 There are .... people in most of the world's big cities nowadays. (HOME)

10 The safari park was a bit of a .... as there were too few animals. (APPOINT)

Listening: gap fill

> **Paper 4, Part 2**

About the exam
In Paper 4, Part 2 you listen to a talk or conversation and complete short sentences with a word or phrase.

Strategy
Always spend at least 45 seconds looking carefully at the instructions and questions before you listen.

1 Read the following instructions and notes and then mark the statements below **T** (true), **F** (false) or **?** (don't know).

Listen to a young traveller giving a report on a place she visited. Match the numbered phrases in Column A with a word or phrase in Column B. Write the appropriate letter in the gaps. There are two extra items in Column B which you do not need to use.

Reporter: Diane Pilgrim **Destination:** Gozo, Malta

Column A

1 She got to Gozo by ....

2 To explore the island she ....

3 There is an old castle on the island that is used ....

4 Marsalforn, Ramla bay and San Blas bay are best for ....

5 The church in Tapinu has been used ....

Column B

a) as a disco.

b) plane and ferry.

c) in a film.

d) swimming.

e) hired a moped.

f) water-skiing.

g) restaurants.

Statements

1 You will hear more than one person speaking on the cassette. ....

2 You will hear somebody telling a story. ....

3 You only have to write in the letters 'a', 'b', 'c', etc. ....

4 The speaker will give her opinion about the place. ....

5 It would be a good idea to listen carefully for words for types of transport and the places mentioned. ....

2 Now listen to the cassette and do the exercise.

Writing: transactional letter

Paper 2, Part 1

About the exam
Part 1 of Paper 2 is **compulsory**. There is no choice. You always write a letter to ask for or give information of some kind.

1 A **formal** letter is a letter you write to someone you don't know or don't know very well, especially companies and institutions. An **informal** letter is the kind of letter you write to friends, members of your family and other people you know well. Which of the following phrases and sentences would you expect to find in a formal letter? Which would you expect to find in an informal letter? Mark them **F** (formal) or **I** (informal).

1 Dear Sir/Madam, ...

2 *Love,*
   Eleni   ....

3 *See you next week. I can hardly wait!*   ....

4 I look forward to receiving
   your reply.   ....

5 *Yours faithfully,*
   Ana García Herrera   ....

6 I am writing in reply to your
   letter of 15 May.   ....

7 Give my love to your parents.   ....

8 Should you require any further
   information, do not hesitate to
   contact us at the above address.   ....

9 *Write back soon and tell me all your news.*   ....

10 I'm sorry I haven't written
   for such a long time, but I've
   been really busy.   ....

11 *I would be most grateful if you could send*
   me any further relevant information.   ....

Strategy
Always read the instructions carefully and decide what kind of letter you are supposed to write. Formal or informal? To a friend or to someone you don't know?

2

1 Look at this task and the underlined words. Will your answer be formal or informal?

Some <u>young people you met last summer</u> are planning to visit your country on holiday and have asked you to suggest some places of interest to see. Write a letter of reply using the notes below.

– when?
– how long?
– come and stay?

2 Now look at this plan for the above task and put the points in a logical order. Write the numbers 1–7 in the gaps.

a) *Apologise for not replying sooner.* ....
b) *Thank them for their letter.* ....
c) *Ask when they will be coming.* ....
d) *Tell them to write again.* ....
e) *Invite them to stay for a few days.* ....
f) *Suggest places to visit/things to do.* ....
g) *Say why you haven't replied sooner.* ....

3 Think of ideas: a reason for not replying; places to visit; things they might enjoy doing and seeing. Is there a particularly good time of year to visit these places? What can your friends do there?

4 Write your letter in 120–180 words.

5 Check it carefully for any grammar, spelling or vocabulary mistakes your teacher has corrected in your written work before. If necessary, write your letter out again.

Strategy
Read the instructions very carefully, write a plan, think of ideas and check your work thoroughly.

Vocabulary: feelings

1 Match the following words with a definition below. Write the appropriate letter in the gaps. There is one definition which you do not need to use.

1 terrified .... 5 nervous ....
2 confused .... 6 cross ....
3 miserable .... 7 depressing ....
4 astonishing .... 8 thrilled ....

a) causing anger or impatience
b) very pleased or satisfied
c) making you feel very sad
d) causing great surprise
e) in a state of extreme shock or fear
f) worried about what might happen
g) uncertain about what to think or do
h) unhappy, tired and uninterested
i) angry, bad-tempered

2 Now look at this letter a student wrote in answer to the writing task on page 11 and find six mistakes with the form of adjectives. Write the sentences out again correctly in your notebook.

Dear Lucy and Tim,

I'm sorry I haven't replied to your letter sooner, but I've been too worried about my exams to think about anything else. I've just heard that I passed everything so I'm feeling pretty pleasing.

I was thrilling to hear that you are planning to come here. My family and I would be delightful to have you both stay.

You asked about interesting places to visit. The mountains are really amazed in spring with all the wild flowers. I went climbing there with some friends last summer, but one of them was terrified of heights so we had to come home early.

Another good place to visit is the provincial capital. There are lots of fascinated old streets with wonderful eighteenth century architecture. It's worth visiting at any time of year, though the summers can be a bit exhausted with the extreme heat.

Well, I had better finish. Write soon and let me know exactly when you plan to come.

Love,
Ruben

Grammar: questions

1 Put the words in the correct order to make questions. Write the sentences out in your notebook. Then match each question to an answer below and write the appropriate letter in the box.

1 people how learn do new words? ☐
2 do what we have do to? ☐
3 you do agree you don't? ☐
4 do you like in what spare doing time your? ☐
5 do you where want go to this weekend? ☐
6 why get you do nervous so? ☐
7 who you angry were with? ☐
8 what mean does 'miserable'? ☐
9 each you translate are word going to? ☐
10 you did definition write a 'cruise' of? ☐

a) The dictionary says 'very unhappy'.
b) My brother. He drives me crazy sometimes.
c) Yes. I copied it from the dictionary.
d) Playing basketball and going to the cinema.
e) By finding a good way of recording them.
f) I have to describe my photograph while you listen.
g) I think I'd like to stay here, actually.
h) I don't know. Exams always make me feel like this.
i) No, I'm afraid I don't.
j) No, just the important ones.

2 Fill in the gaps in the following sentences with an appropriate question tag. Then match each question to an answer below and write the appropriate letter in the box.

1 You're Polish, ... ? ☐

2 I've seen you somewhere before, ... ? ☐

3 Janusz is your older brother, ... ? ☐

4 Your sister studies English, too, ... ? ☐

5 You went on the trip to Oxford, ... ? ☐

6 Janusz really enjoyed it, ... ? ☐

7 He'd been there before, ... ? ☐

8 You used to live in Germany, ... ? ☐

9 You'll be at school tomorrow, ... ? ☐

10 You wouldn't know which bus I get to Piccadilly, ... ? ☐

a) That's right. He went a couple of years ago.

b) I think you get the number 14.

c) No, I didn't actually. I hear it was really good.

d) Yes. He wants to go again next weekend.

e) Yes, I am. How did you guess?

f) Yes, that's where my father's from.

g) Maybe. You look slightly familiar, too.

h) Oh, so you're a friend of his, are you?

i) No, not any more. She's gone back to Poland.

j) I'm afraid not. I'm taking my First Certificate exam.

3 Now listen to the questions Sam asks above and check your answers. Does his voice go up or down on the question tags? Is he fairly sure or not very sure that the information is correct? Mark the tags ↗ (up) or ↘ (down). Then practise saying them yourself.

4 Write indirect questions using the words given.

1 What am I going to do? (*I don't know*)
   I don't know what I am going to do.

2 Why did she say that? (*I wonder*)

   ....

3 How many tourists visit your country each year? (*I'd like to know*)

   ....

4 Does this bus go to Oxford Street? (*I wonder*)

   ....

5 Where is the tourist office? (*Could you tell me*)

   ....

6 Are there any museums near here? (*Do you know*)

   ....

7 What are we supposed to do? (*Would you mind telling me*)

   ....

8 Is she English or American? (*I don't know*)

   ....

Speaking: interacting

▶ **Paper 5, all parts**

About the exam
Paper 5 is a conversation between you and another candidate and/or the interlocutor/examiner.

Strategy
In Paper 5 you have to answer questions, but you also have to **ask** them.

Two candidates doing Part 3 of Paper 5 have been asked to discuss suitable holidays for three families. The candidates make four mistakes with questions. Find the mistakes.

SYLVIE: Are you ready to start?
KATRINA: What we have to do?
SYLVIE: Choose holidays for these three families.
KATRINA: OK. Where you think would the Smith family like to go?
SYLVIE: I think the Channel Islands would be good for them because there are safe beaches and they have small children. Where we will send the Jones family?
KATRINA: Do you know when are they taking their holiday?
SYLVIE: Probably in August like everyone else.

13

2 Work and play

Vocabulary: multiple choice cloze

Paper 3, Part 1

About the exam
In Paper 3, Part 1 you choose between four alternatives to fill gaps in a text.

Strategy
Sometimes the correct alternative is a word that goes with the word after the gap. Here is an example:

First Certificate Exam success .... on adopting the right strategies.

A consists **B** revolves **C** depends **D** results

Alternative C is the correct choice because the verb *depends* is the only one that goes with the preposition *on*. The other verbs go with these prepositions: *consists* **of**, *revolves* **around**, and *results* **in**.

Always look at the words before and after the gap. They will help you choose the correct alternative.

1 Fill in the gaps in the following sentences with *on, from, of, for* or *to*.

1 At the beginning of my English class, I spent ages searching .... my favourite pen, but I couldn't find it anywhere.

2 Eventually I borrowed one .... the girl sitting next to me.

3 However, I was still worrying about the pen and I couldn't concentrate .... the lesson properly.

4 When I got home I saw my brother using a pen that reminded me a lot .... mine.

5 'Don't use things that don't belong .... you!' I said, taking the pen.

6 'And don't accuse me .... things I haven't done!' he said. 'This is *my* pen. Mum bought it for me this morning.'

2 Fill in the gaps in the following sentences with an appropriate word from the box.

ashamed	good	responsible	proud	suspicious
satisfied	keen	terrified		

1 Don't ask me to climb up there. I am .... of heights.

2 In this house I am .... for making sure everyone helps with the washing-up.

3 You must be very .... of her for doing so well in the examinations.

4 I was not very .... with my results in the test.

5 He is not .... on high risk sports.

6 The guard seemed to be .... of the museum visitors and never took his eyes off them.

7 I think athletes who use drugs should be .... of themselves.

8 She speaks five languages, but she is not very .... at mathematics.

3 Read the following job advertisement and then choose the correct alternative to fill in the gaps.

1 **A** seeking
   B looking
2 **A** interested
   B keen
3 **A** qualified
   B good
4 **A** keen
   B interested
5 **A** in charge
   B responsible
6 **A** capable
   B suitable
7 **A** specialised
   B satisfied
8 **A** join
   B belong

WANTED Young People

We are (1) .... for young men and women to work as tour guides. We are (2) .... in interviewing young people of all nationalities who are (3) .... at communicating with people of all ages and (4) .... on travelling. Successful candidates will be (5) .... for meeting our clients at the airport and escorting them on tours of the area. You will be (6) .... for the job if you have finished secondary school and have (7) .... in foreign languages. Applicants who (8) .... to the Association of Professional Tourist Guides will be given preference.

Reading: gapped text

Paper 1, Part 3

About the exam

In Paper 1, Part 3 you look at some sentences or paragraphs that have been removed from a text. You read the text and decide where the sentences fit. There is always one extra sentence which you do not need to use.

Strategy

Look at words like pronouns (e.g. *it*, *she*) demonstratives (e.g. *this*, *that*) and possessive adjectives (e.g. *my*, *her*) in the sentences that have been removed from the text and decide what they refer to.

1 Read these paragraphs from the article '**Why do we risk it?**' (*First Certificate Gold Coursebook*, page 8) and decide what the underlined words refer to. Write the word or phrase in the gaps.

RISK SPORTS are one of the fastest-growing leisure activities. Daredevils try anything from organised bungee jumps to illegally jumping off buildings. These people never feel so alive as when <u>they</u> are risking their lives. (1) ....

Some say that people who do risk sports are reacting against a society which <u>they</u> feel has become dull and constricting. (2) ....
David Lewis, a psychologist, believes that people today crave adventure. In an attempt to guarantee safety, our culture has eliminated risk. 'The world has become a bland and safe place,' says Lewis. 'People used to be able to seek adventure by hunting wild animals, or taking part in expeditions. Now <u>they</u> turn to risk sports as an escape.' (3) ....

Risk sports have a positive side as well. <u>They</u> help people to overcome fears that affect them in their real lives. (4) .... This makes risk sports particularly valuable for executives in office jobs who need to stay alert so that <u>they</u> can cope when things go wrong. (5) ....

2 The following sentences have been removed from the text below. Read the text and decide which sentence goes in each of the numbered gaps.

A Since starting his new firm – Rent-A-Call – Mr Benz has received hundreds of calls from potential clients.

B One man wanted to be telephoned by a woman asking him out to the theatre in order to make his wife feel jealous.

C This idea came to him earlier this year after noticing how many Germans have mobile phones – but that very few ever get called on them.

Rent-A-Phonecall

Joachim Benz, a German businessman, will telephone customers on their mobile phones when they want to talk about whatever they want.

(1_____) Mr Benz, who is twenty-nine, said, 'It struck me that although the reason for displaying these phones was to create an impression of being incredibly important and busy, there was no point in having one if it never rang.'

(2_____) Most have been businessmen anxious to impress colleagues or clients by having their mobile phone ringing at a vital moment in the negotiations.

Inquiries have also come from people wanting to put on an act for a new boyfriend or girlfriend. (3_____)

from *The Age* newspaper

🎧 Listening: note taking

Paper 4, Part 2

About the exam
In another type of exercise in Paper 4, Part 2 you listen and complete notes.

Hot tip! ◄
DON'T write more than three or four words in note-taking exercises!

Listen to an interview in which a woman talks about an unusual occupation and complete the following summary of what she says.

Occupation: (1)
....

Relative with same occupation: (2)
....

Compares racing to: (3)
....

Occasional reactions of hostility from: (4)
....

Reason for becoming a driver: (5)
....

Father's attitude to her racing: (6)
....

Boyfriend's attitude to her racing: (7) ....

Boyfriend's country of origin: (8)
....

Location of boyfriend's hotel: (9)
....

Circumstances in which she met boyfriend: (10) ....
.... in his hotel.

Word formation

Paper 3, Part 5

1 The following sentences come from the interview with Meregan Turner. Look at the underlined word in each sentence and decide if it is an adjective, adverb or noun.

1 I just couldn't believe that anything could be so <u>wonderful</u>. (..........................)

2 It's <u>completely</u> (..........................) taken over my life.

3 Were men <u>protective</u> (..........................) of you on the track?

4 But sometimes you get real <u>hostility</u>. (..........................)

5 When I <u>finally</u> (..........................) succeeded, he <u>actually</u> (..........................) turned into my wheels.

6 I suppose because he understands what it's actually like he's less likely to think it's <u>dangerous</u>. (..................)

2 A suffix is added to the end of a word to change it to another part of speech. Study the suffixes in *italics* in the words in Exercise 1 and complete the following information.

1 If you add -ly to adjectives like ...., ... or ...., you make adverbs.

2 If you drop the -e and add .... to adjectives like *hostile,* you can make nouns.

3 If you add .... to verbs like *protect* that end in -tect, you can make adjectives or nouns (e.g. *detect*........).

4 If you add -ous to nouns like ...., you make adjectives.

3 The following extracts come from the listening *Unpopular jobs* on page 17 of the *First Certificate Gold Coursebook*. Read the extracts and then fill in the gaps with an appropriate form of the words in capitals at the end of each line.

PRIVATE INVESTIGATOR	
It can be quite a (1) ..... job and you can meet some really	**DANGER**
nasty types. I suppose it's not really very (2) ....., but some	**SURPRISE**
people don't like it much if they find out you've been	
spying on them ... – they can get pretty (3)	**PLEASANT**

DEBT COLLECTOR	
I think it's very (4) ..... that this kind of work has such a bad	**FAIR**
reputation. In fact, we all have to be licensed and follow	
strict guidelines. The worst part about the job? Well, I've	
had several (5) ..... phone calls in the office. ... What do I	**ABUSE**
like most about it? ... lunch hours probably ... no, (6) ....., I	**SERIOUS**
think it's the fact that there's lots of (7) ..... . I'm certainly	**VARY**
always busy.	

Vocabulary: jobs/employment

1 Match the jobs in Column A with a phrase from Column B. Be careful! The word *conductor* has more than one meaning. Write the appropriate letter in the gaps.

Column A

1 Bouncers   ....

2 A traffic warden   ....

3 A stockbroker   ....

4 The conductor   ....

5 Referees   ....

6 An editor   ....

7 A plumber   ....

8 The dustmen   ....

9 Nurses   ....

Column B

a) doesn't drive the bus. S/he collects the fares.

b) prepares books and newspapers for printing.

c) are always leaving the lid off our rubbish bin.

d) buys and sells stocks and shares.

e) are always awarding penalties against our team.

f) keep troublemakers out of clubs or discotheques.

g) checks that vehicles are not parked in the wrong place.

h) are going on strike next month over conditions in hospitals.

i) is coming round to fix the leaking tap in the bathroom.

j) is picking up her baton and looking at the first violinist.

2 Mark where the main stress falls in the following jobs then check your answers in the dictionary.

EXAMPLE: commercial 'artist

1 debt collector   6 nightclub bouncer

2 social worker   7 plastic surgeon

3 traffic warden   8 bus conductor

4 private investigator 9 senior librarian

5 tax inspector   10 newspaper editor

3 Find words in the grid below to match the following definitions. The first letter of each word has been given to help you.

1 money paid for professional job   s...................

2 announce formally that you are going to leave a job   r...................

3 a period of time when workers stop work to try to get better pay and conditions   s...................

4 money paid to a salesperson for each sale s/he makes   c...................

5 stop working because you are old   r...................

6 an amount of money added to your usual pay usually because you have worked hard   b...................

7 dismiss from a job   s...................

8 the ability to do something well   s...................

9 a person who is paid to work for somebody or a company   e...................

10 get money by working   e...................

C	B	X	H	S	K	I	L	L	C
L	O	N	R	S	A	P	Q	S	O
M	N	M	O	T	P	C	C	D	M
E	U	S	M	R	C	R	K	K	M
A	S	F	T	I	Z	E	C	R	I
R	G	U	B	K	S	T	X	E	S
N	W	H	V	E	Y	I	F	S	S
S	A	L	A	R	Y	R	O	I	I
K	I	J	X	E	D	E	G	G	O
E	M	P	L	O	Y	E	E	N	N

Speaking: collaborative task

Paper 5, Part 3

About the exam
In Paper 5, Part 3 you talk to the other candidate or the examiner about some pictures, maps or plans. Often you talk about putting things in order of priority.

Strategy
Ask the other person what s/he thinks and say whether you agree or disagree with what s/he says.

┌─ **Hot tip!** ◄─ ─ ─ ─ ─ ─ ─ ─ ─ ─ ─ ─ ─┐
│ DON'T make a speech!   │
└ ─ ┘

1 Listen to some students doing a task in Paper 5, Part 3 and look at the pictures.

2 Now listen to Petra and Stefan again and complete the following questions which they ask each other.

1 .... put dustmen after nurses?

2 What shall we .... ?

3 .... editors?

4 Let's see. .... ?

5 .... to put them before editors?

3 Listen once more and write down three words or phrases they use for agreeing and one word or phrase they use for disagreeing.

1 ....

2 ....

3 ....

4 ....

Grammar: present tenses

1 Fill in the gaps in the following sentences with the correct Present Simple or Present Continuous form of the verbs in brackets. Put the adverbs in the correct position.

1 I .... *(not/like)* getting up in the morning.

2 My brother and I .... *(have)* to get up quite early to get to school on time.

3 Our father .... *(sometimes/drive)* us, but on other days we .... *(get)* the school bus.

4 We almost .... *(never/get)* to the bus stop on time and the bus .... *(always/wait)* when we .... *(turn)* the corner.

5 The bus driver .... *(tell)* us to hurry up and we .... *(jump)* on the bus.

6 We .... *(not/go)* to school next Monday because it's a holiday.

7 Instead all the people from my class .... *(meet)* in the mountains for a picnic.

8 I .... *(make)* a chocolate cake, my friend Ioanna .... *(bring)* a salad and the others .... *(bring)* meat, bread and soft drinks.

9 Ioanna .... *(ring)* me up every evening and asks, 'What .... *(have)* to do for homework?'

10 She .... *(not/listen)* when the teacher .... *(give)* us our homework for that night.

11 She .... *(always/talk)* in class which .... *(drive)* all the teachers crazy.

12 When Ioanna .... *(ring)* me up, she .... *(always/say)*, ''What .... you .... ?' *(do)*

13 And I .... *(answer)* ' I .... *(talk)* to you, silly!'

2 Look at Column B in the jobs vocabulary on page 17 again and write the numbers of the sentence or sentences that:

● are complaints about an irritating situation that occurs regularly. 1 ....   2 ....

● are explanations of the meaning of the word. 3 .... 4 .... 5 .... 6 .... 7 ....

● is said by a radio announcer while watching what is happening on stage. 8 ....

● are statements about events that will definitely take place in the future. 9 ....   10 ....

3 Now look at what Luca, an FCE candidate, said about the two photos he was asked to compare and contrast in Part 2 of Paper 5. Look at the photos and fill in the gaps with the correct Present Simple or Present Continuous form of the verbs in brackets.

These two photographs show different places where people (1) .... *(go)* on holiday. In the first photograph there are people on a beach. Some of them (2) .... *(sunbathe)* and others (3) .... *(swim)* or (4) .... *(walk)* along the beach. A big difference between the two photographs is that in the first one there are a lot of people, but in the second one I can only see one person. I (5) .... *(not know)* if it is a man or a woman, but she or he (6) .... *(ski)* and seems to be completely alone in this beautiful landscape.

A

B

Writing: transactional letter

Paper 2, Part 1

1 Look at the following task. Are you asked to write a formal or an informal letter?

> Look at the advertisement and the notes you have made below it. Then write a letter of **between 120 and 180 words** in an appropriate style asking for more information covering the points in your notes. Do not write any addresses.
>
> ## WANTED NEW MEMBERS
>
> For water sports club. Water-skiing, scuba diving, jet ski, windsurfing! You name it – if it's a watersport, we offer instruction and facilities for it. Plenty of opportunity to practise your chosen sport with other enthusiasts at Club Aquarius! For your membership application form write to:
>
> *The Secretary*
> *Club Aquarius*
> *P.O. Box 312*
> *Littlehampton*
> *Sussex, SU3 9JT*
>
> – *Membership fee?*
> – *Annual or monthly payment?*
> – *Use of facilities free to members?*
> – *Sports not mentioned in advertisement?*

2 Are the following statements true or false? Mark them **T** (true) or **F** (false).

In a formal letter:

1 you include your name in your address.   ....

2 you include the name and title (Managing Director, Head Teacher, etc.) of the person you are writing to in her/his address.   ....

3 you write the whole date in words, like this: 'fifteenth of November, nineteen ninety-nine'. ....

4 if you begin the letter *Dear Sir/Madam*, you finish it with *Yours faithfully*, ...

5 you can begin your letter with *Dear* + the addressee's title, for example *Dear Secretary*, ...

3 Now write the letter in Exercise 1 in 120–180 words. You should follow this procedure.

1 Look at the instructions and underline the words and phrases that tell you exactly what you have to do.

2 Think of four questions you want to ask in your letter.

3 Decide what order you want to put them in.

4 Write your letter. Use linking words such as *first of all, also, as well as this, finally.*

5 Check your letter carefully for any grammar or spelling mistakes. Make sure your letter is properly laid out.

Strategy
You have 1 hour and 30 minutes to write two answers.
Spend **45 minutes** on each question. Divide the 45 minutes like this:
- **5 minutes** reading the instructions very carefully, underlining key words and checking how many things you have to do.
- **10 minutes** thinking of ideas and writing a plan.
- **25 minutes** writing your answer.
- **5 minutes** checking your work carefully and correcting any mistakes.

Hot tip! ◄
DON'T waste time writing your answer out again! Write on every second line so that you can make corrections easily. If your work is clear and easy to read, it is not necessary to write it out again.

Vocabulary: describing people

1 Match a word in Column A with a word with the opposite meaning in Column B. Be careful! There are two extra words in Column B which you do not need to use. Write the appropriate letter in the gaps.

Column A		Column B
1 hard-working	....	a) mean
2 kind	....	b) silly
3 generous	....	c) well-behaved
4 stubborn	....	d) lazy
5 naughty	....	e) tough
6 sensible	....	f) cruel
7 modest	....	g) flexible
		h) narrow-minded
		i) arrogant

2 Fill in the gaps in the following sentences with an appropriate word from Exercise 1.

1 He's rather .... and never stops telling you how wonderful he is.

2 If you don't stop being ...., you won't get an icecream.

3 I wish you weren't so .... Why can't you pay for the coffee for once?

4 Going out in the middle of winter without a jacket was a rather .... thing to do.

5 They're very .... They let us stay in their house and lent us a car.

6 There's no need to be so .... You deserve to be proud of yourself.

7 If you were a bit more .... and tried to see his point of view, I'm sure you'd get along.

8 People who live in small communities can be a bit .... and afraid to accept new ideas.

Listening: multiple matching

> **Paper 4, Part 3**

About the exam
In Paper 4, Part 3 you hear short extracts. You listen to people speaking about a theme. You select information from each extract to go with statements or questions.

Strategy
Note key words and phrases when you listen to the cassette for the first time.

1 Listen to four people talking about how their position in the family has affected their personality. Which of the following adjectives are used to describe each position in the family? Mark them **E** (eldest child), **M** (middle child), **Y** (youngest child) or **O** (only child).

1 open-minded	....	6 ambitious	....
2 serious	....	7 aggressive	....
3 independent	....	8 adaptable	....
4 self-confident	....	9 relaxed	....
5 selfish	....	10 responsible	....

2 Listen to the speakers again and answer the following questions. Write the number of the speaker (1, 2, 3 or 4) in the gaps.

a) Who tries to do what people expect? ....

b) Who probably works best in a team or group? ....

c) Who probably had the most freedom as a child? ....

d) Who may try to dominate others? ....

e) Who may be a bit irresponsible? ....

f) Who may blame other people for her/his own mistakes? ....

Reading: multiple choice

About the exam

In Paper 1, Part 2 you choose between four alternatives to answer questions about a text.

Strategy

- Read the text once quickly.
- Read it again.
- Answer the questions without looking at the alternatives.
- Find an alternative that is like your answer.

1 Read the following article and decide which of these adjectives best describes Janet Jackson.

A unhappy   **B** positive **C** aggressive **D** sophisticated

The *Other* Jackson

Janet Jackson, the youngest of nine children, was born in 1966. She became a child star of American TV soaps after being spotted in a television appearance with her brothers, The Jackson Five. In the past ten years she has recorded five albums, the last two of them providing her with twelve American Top Five singles.

Initially overshadowed by her brothers and sisters, she has now become famous in her own right. As a female singing star, only a handful of other artists – Madonna, Whitney Houston and Gloria Estefan, for example – provide her with serious competition.

Janet has managed to create a new art form, a mixture of music, dance and fashion which is perfect for the video age. She is small and rather shy which makes her seem vulnerable. She is also much more natural than many of today's stars.

Janet was born in Gary, Indiana, but moved with her family to the West Coast when she was two. She was brought up in the deluxe Jackson compound in Encino, California, with its own zoo and private cinema. She would turn on the TV to find cartoon likenesses of her brothers dancing to 'ABC' and 'I want you back'.

By the age of seven she was performing in the family's live stage act. Janet and her brother Randy would do impressions of Sonny & Cher, W.C. Fields and Mae West. Then came her enrolment in Valley Professional, a school for children in the entertainment business, small parts in TV series and a recording contract with A&M Records.

At the age of eighteen she moved away from the family to live in New York. She then secretly married Motown singer James DeBarge. The marriage only lasted sixty days and ended in annulment. 'All my life I had people telling me what to do. I wanted to do something on my own. So I ran away to get married.'

Janet came from a large, tight-knit family with a dominant and ambitious father who turned from his own minor music career to direct those of his children. Trying to become independent and gain control of her life must have been very difficult. It would be understandable if she had had to give up some things. Does she have any regrets?

'No. None. If I had my life to live all over again, I'd do it exactly the same. Everything I experienced, good or bad, was for a reason, and that was to prepare me for today and tomorrow.'

from *The Observer* magazine

2 Write answers to the following questions using information from the text.

1 How did Janet Jackson become a TV star?

....

....

2 Why was her childhood unusual?

....

....

3 Why did she move away and get married?

....

....

4 How does she feel about her life so far?

....

....

3 Now look at these alternative answers to each of the questions above and choose the correct answer, A or B.

Question 1
A Someone saw her performing with her brothers on TV.
B Her brothers saw her performing on TV.

Question 2
A It was exciting because her family moved so often.
B It was unusual because her family were very rich and famous.

Question 3
A Because she wanted to be independent.
B Because she didn't want anyone to come to the wedding.

Question 4
A She feels that the things that have happened to her have prepared her well for the life she leads.
B She feels sorry about some things that happened in the past and wishes she could change them.

4 Alternative B in Question 1 is wrong. The text says she was 'spotted in a television appearance *with* her brothers' NOT *by* her brothers. Look at the other questions again and match the following statements to the incorrect alternatives. Write the question number and the letter of the incorrect alternative in the gaps.

1 This is wrong because it says the **opposite** of what the text says.   ....

2 This is wrong because it says something that might be true which is **not** in the text.   ....

3 This is wrong because it says something the text does **not** say.   ....

┌─ **Hot tip!** ◄ ─ ─ ─ ─ ─ ─ ─ ─ ─ ─ ─ ┐
If you don't know which alternative is correct, guess! NEVER leave a question unanswered!
└ ─ ─ ─ ─ ─ ─ ─ ─ ─ ─ ─ ─ ─ ─ ─ ─ ─ ─ ┘

5 Look again at the text and find words with the following meanings.

1 made to appear less important *(para. 2)*

....

2 a small number (of people) *(para. 2)*

....

3 can be understood *(para. 7)*

....

'I bet other people's parents don't put their kids under this much pressure.'

23

Word formation

Paper 3, Part 5

Learner training
Pay attention to the beginnings and endings of words. You can often work out the meaning of new words if you can break them up into parts. For example: *un-believ-able*.

1 Look at the words in Exercise 5 on page 23 that you found in the text on Janet Jackson and find:

1 a suffix that can be added to a verb to make an adjective. ....

2 a suffix that means 'the amount contained in'. ....

3 a prefix that means 'from above' or 'too much'. ....

2 Read the following text and then fill in the gaps with an appropriate form of the word in capitals at the end of each line.

Strategy
- Read the text all the way through once quickly.
- Decide what part of speech goes in each gap.
- Think of possible words to fill each gap.
- Form words from the words in capitals.
- Check that each word is the right part of speech.
- Check that each sentence makes sense, for example that you have used a negative prefix in a sentence with a negative meaning.

Although my two sisters and I have (0) .....*different*.....	**DIFFER**
mothers, we are definitely (1)	**LIKE**
This is not just a matter of (2) ...., though	**APPEAR**
we are all small with curly hair and a (3)	**TEND**
to (4) .... and put on weight. The resemblance	**EAT**
goes much further than that. Throughout our (5)	**CHILD**
we were brought up to be very (6) .... and our	**ADAPT**
ability to accept change is another (7)	**CHARACTER**
we share. Another would be (8) .... We all hate	**SHY**
parties where you have to walk into a (9)	**ROOM**
of strange faces. Being (10) .... like this means	**CONSCIOUS**
we are all interested in wearing (11) .... clothes.	**FASHION**
We often share our clothes. (12) .... this causes	**FORTUNATE**
arguments. We really should come to some (13)	**AGREE**
about who can borrow what from whom – and when.	

Grammar: making comparisons

1 Read the article opposite. Which of the families is most like your own?

2 Read the article again and mark the following statements **T** (true) or **F** (false).

1 Peter Menzel and his team visited the same number of families as countries.

2 The Carballo family is smaller than any of the other families.

3 They have fewer domestic appliances than the Pfitzners or the Ukitas.

4 The Ukitas have the same number of children as the Pfitzners.

5 The Ukitas' daughter Miyo is older than both of the Pfitzners' sons.

6 The Pfitzners seem to have a bit more free time than the other families.

7 In some ways the Carballos seem to be happier than the other families.

8 They seem to be more concerned about the future of their country than the other families.

3 Now write five more sentences like the ones in Exercise 2 comparing the families in the text.

FAMILIES AROUND THE WORLD

In 1994, the International Year of the Family, Peter Menzel, an American photographer, decided to take photographs to show the many different ways families live around the world. With a team of photographers and journalists he visited thirty average families in thirty different countries. They got to know the families and took photographs of them outside their homes surrounded by their possessions. Here are some of the results:

The Carballo family, Argentina

Family members:
Juan Carlos, husband, 42
Marta Elizabeth, wife, 31
María Pía, daughter, 6
María Belén, daughter, 8
Nahuel, son, 9

Mr and Mrs Carballo both work as photographers. They are not rich, but they could afford to buy a new stereo, television and video recently. But times are not easy and they have had to move in with one of Mrs Carballo's aunts. Sunday afternoon is their favourite time of the week. They all get together round the barbecue to eat, dance and laugh.

Size of family home: 3 rooms in Mrs Carballo's aunt's house.
Working week: husband 30 to 35 hours, wife 40 hours.
Domestic appliances: 1 radio, 1 telephone, 1 television, 1 video, 1 stereo.
What they want for the future: a more stable situation in Argentina.

The Ukita family, Japan

Family members:
Kazuo, husband, 45
Sayo, wife, 43
Miyo, daughter, 9
Maya, daughter, 6

Mr Ukita and Mrs Ukita and their children have very busy lives. Miyo, the older daughter, dreams of taking part in the Olympic games. Five days a week she rides her bicycle to the local sports centre where she spends two hours swimming lengths of the pool. She also goes to extra classes to prepare for the difficult national exams. This leaves her a little time left for watching television and the Ukitas have one with a special button so that they can watch foreign programmes in the original language.

Size of family home: a flat measuring 132 square metres, including living room, dining room, kitchen and bathroom.
Working week: husband 40 hours, wife 60 hours (housework).
Domestic appliances: 3 radios, 1 telephone, 1 television, 1 video, 1 microwave oven, 1 computer.
What they want for the future: a bigger house with more space.

The Pfitzner family, Germany

Family members:
Bernhard, husband, 38
Brigitte, wife, 36
Manuel, son, 7
Christian, son, 4

Bernhard Pfitzner works as a physiotherapist in Neuss, a city near Cologne. He works hard, gets home late and is often tired. He would like to be able to spend more time with his sons and dreams of owning a house in the country. Mrs Pfitzner works hard, too. She is very concerned about environmental issues. She does not want her two sons to grow up heavily influenced by television so she only lets them watch for between half an hour and an hour a day.

Size of family home: a rented flat measuring 83 square metres with four bedrooms, kitchen, hallway and bathroom.
Working week: husband 40 hours, wife 50 hours (housework).
Domestic appliances: 3 radios, 1 radio cassette, 1 television, 1 video, 1 video camera.
What they want for the future: a bigger fridge, a house in the country and a cleaner natural environment.

▲ The Carballo family

The Ukita family ▶

The Pfitzner family ▶

Writing: transactional letter

Paper 2, Part 1

Hot tip! ◄

DON'T waste time in the exam counting words! Work out how many words you normally write on a line and multiply this by the number of lines you have written.

1 Read the following task and the answers that two candidates wrote.

> Your younger sister/brother is going to visit relatives in an English-speaking country. Your relatives have not met her/him before. Write telling them about her/his travel arrangements and explaining how they should recognise her/him.
>
> Include these notes in your answer:
>
> – check flight times
> – describe clothes
> – gift from here?

Candidate A

Dear Susan and Nick,

We collected Stavros's ticket yesterday so I'm writing to give you his travel details.

He leaves Athens on December 13 on Flight OM 197 and arrives to Melbourne the next day at 11.20 in the morning. The airline says there are sometimes delays so it's worth phoning them at the airport to check the flight is on time.

I've enclosed a recent photograph, but just in case you have problems recognising him, he's quite tall for his years with a straight light brown hair and green eyes. He'll be wearing a light grey T-shirt, jeans and black trainers.

Is there anything you would like him to bring from Greece? The honey is delicious, you know it, and so are the olives. I ask you to tell us what would you like.

I think that's all for the moment.

All the best,

Giorgos

Candidate B

Hello my friends,

I writting inform you about my sister travel. She is leave on fly IB264 from Barcelona and arive your country at 6 o'clock.

She is very pretty with a blonde hair and blue eyes. She is good student. She is studying very hard every day. Sometimes she uses glasses but she will use contact lens this day. She will be dressing a blue trouser and a yellow bluse. I send you one foto.

Do you want that she bring you a gift? She can bring a tipical food or clothes. You must say me what do you like.

Goodbye,

Carlos

2 Now look at the following examiner's reports and decide which is for Candidate A and which is for Candidate B.

Report 1

Candidate: ....

Grade: **unsatisfactory**

* Some points in instructions not covered.
* Beginning and ending of the letter are inappropriate.
* Letter is quite well-structured.
* Basic errors (spelling, grammar and vocabulary).
* Inappropriate vocabulary for an informal letter.
* Not enough information about flight details.

Report 2

Candidate: ....

Grade: **very good**

* Clear paragraphs covering all the points in the instructions.
* Appropriate beginning and ending to the letter.
* Some good structures.
* Wide vocabulary.
* Some poor expression, but almost no errors.
* People reading letter would know exactly what to do.

3 Find five spelling mistakes in Candidate B's letter and write the words out again correctly in your notebook.

4 Find five sentences in Candidate B's letter which contain mistakes with verb forms and write them out again correctly in your notebook.

5 Find five sentences in Candidate B's letter which contain mistakes with articles (*a/an, the*) and write them out again correctly in your notebook.

6 What verb normally goes with the words *glasses, contact lenses* and *trousers?* ....

7 Rewrite the unsatisfactory letter using the good letter as a model.

Learner training
Do extra writing exercises and exchange them with a friend. Get your friend to correct your mistakes. Correct your friend's mistakes.

4 Seeing is believing

Reading: multiple matching

Paper 1, Part 1

About the exam
In Paper 1, Part 1 you read a text and either match headings or summary sentences to each paragraph.

Strategy
Learn to recognise the structure (like a plan) of the text. This will help you decide on the paragraph headings or summary sentences.

1 Read the following article about computer errors and decide which of these two plans the writer followed.

A

- Describe the situation.
- Describe a problem.
- Describe unsatisfactory solutions.
- State the problem again.

B

- Ask a question.
- Answer the question.
- Give specific examples.
- Ask another question.

When a computer error is a fatal mistake

Our lives depend on computers. They control our money, transport, our exam results. Yet their programs are now so complex that no one can get rid of all the mistakes.

(0 _G_)
Life without computers has become unimaginable. They are designed to look after so many boring but essential tasks – from microwave cooking to flying across the Atlantic – that we have become dependent on them.

(1___)
But as the demands placed on computers grow, so have the number of incidents involving computer errors. Now computer experts are warning that the traditional ways of building computer systems are just not good enough to deal with complex tasks like flying planes or maintaining nuclear power stations. It is only a matter of time before a computer-made catastrophe occurs.

(2___)
As early as 1889, a word entered the language that was to become all too familiar to computer scientists: a 'bug', meaning a mistake. For decades bugs and 'de-bugging' were taken to be part of every computer engineer's job. Everyone

accepted that there would always be some mistakes in any new system. But 'safety critical' systems that fly planes, drive trains or control nuclear power stations can have bugs that could kill. This is obviously unacceptable.

(3____)

One way to stop bugs in computer systems is to get different teams of programmers to work in isolation from each other. That way, runs the theory, they won't all make the same type of mistake when designing and writing computer codes. In fact research shows that programmers think alike, have the same type of training – and make similar mistakes. So even if they work separately, mistakes can still occur. Another technique is to produce back up systems that start to operate when the first system fails. This has been used on everything from the space shuttle to the A320 airbus, but unfortunately problems that cause one computer to fail can make all the others fail, too.

(4____)

A growing number of computer safety experts believe the time has come to stop trying to 'patch up' computer systems. They say programmers have to learn to think clearly and to be able to demonstrate through mathematical symbols that the program cannot go seriously wrong. Until programmers learn to do this, we will probably just have to live with the results of computer bugs.

(5____)

Of course, more often than not the errors are just annoying, but sometimes they can come close to causing tragedies. On the Piccadilly line in London's Underground a driver who was going south along a track got confused while moving his empty train through a cross-over point. He started to head north straight at a south-bound train full of people. The computerised signalling system failed to warn him of impending disaster and it was only his quick human reactions that prevented a crash.

from *Focus* magazine

2 Now read the article again and choose a heading for each paragraph from the list below. There is one extra heading which you do not need to use. The first one has been done for you.

A An old problem with serious consequences.
B Two new approaches, but can they solve the problem?
C A potentially tragic error.
D But are they here to stay?
E Experts say 'Bring back maths!'
F Old methods are no longer satisfactory.
G We couldn't live without them.

3 Find words or phrases in the text with the following meanings:

1 impossible to imagine (*para. 0*) ....

2 needing support from (*para. 0*) ....

3 long-established, conventional (*para. 1*) ....

4 sudden great disaster (*para. 1*) ....

5 often seen or heard (*para. 2*) ....

6 not good enough (*para. 2*) ....

7 separately (*para. 3*) ....

8 support (*para. 3*) ....

9 terrible events that cause great sadness (*para. 5*) ....

10 about to happen (*para. 5*) ....

Grammar: *like*

Paper 3, Part 3

About the exam

In Paper 3, Part 3 you read sentences and complete new sentences so that they have a similar meaning. You have to use a word that is printed in **bold** to complete the new sentence.

Hot tip!

Check for third person singular 's' in the Present Simple.

1 Complete the second sentence so that it has a similar meaning to the first sentence. Use the word in **bold** and other words to complete each sentence.

EXAMPLE: I am very similar to my brother.
like
My brother .... *is very like* .... me.

1 Do you want me to help you tidy up?
like
Would *you like me to help* .... you tidy up?

2 Can you describe him for me?
tell
Can you *Tell me How is* .... like?

3 I think it must be a dog barking.
like
It *is like* .... a dog barking.

4 She plays racket sports, such as tennis and squash.
like
She .... tennis and squash.

5 They enjoy going to the beach at the weekends.
like
They........................ at the weekends.

6 I think I can smell smoke.
like
That .... smoke.

7 My sister and I are very alike physically.
look
I .... my sister.

8 Can you tell me about the course?
like
I .... know about the course.

2 The following dialogue contains nine mistakes with the use of *like*. Find the mistakes and write the sentences out again correctly in your notebook.

JOAQUÍN: How is your sister like?
HEIDI: She's the same height like me and she's blonde, too. She looks so much like me you'd think we were twins.
JOAQUÍN: By the way, would you like going to the cinema at the weekend?
HEIDI: That sounds as a good idea.
JOAQUÍN: Do you like to see anything in particular?
HEIDI: Let's see something funny. I'd like comedies.
JOAQUÍN: OK. I'll come round to your house at five, if you like it.
HEIDI: Fine. Are you as your brother, always late?
JOAQUÍN: No. I like my mother, always on time.
HEIDI: Good, I like punctual people. I'll be ready at five o'clock.
JOAQUÍN: Perhaps your sister would like to come, too.
HEIDI: No, I don't think so. She's already going out on Saturday night.
JOAQUÍN: OK. See you on Saturday.
HEIDI: See you then.

Vocabulary: phrasal verbs (*take*)

1 Match the first half of the sentence in Column A with the second half of the sentence in Column B. Write the appropriate letter in the box. Then fill in the gaps with *on, off* (x3), *up* (x2), *in* or *over*.

Column A

1 I really should take a day .... ☐
2 The manager said they were not taking .... ☐
3 I'm sorry to have taken .... ☐
4 My older sister was always taking .... ☐
5 It was hilarious! He was taking .... ☐
6 Take .... ☐
7 We thought these virtual reality things would really take .... here, ☐
8 I wasn't taken .... ☐

Column B

a) for a moment when she said she had been ill.
b) volleyball. It'll do you the world of good.
c) so much of your time.
d) work and paint the kitchen.
e) our games when we were children.
f) but they've been a complete financial disaster.
g) any more bar staff for the time being.
h) one of the teachers when she walked in.

2 Fill in the gaps in the following sentences with an appropriate phrasal verb from Exercise 1.

1 You can use ...., with words like *a sport* or *a hobby* or names of specific sports and hobbies.

2 You can use .... with the word *staff* or with words for specific jobs.

3 People who study or work can .... *a few days, two weeks, a month*, etc.

4 Activities, things or people can .... *too/so much/a lot of time/space*.

5 Bossy people often .... other people's *jobs/games/conversations/meetings*, etc.

3 There are mistakes in four of the following sentences. Find the mistakes and write the sentences out again correctly in your notebook.

1 She took off me so well I had to laugh.

2 The meeting had only been going for a few minutes and he'd taken it over completely.

3 The doctor said I should swim, so I've taken up it.

4 They've already made them redundant and they only took on them a month ago.

5 We won't be very busy this week so why don't you take off it?

6 She's such a clever liar she always takes me in.

Listening: multiple matching

Paper 4, Part 3

About the exam
In Paper 4, Part 3 you listen to short extracts. You match each extract to a question or statement.

Strategy
Once you have matched a statement to a speaker, cross it out and concentrate on the others.

You are going to hear five people talking about problems they have had with machines and electronic devices of various kinds. Listen and match one of the following statements **A–E** to one of the speakers. There is one statement which you do not need to use.

A She/he was frightened.
B She/he found herself/himself in the wrong place.
C She/he disturbed some other people.
D She/he said something she/he didn't mean to say.
E She/he asked someone to help her/him.
F She/he almost forgot where she/he was.

Speaker 1 ....

Speaker 2 ....

Speaker 3 ....

Speaker 4 ....

Speaker 5 ....

Writing: narrative

> **Paper 2, Part 2**

> **About the exam**
> In Paper 2, Part 2 you choose one question to answer out of four. One of the questions may ask you to write a story.

1   Below are the first two paragraphs from a story, but the sentences are in the wrong order. Put the sentences in the correct order. Write the numbers 1–11 in the gaps. Use the words and phrases in bold to help you.

Paragraph 1

a) A search party went out to look for **the men** and found **them** two hours later more than 100 kilometres away. ....

b) **In 1970 an army battalion** were doing basic training on an enormous plain in the north-west of China. ....

c) **They** seemed dazed and confused and their uniforms were badly torn. ....

d) One morning a thick fog came down and **three soldiers** became separated from the others and were reported missing at about ten o'clock. ....

e) **They** gave **the following** explanation of what had happened to them during their two-hour absence. ....

f) **Nevertheless**, they were in perfectly good health and did not have any physical injuries. ....

Paragraph 2

g) Apparently the three men lost consciousness **at this point** though they all reported feeling they were inside some kind of aircraft and they all remembered seeing coloured flashing lights. ....

h) **Suddenly** they heard **a loud whirring noise** as if an enormous helicopter were somewhere overhead. ....

i) **As the three soldiers looked around for the rest of the battalion** they realised they were alone though they felt as if someone or something was watching them. ....

j) **Moments later** they felt themselves being drawn upwards towards **the light** by an irresistible force. ....

k) When they looked up to see where **the noise** was coming from they were almost blinded by **an intense yellow light**. ....

2   Here is the last paragraph of the story, but it contains six mistakes with verb tenses. Find the mistakes and write the paragraph out again correctly in your notebook.

> The captain has not believed their story at first. After all they could have easily hitched a ride with a passing lorry driver. What was more difficult to explain was the fact that even though they have been missing for only a few hours, when they had been found they all have long beards as if they have not shaved for six months or more. They had all been absolutely clean shaven when they had disappeared.

3 Read the following task.

> Write **a story** that begins or ends with the following words:
>
> *I stared in amazement as the strange object disappeared beneath the surface of the lake.*

1 Decide whether you want to begin or finish your story with the words provided.

2 Think of ideas. Ask yourself questions like: *What disappeared? Where did it come from? Who else saw it?*

3 Write a plan with your ideas in order.

4 Write your story in 120–180 words.

5 Check your work very carefully for errors with verb tenses.

> **Strategy**
> If you can't think of any ideas, ask yourself questions like:
> - When did it happen?
> - Where did it happen?
> - What happened first?
> - What happened after that?

'For heaven's sake Maureen, not everybody wants to see photographs of our grandchildren.'

Vocabulary and grammar:
open cloze

> **Paper 3, Part 2**

> **Strategy**
> Remember to read the text all the way through first. Then decide what part of speech is missing from each gap.

Read the following text and then fill in the gaps with an appropriate word. You have been given the first three letters of each word to help you.

> When you read magazine articles about
> (1) sci.................... discoveries or
> (2) tec.................... advances, you can get a very false impression of the way scientists and technicians actually work in (3) lab.................... .
> Of course the (4) res.................... they do solves
> (5) pro.................... or leads to the
> (6) dev.................... of new theories. But it is not all as carefully planned as we might imagine. A lot of the discoveries that have (7) rev.................... the way a disease is treated or a crop grown were made by chance. A chemist might add a
> (8) che.................... to a test tube and
> (9) pro.................... a new substance. A professional (10) inv.................... might try out all sorts of unsuccessful designs before coming up with a brilliant invention almost by accident.

> **Hot tip!**
> If you don't know what word goes in the gap, think of any word which is the right part of speech. NEVER leave a gap blank! You cannot lose marks for wrong answers.

> **Learner training**
> Make your own gap filling exercises. Use the reading texts and tapescripts from this book. Get a friend to take out a word every six or seven words.

Speaking: picture prompts

Paper 5, Part 2

About the exam
In Part 2 of Paper 5 you talk about some photographs and say how you feel about them.

Strategy
If you do not know the English word for something in the picture, paraphrase. Say things like: 'It's a thing you use for ...' or 'It's a kind of ...'.

1 Listen to two candidates doing this part of the interview and look at the photos below. Which candidate did well, Laura or Ahmet?

1

2

4

2 Listen to the first candidate again and complete the following sentences with the words Laura uses.

1 .... a 'parabolic antenna' or aerials.

2 .... dish.

3 .... receiving satellite TV.

Hot tip! ◄
DON'T say things like 'That's all. I don't know what else to say.'! The examiner wants to hear you speak.

5 All you need is love

Grammar: reported statements

1 Read the following conversation between a doctor and a young patient and then complete the doctor's notes below.

DOCTOR: Well, what seems to be the trouble?

LAURA: I feel fine, but my parents are worried about me. They think I'm acting strangely.

DOCTOR: Are you sleeping well at night?

LAURA: I sleep well, but I wake up very early.

DOCTOR: And what about meals? Are you eating normally?

LAURA: No. I haven't eaten a full meal for a week. I never feel hungry.

DOCTOR: And has anything happened to upset you? A problem at school or perhaps at home?

LAURA: It's not really a problem. But there's a new student at school and ... well, doctor, he's the most wonderful person I've ever met. He's kind, intelligent and so good-looking. I can't think about anything else. His name's Steve and he's got a motorcycle ...

DOCTOR: Well, young lady, I don't think there's really very much the matter with you.

Case notes

The patient said she (1)_____, but that her parents (2)_____. She said they (3)_____. When I asked about her sleeping patterns, she said she (4)_____, but (5)_____. Her eating patterns are also irregular. She said (6)_____ a full meal for a week and that she never (7)_____. When I asked if something was worrying her, she said there (8)_____ at school. My diagnosis is that the patient is in love.

2 Read the following extract from a letter Laura wrote to her friend Suzie and complete the dialogue.

I couldn't believe it. He came up to me as I was getting on the school bus. He asked me if I was doing anything next weekend. I said I had to go out to lunch with my parents on Sunday, but that apart from that I didn't have any special plans. Then he asked if I'd seen the new Harrison Ford film. I said I hadn't, but that my brother had told me that he had really enjoyed it. He asked if I wanted to go and see it with him on Saturday night and I said that sounded great. He asked what time I wanted to go to the movie and I said I thought the 6.00 session was usually less crowded, so he suggested we meet at the cinema at about 5.45 and that we could have a pizza afterwards. I haven't decided what to wear yet, but Nicki says I can borrow her new top.

STEVE: Hi, how are you?

LAURA: Oh, hi. Fine.

STEVE: Listen. I was wondering ... Are you doing anything next weekend?

LAURA: Well (1).., but apart from that (2).. .

STEVE: Have you seen the new Harrison Ford film?

LAURA: No, (3).., but my brother (4).. .

STEVE: Yes, everyone says it's brilliant. Would you like to go and see it on Saturday night?

LAURA: That (5).. .

STEVE: What time do you want to go? At six or at eight?

LAURA: (6).. the six o'clock session (7).. .

STEVE: OK. Shall we meet at the cinema at about 5.45? Perhaps we could go for a pizza after the film.

Grammar: reported questions

Laura got home from her evening out with Steve very late and her mother was angry. Read their conversation and then complete Laura's diary.

MOTHER: What's his name?
LAURA: Steve.
MOTHER: Steve what? What's his surname?
LAURA: I don't know.
MOTHER: Well how did you get to know him?
LAURA: He goes to school.
MOTHER: What year is he in at school?
LAURA: Err ... I'm not sure. He's a bit older than me.
MOTHER: How much older is he?
LAURA: A couple of years. I think he's about sixteen or seventeen.
MOTHER: I see. So he's a lot older than you. And where did you go?
LAURA: I told you. We went to see a movie.
MOTHER: What time did the movie finish?
LAURA: At about eight o'clock.
MOTHER: And what did you do after that?
LAURA: We went to have a pizza.
MOTHER: How long were you in the restaurant? It doesn't take four hours to eat a pizza!
LAURA: It took quite a long time to get home.
MOTHER: And how did you get home?
LAURA: On Steve's motorcycle, but it broke down on the way.
MOTHER: On Steve's motorcycle! Listen my girl – that's the last time you go out with this Steve. Just think yourself lucky your father hasn't heard about this!

Dear Diary,
Mum is really angry with me. She says I'm not allowed to go out with Steve ever again and all because I got home a bit late. The next morning she wouldn't stop asking me questions. Honestly it was just like a police interrogation! She asked me what (1)_____. and how (2)_____ . When I said he went to school, she wanted to know (3)_____ . I didn't want her to find out that he's eighteen, so I just said he was a bit older. But she wasn't happy with that, she wanted to know (4)_____ . And then we started on what happened that night. She questioned me about where (5)_____ , what time (6)_____ and what (7)_____ after the movie. When I said we went to have a pizza, she asked (8)_____ . And of course she wanted to know how (9)_____ . When I told her Steve had a motorcycle, she nearly had a fit!

'Mum'll be down in a minute.
While you're waiting would you like to see
the video of her first wedding?'

Grammar: key word transformations

Paper 3, Part 3

Hot tip! ◄

DON'T change the word given! You must use the same form of verbs and nouns.

Complete the second sentence so that it has a similar meaning to the first sentence. Use the word in **bold** and other words to complete each sentence.

EXAMPLE: 'I'm sorry I got home so late,' said Laura.
apologised
Laura ..*apologised for getting*.. home so late.

1 'I won't tell anyone about it,' said Suzie.
promised
Laura's friend Suzie .... anyone about it.

2 'Laura, you should try being honest with your parents,' said the doctor.
advised
The doctor .... honest with her parents.

3 'Don't go out with that boy again!' said Laura's father.
warned
Laura's father .... go out with Steve again.

4 'You've been meeting your boyfriend after school, haven't you?' said Mum.
accused
Laura's mother .... her boyfriend after school.

5 'Lend me your gameboy, or I'll tell Mum and Dad,' said Laura's brother.
threatened
Laura's brother .... her parents unless she lent him her gameboy.

6 'I haven't seen Steve since Saturday night,' said Laura.
denied
Laura .... Steve since Saturday night.

7 'But I tried to phone him yesterday,' said Laura.
admitted
Laura .... him the day before.

8 'Perhaps I could meet your parents,' said Steve.
suggested
Steve .... Laura's parents.

9 'No, I will not speak to him,' said Laura's mother.
refused
Laura's mother .... Steve.

10 'Try being a bit more understanding, Mrs Carter,' said the doctor.
encouraged
The doctor .... a bit more understanding.

11 'I've made up my mind. I'm going to ask Steve to lunch on Sunday,' said Laura's mother.
decided
Laura's mother .... Steve to lunch on Sunday.

12 'Would you like to have lunch with us on Sunday, Steve?' said Laura's mother.
invited
Laura's mother .... lunch with them on Sunday.

13 'I think you're right. Laura is too young to stay out so late,' said Steve.
agreed
Steve .... too young to stay out so late.

14 'Next time we could take Andrew with us,' said Steve.
offered
Steve .... Laura's younger brother with them the next time.

15 'Perhaps it would be better to go out in the afternoons,' said Laura's father.
recommended
Laura's father .... in the afternoons.

37

Grammar: error correction

Paper 3, Part 4

About the exam

In Paper 3, Part 4 you read a text in which each line is numbered. Some lines are correct and other lines have an extra, unnecessary word. For the correct lines you put a tick (✔) at the end of the line. For the incorrect lines you circle the extra word and write it at the end of the line. In the actual exam you will transfer your answers from the question booklet to the separate answer sheet.

Strategy

If you see any of the following in a line, check that they should be there:

- definite and indefinite articles e.g. I go to school by (the) bus.
- auxiliaries (*do, have, are*, etc.) e.g. She asked me where (did) I put the keys.
- the word 'more' e.g. He is (more) taller than me.
- prepositions e.g. My parents gave (to) me a book.
- pronouns e.g. The man who (he) told me to come back today sounded German.

Read the following text and decide which lines are correct and which have an additional incorrect word. There are two examples at the beginning (**0** and **00**).

0	I (have) received a really nice long letter last week.	*have*
00	from a girl called Laura I met on holiday last summer.	✔
1	In the letter she told to me about her new boyfriend.	
2	He goes to her school, but is quite a lot more older.	
3	At first her parents did not like to him very much	
4	because they went out together and she got home late.	
5	When she told her mother he had a motorcycle, she was	
6	very upset and refused that to allow Laura to go out with	
7	him again. Laura was very upset and went to the family doctor	
8	for to discuss her problem with her. The doctor suggested	
9	that Laura should to be more honest with her parents. She spoke	
10	to my friend's mother and advised her to be more of understanding.	
11	Eventually my friend's parents met her new boyfriend and	
12	got on quite well with him. He promised to make sure Laura	
13	always gets at home before eleven o'clock and suggested	
14	taking Laura's younger brother when they go out.	
15	Laura says me her parents really like her boyfriend now.	

Vocabulary: love and marriage

Read the following letter to a problem page. Then fill in the gaps with an appropriate word or phrase from the box. Use the correct form of the verbs.

best man   infatuated
get married   fall in love
anniversary   go out
get engaged   choir   vicar
aisle   have an affair
bridesmaid   bouquet
have a baby   have rows
get a divorce

Dear Madge,

Tom and I met at a dance about five years ago. We started (1).............................. together and although at the beginning I thought I was just (2)............................ with him, before long we both realised we (3)............................. .

We wanted to wait until he had finished his military service before we (4)............................, but we (5)............................. anyway, before he went into the army.

The wedding was all the more wonderful because we had had to wait. Tom asked his oldest friend to be (6)............................ . As I walked down the (7)............................ I felt so happy I thought I would die. When the (8)............................ said, 'I now pronounce you man and wife.' and the (9)............................ sang 'Ave Maria' everyone could see how happy I was. Outside the church I threw my (10)............................ as high as I could and my sister Mary caught it.

But not long after that things started to go wrong. We started to (11)............................ about silly things and not long after little Lucy was born I found out that Tom (12)............................. .

I don't know what to do. I still love him, but he wants (13)............................ . Should I agree?

Yours,
CONFUSED

📼 Listening: multiple choice

Paper 4, Part 1

About the exam
In Paper 4, Part 1 you will hear people talking in different situations. You choose the best of three answers to questions.

Strategy
Listen for clues about:
- what the people are talking about.
- how they feel about what they are saying.
- the relationships between the people e.g. friends, business colleagues.

Listen to the extracts on the cassette and choose the correct alternative to complete the following statements.

1 You are watching television. You hear this woman talking. She is talking about

  A a film she didn't enjoy very much.
  B a play that she didn't think was very good.
  C a book that she found very exciting.

2 You are listening to the radio. You hear this man speaking. He thinks people listening

  A speak Spanish.
  B may not speak Spanish.
  C do not speak Spanish.

3 You overhear this girl talking on the telephone. She is

  A politely refusing to go out with the person who phoned her.
  B accepting an invitation from the person who phoned her.
  C inviting the person who phoned her to go out.

4 You hear this woman talking about her husband. They met

  A at a cinema.
  B on a picnic.
  C in class.

5 You overhear these two boys talking on a bus. The first boy

  A doesn't mind meeting the girl's parents.
  B is afraid of meeting the girl's parents.
  C has met the girl's parents before.

Writing: background reading texts

Paper 2, Part 2

About the exam
In Paper 2, Part 2 there is always a question on the background reading texts. This question is **optional**.

⌐ Hot tip! ◄
DON'T attempt this question if you have not read any of the books! Reading a summary is **not** enough.

Strategy
Read the book once all the way through. Then read the book again and keep notes of:
- what happens in the story.
- the characters.
- the places.
- the way you feel about the things that happen.

Read the book again quickly a week or two before the exam.

Think of a book or story that you have read recently in English or in your own language. Write a composition retelling the story in your own words so that a friend of your own age could decide whether to read it or not.

1 Underline the important words in the instructions.

2 Make a list of the important events in the story.

3 Plan your composition. Decide how many paragraphs you are going to write and which events you will mention in each paragraph. Will you write about what happens at the end?

4 Write your composition in 120–180 words.

5 Check your composition for spelling and grammar mistakes. Be particularly careful with reported speech.

Learner training
There are film versions of many of the books that are set as background reading texts. If you see the film (preferably in English) before you read the book, it will make it easier to understand.
Remember that it will still be **absolutely necessary** to read the book several times as well.

Reading: multiple choice

About the exam

In another type of multiple choice question in Paper 1, Part 2 you say what words like pronouns (e.g. *it, she, they*) and possessive adjectives (e.g. *his, our, their*) in the text refer to.

Strategy

To work out what a word refers to:
- look at the sentences before or after the word.
- remember that words like 'it' and 'this', or 'do' and 'so' can refer to verbs, nouns, adjectives and adverbs, or to phrases and clauses.

1 The following lines all come from Elton John's *Your Song* (page 47 of the *First Certificate Gold Coursebook*). Look at the underlined words and write what they refer to.

1 It's a little bit funny,
   This feeling inside,

   ....

2 Don't have much money,
   But boy if I did,

   ....

3 And you can tell everybody this is your song.
   It may be quite simple, but now that it's done,

   ....

4 But, the sun's been quite kind while I wrote this song,
   It's for people like you that keep it turned on.

   ....

5 So excuse me forgetting, but these things I do,

   ....

2 Read the article opposite and then choose the best title from the list below.

A So, love, this is your song.
B The successful pop song: a recipe.
C What's in a name?: what to call your baby.

THE WORLD is divided into the 'haves' and the 'have nots': those who have had their names used in popular songs and the rest. The 'haves' include anyone named Eleanor, Carol, Bernadette, Maria, Frankie or Johnnie. Girls called Sue or Suzie are especially fortunate, what with 'Wake up Little Suzie' and so on. The 'have-nots', a large and unhappy group, include people named Graham, Bruce, Jacqueline and a great many others. Anyone
10 with a name like these is likely to go through life without ever hearing their name in a song on the radio or anywhere else.

But help is at hand. Serge Romano has started a business called 'Songs for You' in Melbourne, Australia. Anyone can have a song written, recorded, preserved and presented to fit their specifications.

Serge got the idea for 'Songs for You' about a year ago when he and his wife Cathy were at a
20 wedding. 'The groom had got a song done for his bride. The reaction from her and the bridesmaids and other guests was fantastic. A little while later I was discussing it with friends, and it struck me that this could really take off.'

Aiming at the wedding and engagement market, the Romanos advertise on cards in florists and photographers' studios, but they will also take requests for songs for birthdays, Christmas and anniversaries. The minimum fee is $300. For this,
30 clients get a recorded version of their song on cassette (a CD is extra), plus a framed copy of the lyrics.

The creative process begins with a client filling out a questionnaire: About your song. This seeks details of the special occasion, relationship with the person to be immortalised in song, how they met, habits and most memorable moments. The musical style can be tailored to suit the client. For lovers, something romantic; for a younger listener a heavy-
40 metal feel might be more appropriate.

Each client gets a different song, though Serge admits that they may repeat a line from time to time. They try to avoid this as there is always the danger that two clients may meet and compare songs, but most songs are so personal, they couldn't be about anyone else. They might include nicknames or references to some special habit.

Most of Serge's customers are very satisfied with their songs. 'Yesterday I met a girl who'd had a song
50 done for her for Christmas. She played it in the bank where she works. She was nearly crying, explaining to me how much it meant to her. She knows the words by heart,' says Serge. 'To anyone else', he suggests, 'it might seem just like any other song, but Mary certainly doesn't think so.'

Are there any situations that Serge and his songwriters couldn't deal with? For example a woman about to split up with a man who wants to leave him a song to remember her by? Could Serge
60 and his team come up with something appropriate? 'Sure. We could do that. Though it's not a situation we've ever been presented with. Thank goodness!'

from *The Age* newspaper

3 Choose the correct alternative to answer the following questions.

1 Does the word 'these' in *line 10* refer to

   A names like Maria, Frankie or Johnnie?
   B names like Graham, Bruce or Jacqueline?
   C names like Eleanor, Carol or Bernadette?
   D names like Sue or Suzie?

2 Does the word 'her' in *line 21* refer to

   A Serge's wife Cathy?
   B the groom?
   C Serge?
   D the bride?

3 Does the word 'this' in *line 43* refer to

   A repeating a line from time to time?
   B two clients meeting?
   C writing different songs for each client?
   D clients comparing songs?

4 Does the word 'so' in *line 55* refer to the fact

   A that there are situations that Serge and his songwriters couldn't deal with?
   B that it meant a lot to her?
   C that it seems just like any other song?
   D that she knows the words by heart?

5 Does the word 'that' in *line 61* refer to

   A leaving him with a song to remember her by?
   B coming up with something appropriate?
   C being presented with a situation?
   D dealing with the request?

Learner training

You can improve your English and do well in FCE if you read newspapers, magazines and books in English. When you read widely like this, you will see words that are new to you. Sometimes it is necessary to look them up in a bilingual dictionary. Sometimes it is better to work out the meaning using your general knowledge and the words and sentences around the new word.

---

4 Use your general knowledge and the context to work out what the following words from the above article mean. Circle the correct alternative.

1 Often people have ideas very suddenly. So 'struck' *(line 23)* means

   A hit sharply or forcefully.
   B came immediately to the mind.

2 A song is a combination of words and music. So 'lyrics' *(line 32)* means

   A the words of a song, especially a modern popular song.
   B a musical instrument.

3 Something that only friends usually know about a person is the special name they like to be called. So 'nickname' *(line 47)* means

   A the same as surname.
   B a name used informally instead of a person's real name.

4 If you listen to a song a lot you eventually remember the words. So 'she knows the words by heart' *(line 53)* means

   A she has memorised the words.
   B she feels strongly about the words.

5 Find words in the text *So, love, this is your song* with the following meanings.

1 A word meaning 'man about to be married'. ....

2 A word meaning 'woman about to be or recently married'. ....

3 A word meaning 'unmarried girls who help the woman getting married at a marriage ceremony'. ....

4 A word meaning 'agreement to marry'. ....

5 A word meaning 'a date that is remembered because it is an exact number of years after an event'. ....

6 It's all in the mind

Grammar: gerunds and infinitives

1 The following sentences come from a story called *Lady Musgrove's necklace*. There are grammatical mistakes in seven of them. Find the mistakes and write the sentences out again correctly in your notebook.

1 At first Mary denied to steal the necklace.

2 Even when her fingerprints were found all over Lady Musgrove's dressing room, she continued to claim she was innocent.

3 She pretended not to hear when they asked her where she had been the evening the necklace vanished.

4 But eventually she admitted to take it.

5 The astonishing thing was that she refused saying where she had hidden it, even when Lord and Lady Musgrove offered to drop the charges.

6 Finally, when the police were arranging take her to the station, she agreed returning it.

7 She seemed to be genuinely sorry, and Lord and Lady Musgrove promised to let her keep her job.

8 However, she said she would prefer to work as a shop assistant and that she intended to go to London.

9 She hoped finding a job there.

10 Lady Musgrove said she would try helping her find work.

11 Mary stopped to cry and thanked her for her kindness.

2 Fill in the gaps in the following sentences with the correct form of the verbs in brackets.

1 If they're too big, try .... *(wear)* them with thicker socks.

2 I'd like .... *(know)* more about how the brain works.

3 I remember .... *(wake up)* very early on my fifth birthday.

4 Try not .... *(make)* mistakes with verb tenses in the exam.

5 I was late for class because I stopped .... *(talk)* to a friend I met on the way.

6 Today is a holiday, but luckily I remembered .... *(go)* to the bank yesterday.

7 I stopped .... *(smoke)* three years ago.

8 I like .... *(go)* to the beach at the weekends, but it's seldom warm enough.

Listening: note taking

Paper 4, Part 2

About the exam
In this type of exercise in Paper 4 you listen for:
- the main points.
- specific information.

Strategy
Study the incomplete notes before you listen to work out what kind of information you need to listen for.

1 You are going to hear a scientist talking about the body clock. First look at the sentences and think about the kind of information you need to complete them.

1 It is only when our normal routine is interrupted that we notice our physical or .....*psychological rhythms.*.....................

2 Everyone's biological rhythms are determined by .... of day into night, night into day.

3 .... works best around midnight.

4 Short term memory lasts about ....

5 The best time to do problem solving tasks is around .... in the morning.

6 Three in the afternoon is when .... works best.

7 A person's reflexes are at their peak between .... o'clock.

8 A splash of cold water and a blast .... can help you wake up in the morning.

9 Inside the brain two tiny structures connected to .... control our body clock.

10 Exposure to sunlight helps people recover ....

2 Now listen and complete the sentences.

Hot tip!
REMEMBER! You don't have to write complete sentences.

Grammar: key word transformations

Paper 3, Part 3

Complete the second sentence so that it has a similar meaning to the first sentence. Use the word in **bold** and other words.

1 He didn't want to take the books back to the library.
feel
He .... the books back to the library.

2 That overcoat costs too much.
afford
I .... that overcoat.

3 He hates it if he has to study on Saturday afternoons.
stand
He .... on Saturday afternoons.

4 She said she would accept my FCE registration a few days late.
agreed
She .... my FCE registration a few days late.

5 Do you think I should buy a bilingual dictionary?
suggest
Would you .... a bilingual dictionary?

6 She wouldn't lend me her notebook.
refused
She .... her notebook.

7 The burglars said they were plumbers.
pretended
The burglars .... plumbers.

8 Do you think you will pass the exam?
expect
Do you .... the exam?

9 'Why don't you do the exam again?' he said.
encouraged
He .... the exam again.

10 I haven't smoked for three years.
gave
I .... three years ago.

Vocabulary: multiple choice cloze

About the exam
Apart from adjectives and verbs that are followed by prepositions, you will be tested on your knowledge of which words to use in particular contexts.

Strategy
Check that each of the alternatives can be used in the context. For example, look at these words:

A agenda   **B** timetable   **C** programme

All of the words refer to time that is planned. But 'timetable' is the most likely alternative in a text about classes in a school, 'agenda' would be best in a text about meetings and 'programme' in a text about concerts.

Read the following text and then choose the correct alternative below for each of the numbered gaps. Remember that in the exam there will be **four** alternatives for you to choose from.

1 **A** attend   **B** assist   **C** go
2 **A** brought up   **B** educated   **C** trained
3 **A** personal   **B** private   **C** particular
4 **A** matters   **B** courses   **C** subjects
5 **A** succeed   **B** pass   **C** approve
6 **A** degree   **B** curriculum   **C** career
7 **A** pupils   **B** trainees   **C** students
8 **A** lectures   **B** conferences   **C** talks
9 **A** lectures   **B** reading   **C** training
10 **A** lecturer   **B** professor   **C** teacher

EDUCATION IN AUSTRALIA

In Australia most children (1).................... primary school from the age of five. Only two per cent of children of primary school age are (2).................... at home. Some children who go to school also take up extra activities such as learning to play a musical instrument or dancing, and they go to (3).................... classes for these and for school (4).................... they find difficult or particularly interesting, such as languages, mathematics or computing. Ninety-five per cent of the population go on to secondary school, but a much smaller percentage (5).................... the final year of secondary school examinations and complete a university (6).................... . At the moment university (7).................... and graduates make up less than a third of the total population. Australian universities are modern and well-equipped. Most teaching is by a combination of (8)...................., tutorials and practical classes. The humanities courses like History and Philosophy, usually involve a lot of extra (9).................... in the library. To become a primary or secondary school (10)...................., it is usually necessary to study at a university for three years or more.

Learner training
'False friends' are words in English that look very similar to words in other languages, but mean something different. 'Sympathetic' is an example. If you say: 'She was very sympathetic.' in English, you mean: 'She showed that she understood someone else's suffering.' In many other European languages it would mean that you thought she was a nice person. It is a good idea to make a list of 'false friends'.

Hot tip!
The incorrect alternatives are sometimes 'false friends'.

Vocabulary: education

1 Find ten words in the grid below to do with education. Then write a definition of each word.

EXAMPLE: *truant*: a student who stays away from school without permission

C	A	P	R	C	H	E	A	T	L
L	M	T	G	M	B	A	F	Z	R
A	Y	E	S	E	C	K	P	K	P
S	B	R	M	Q	W	M	A	R	K
S	O	M	T	O	T	X	S	E	L
B	H	V	D	I	R	Z	S	V	E
G	F	V	H	Q	U	I	P	I	S
C	N	A	E	D	A	Y	S	S	S
W	J	F	I	X	N	J	N	E	O
R	Y	K	O	L	T	M	Z	X	N

2 Match a word in the box below with an object in the picture.

> bookcase   calendar   lamp   stapler   pencil
> sharpener   highlighter   calculator   notebook
> waste-paper bin   paper clips

Speaking: short responses

About the exam
At the beginning of Paper 5 the interlocutor encourages you to give personal information about yourself.

Strategy
Make sure you know how to talk about:
- why you are learning English.
- subjects you study/studied at school/university.
- free time activities.
- your family.
- the area where you live.
- your plans for the future.

1 Here are some examples of candidates doing the first part of Paper 5. Who gives the best response in each case?

1

INTERLOCUTOR: So you are Daniel and Nilgün. First of all we'd like to know something about you, so I'm going to ask you some questions about yourselves. What do you like most about your school?

DANIEL: I like ... I don't know how to say it in English ... informatic? ... and sport.

INTERLOCUTOR: What do you like most, Nilgün?

NILGÜN: I like everything really. The things I find most interesting are maths and science subjects. Chemistry is my favourite.

2

NTERLOCUTOR: What will you do when you leave school, Nilgün?

NILGÜN: I don't know.

INTERLOCUTOR: What will you do, Daniel?

DANIEL: I'd like to go to university to study engineering or computer science.

2 Now roleplay this part of Paper 5 with two friends. You should each take it in turns to play the part of the examiner.

Writing: discursive

About the exam
In Paper 2, Part 2 you may be asked to write an article expressing your opinion about something.

1 Look at the following task and the answer one candidate wrote. He has made six mistakes with the language of giving opinions and agreeing and disagreeing. Find the mistakes and write the sentences out again correctly in your notebook.

An international magazine has asked you to write an article expressing your opinion about the following statement:

Co-education is a disaster for girls.

Write a short **article** for the magazine, based on your own experience.

I am not agree with the statement 'Co-education is a disaster for girls.' On my opinion co-educational schools have both advantages and disadvantages for both sexes.

It is often suggested that girls do not do as well because they are more self-conscious in the company of boys. But girls and boys will never learn to get over their shyness unless they actually have a chance to get to know people of the opposite sex.

I am agree up to a point that girls learn to be more passive in co-educational schools, but the two sexes are not normally separated in society and young women must learn to compete with men.

Another argument against co-education is that boys mature more slowly than girls and that this holds the girls back. This is truth up at a point, but surely the boys compensate for this in other ways. The sexes are different after all and as far as I am concerning these differences are a good thing.

So let's not separate boys and girls in our education system. In my point of view we are denying them important opportunities if we do so.

2 Rewrite the following letter with correct punctuation.

1 *dear mr lewis*

....

2 *my daughter helen will not be able to attend school tomorrow morning*

....

3 *she has an appointment with the dentist at nine oclock*

....

4 *dr melroses surgery is about twenty minutes from the centre of cambridge*

....

5 *it is unlikely that i can get helen to school before midday*

....

6 *i would be grateful if you would excuse her from english and mathematics classes*

....

7 *yours sincerely jane warburton*

....

3 Read the following task and then write your answer in 120–180 words. Use the language of agreeing and disagreeing from Exercise 1 and make sure you use correct punctuation.

> You have been asked to write an article for an English language newspaper aimed at parents with young children. Your article should be a response to the following statement:
>
> *Foreign languages should be taught at nursery school level.*

1 Underline key words in the instructions.

2 Make two columns: one headed FOR, the other AGAINST. Think of arguments for or in favour of the statement. Write them in the first column. Think of arguments against and write them in the second column.

3 Choose one of these two plans. (They are both good plans.)

PLAN A
- Introduction: my opinion.
- Paragraph 1: point for the statement; argument against this point.
- Paragraph 2: point for the statement; argument against this point.
- Conclusion: state opinion again.

PLAN B
- Introduction: my opinion.
- Paragraph 1: arguments in favour of the statement.
- Paragraph 2: arguments against the statement.
- Conclusion: state opinion again.

4 Write your article.

5 Check carefully for mistakes with verb forms.

Strategy

If you cannot think of arguments for *and* against, imagine what people you actually know would think about the question. What would your mother think? How about your best friend? And your grandparents?

47

Reading: multiple matching

Strategy
Find the sentence that expresses the main idea in each paragraph. The headings you choose from will also express the main idea.

Read the following article and choose a heading from the list below for each paragraph. The first one has been done for you. There is one extra heading which you do not need to use.

A A very powerful mechanism.
B Two ways of remembering.
C Why we forget our earliest memories.
D Short term and long term memory.
E Healthy body; healthy mind.
F An old approach but a good one.
G Are you forgetful?

Learner training
Label real objects in your room or house with small pieces of paper with the English words written on them. You can learn other words in this way as well. For example, if you want to learn all the words for school subjects, stick pieces of paper with these words on objects in your room. Try to associate the word with the object. When you want to remember the words, imagine yourself walking round the room and seeing the various objects with the labels.

How to boost your memory

(1 _G_)
Perhaps you do badly in exams because you can't recall facts and figures or words and structures in a foreign language. Are you always losing things or forgetting the books you need for school that day? Or do you forget what Mum wanted you to get at the corner shop? Relax! Help is close at hand. There's a tremendous range of methods to boost your memory.

(2___)
Your memory is like a brilliant, but unreliable computer storing a vast amount of information. In fact the memory's capacity is theoretically unlimited. The brain can record more than 86 billion bits of information every day and our memories can probably hold 100 trillion bits in a lifetime.

(3___)
Nevertheless only about 20 per cent of our daily experience is registered, and of that only a tiny proportion is loaded into long term memory. Most of the images and ideas that pass through our minds during a day are held for only 25 to 30 seconds. This is just long enough for us to be able to keep the words of a sentence in our head as we read it so we understand its meaning.

(4___)
We also remember different things in two different ways: declarative and non-declarative. Declarative memory deals with concrete things, specific events and facts such as what we have been doing and our recall of things that have happened. Non-declarative memory includes knowledge of general things, how to ride a bicycle, how to behave and so on. Someone with amnesia will almost always remember how to ride a bike, but may well forget her own name. One sad victim of this type of amnesia announces every ten minutes that he has 'just woken up'. Every time his wife walks into the room he throws his arms around her as if he has not seen her for years, even though she has only been gone for a few minutes. Yet this man, formerly a highly-talented musician, is still able to play the piano and conduct a choir through a long and complicated concert piece.

(5___)
Normal, healthy people can improve their memories very easily. First of all learn to relax if you're trying to memorise something. You may miss important items if your mind is on something else or if you weren't paying attention because of anxiety – you retain information best when you are alert and concentrating. If you're having trouble concentrating, increase the flow of oxygenated blood to the brain. Despite its small size the brain uses 20 per cent of the body's oxygen requirement. So try to combine study with exercise, particularly the kind of exercise that gets you breathing faster. Keep your mind fit as well as your body by doing mental workouts. Crosswords, Scrabble and quizzes all help to keep the mind in shape.

(6___)
You can also train your memory in certain ways. The ancient Greeks invented memory systems called mnemonics, and they still work today. Most systems involve associating the things you want to remember with something you already have safely stored in your head, and the most effective systems make use of visual imagery, smell, touch and sound. If you want to remember someone's name, try to find something distinctive about their hair, nose or eyes to associate with the name, e.g. Jane's wearing jewellery, Tim's tall or Bill's got a beard. If you want to remember numbers try to make associations between numbers in sequence – think of people's ages, special dates, whether they're odd or even.

from *Best* magazine

7 The price of fame

Grammar: error correction

Paper 3, Part 4

> **Strategy**
> As you read the text, 'say' the words in your mind.

Read the following text and look carefully at each line. Some of the lines are correct and some have an extra incorrect word that should not be there. If a line is correct, put a tick (✔) next to it. If a line has a word that should not be there, circle the word and write it at the end of the line. There are two examples at the beginning (**0** and **00**).

	Stagefright	
0	Even the most experienced performers suffer from	✔
00	(the) stagefright. Sometimes this can be so extreme	*the*
1	that it almost completely paralyses the person concerned.	
2	They stand in the wings, their heart beating at a rate of	
3	130 or 135 for a minute and often seriously think about	
4	not going on. Some even they find it impossible to remember	
5	the performance at all after it is over. Others genuinely believe	
6	they have completely forgotten all their lines or one of in	
7	particular. Most have feel ill. They sweat and shiver and their	
8	stomachs are make strange noises. Considering the	
9	agonies that even such as well-known actors as Dustin	
10	Hoffman or Robert de Niro go through, it is surprising	
11	that less experienced performers ever have the courage to walk	
12	on stage at all. So next time that you are feeling nervous before a	
13	job interview or an oral examination, remember you are in	
14	good company. The world's top performers know exactly how do	
15	you feel. They should. They often feel a lot worse.	

🎧 Listening: selecting

Paper 4, Part 4

> **About the exam**
> In Paper 4 you may hear different accents such as Australian and Scottish accents as well as speakers whose first language is not English.

> **Strategy**
> You will hear the cassette twice. Before you listen underline key words in the questions. Listen for mention of these key words the first time you hear the cassette.

Listen to an interview with Alex Dimitriades, the star of an Australian TV series, and mark the following statements **T** (true) or **F** (false).

1 Alex found it easy to get used to being famous. ....

2 Alex has been in several plays. ....

3 Alex wants to get a part in another film. ....

4 Alex hasn't seen all of Robert de Niro's films. ....

5 The interviewer asks Alex a lot of questions about his private life. ....

6 The interviewer is interested in how he feels about being famous. ....

> **Learner training**
> If you have a short wave radio, you can listen to broadcasts in English from all over the world. This will help you get used to the different accents you may hear in Papers 4 and 5.

Vocabulary: entertainment

Look at the following sentences and decide if the people are talking about theatre, music, film, painting or sculpture. Mark the sentences **T** (theatre), **M** (music), **F** (film), **P** (painting) or **S** (sculpture). In some of the sentences more than one category is possible.

1　My audition went really well and I got the part. ....

2　The lead singer also plays guitar. ....

3　His first exhibition opens next week. ....

4　I don't know who composed it, but it's my favourite piece. ....

5　We could only get tickets in the front row so we were much too close to the screen. ....

6　One of the critics said the director should have stuck to acting. ....

7　It had such a sad ending that almost everyone in the audience was crying. ....

8　Are there any well-known heavy metal groups in your country? ....

9　He almost forgot his lines in the performance we saw. ....

10　I thought that young woman conductor was really brilliant. ....

11　He did all the statues in the park. ....

12　The audience went on applauding even after the last curtain call. ....

13　The photography was wonderful, but I didn't think much of the plot. ....

14　Have you heard their latest album? ....

15　They're very modern and the colours are amazing. ....

Vocabulary and grammar: open cloze

Paper 3, Part 2

Strategy
Read the text all the way through and make sure you know what it is about before you begin to answer.

1 Read the following text and answer these questions.

1　Is it about a play or a film? ....

2　How many lines of the text do you have to read before you can be certain? ....

When we got to the booking office, there were very (1).................... tickets left so we couldn't sit (2).................... . George sat in the front (3).................... because he likes to be near the (4).................... and I sat towards the back of the (5).................... .

As soon as it started, I knew I wasn't (6).................... to like it. I really can't (7).................... that kind of thing. Something like ten people were killed in the first ten minutes, and the director (8).................... made sure that he didn't miss a single detail. There was one (9).................... that made me feel quite sick. I don't think they should be allowed to show (10).................... violent films. I'm sure they have a bad effect on people.

I suppose the only good thing about it was the actor who played the (11).................... of the gangster. He was really brilliant. The soundtrack was good, too. There were songs by all the best known (12).................... from the sixties, like the Beatles and the Rolling Stones. I might try and buy the CD when it (13).................... out.

I got the impression the rest of the (14).................... didn't enjoy it much either. It just goes to show you (15).................... never trust what you read in reviews in the press. The critics have such strange taste in films.

2 Now read the text again and fill in the gaps with an appropriate word.

Grammar: Present Perfect

1 Fill in the gaps in the following dialogues with the correct Past Simple, Present Perfect Simple or Present Perfect Continuous form of the verbs in brackets.

A

A: (1)............................. *(see)* the latest Arnold Schwarzenegger film?

B: Yes. I (2)............................. *(see)* it last weekend.

A: What (3)............................. *(think)* of it?

B: I (4)............................. *(like)* it, but I (5)............................. *(think)* it (6)............................. *(be)* a bit violent.

B

A: (7)............................. *(hurt)* your hand? It's all red and swollen.

B: Yes. I (8)............................. *(hit)* it with a hammer this morning. I (9)............................. *(go)* to carpentry classes for the last couple of weeks.

A: (10)............................. *(make)* any furniture yet?

B: Yes, I (11) .... *(make)* a small coffee table for my wife last week. It was her birthday present.

C

A: I (12)............................. *(not/see)* Alex for weeks. (13)............................. *(go)* away somewhere?

B: No. I think he (14)............................. *(study)* for an exam and so he (15)............................. *(not/go)* out very much lately. Hey! (16)............................. *(pass)* your driving test last week?

A: No. I (17)............................. *(fail)* and that's the third time I (18)............................. *(take)* the test!

2 The following sentences were all written by English children. They contain mistakes with the Past Simple and past participle forms of irregular verbs. Find the mistakes and write the sentences out again correctly in your notebook.

1 Our dog has bited me three times.

2 The wind has blowed down all the trees in our street.

3 My daddy builded our house himself.

4 When I throwed the ball yesterday, our dog catched it.

5 My mum and dad buyed me a bicycle.

6 I've falled over at school twice this week.

7 I finded 50p on my way home today.

8 I I spended all my pocket money on sweets.

9 I've writed a story about a boy and a cat.

10 My granny sended me a dolly for my birthday.

Writing: report

About the exam
In Paper 2, Part 2 you may be asked to write a report on a place you have visited and what it offers a particular group of people.

1 Look at the following task and the answers two candidates wrote which the examiner has already marked.

You work in a language school helping to organise excursions and trips for students. The school director has asked you to prepare a report on a museum in your area.

Write your **report** in 120–180 words describing the museum and what it has to offer students of English as a foreign language. Mention both good and bad points in your report.

Candidate A

Last week my classmates and I went on (a) excursion to the Toy Museum in London. We (have left) the school at 10 o'clock and reached (to) the museum at 11, so we (have had) plenty of time to look around.

The section I liked (more) was the dolls. There were dolls from all over the world in national dress. There was even one from my country. There were also beautiful dolls from the last century.

(On the other hand,) Andres and Mehmet really liked the model railway. Jorge and Hiroshi spent most of the time looking at the tin soldiers. We all really loved the collection of teddy bears.

We had lunch in a cafe and travelled back to school by double-decker bus. It was a very nice trip. After I thought that children all over the world are really the same.

Candidate B

Report on the Science Museum
To: School Director
From: Excursions officer
Date of visit: 12 April

(I have visited) the Science Museum last week to decide if (it will) be good for students from the school to see. I will make comments on the following: price, interest, language.

1. Price
           an
It costs £5 for/entrance ticket to the museum. This is ~~much~~ too expensive for most students. There is a special price on Wednesday mornings (£2.50), but most students are in class at this time. However, the museum is very interesting (see next section) so this makes it worth/

2. Interest
There are many exhibits and displays, although the section on astronomy was closed for (reforms). Most people will find something that interests them. I liked (especially) the section on the human body.

3. Language
All of the exhibits have short texts in English ~~expla~~ (explicating) what is shown. Some exhibits had tapes you could listen/. These were a bit difficult sometimes. In spite of this I think many students could ~~improving~~ improve their English listening to these tapes.

Conclusion: I think levels 4 and 5 should visit this museum. The teachers should prepare some activities to do while we are there.

2 Now read the examiner's comments below. Which comments apply to Candidate A and which to Candidate B?

```
1  Comments: Candidate .............

Grade: Good

The task of writing a report has been
done well, with a clear layout and
careful attention to the instructions.

There are some errors of tense and
vocabulary, but the candidate uses
linking words very well.

Although the report contains more than
the minimum number of words, the
candidate could have used a wider range
of vocabulary.


2  Comments: Candidate .............

Grade: Unsatisfactory

There are some good structures and
vocabulary, but there is no attempt to
write a report or to cover any of the
specific points in the instructions.

There is one example of a linking
expression used incorrectly and there
are also two mistakes with verb tenses.
```

3 Look at the two candidates' answers again. The examiner has marked a number of mistakes in orange. Write the sentences with mistakes out again correctly in your notebook.

4 Join the phrases and sentences in Column A with those in Column B using an appropriate linking word/phrase from the following list. Write the complete sentences in your notebook. You will need to use some of the linking words/phrases more than once. Be careful of punctuation.

- despite/in spite of
- although/even though
- However
- but
- On the other hand

Column A

1 Our visit to the museum was enjoyable
2 We managed to see the exhibits on new technologies
3 Most students thought the museum was interesting.
4 Several students bought copies of the guide
5 We found it a bit difficult to understand all the recorded information with some exhibits
6 Visits to museums can be a bit boring sometimes.

Column B

a) the fact that they cost £15.00.
b) some of that section of the museum was closed.
c) they are an excellent way to learn about the world and to practise our English.
d) the high entrance fee and the crowds.
e) our teachers had taught us a lot of the vocabulary.
f) some of us felt that there wasn't enough information about the exhibits.

5 Now write a report in 120–180 words in answer to the task in Exercise 1.

1 Think of good and bad points about the museum, especially in relation to students of English.
2 Join the good and bad points using the linking expressions listed in Exercise 4.
3 Organise your sentences into numbered paragraphs.
4 Write your report following the layout in Candidate B's answer.
5 Check your answer carefully for mistakes with verb tenses.

Strategy
Use numbered points in reports. It is much easier to plan and write like this.

Reading: multiple choice

About the exam
In this part of Paper 1 you may be asked questions about the relationship between words in the text.

Strategy
Apart from words like pronouns (e.g. *it, them*) and demonstratives (e.g. *this, that*), nouns and verbs can refer back or forward to other words in the text. For example:

> Making the **wax models** is a highly skilled and lengthy process. From start to finish it takes months of work for the artists and craftsmen who combine to produce the final **figure**. All the **waxworks** are life-size **replicas** of the real person, down to the last detail.

The words 'wax models', 'figure', 'waxworks' and 'replicas' all refer to the same thing. Look for networks of related words like this. This will help you understand the text.

1 Read the following text about guitars and decide which one of the following subjects is **not** referred to.

A companies that make guitars
B materials guitars are made of
C the role of technology
D other musical instruments

2 Answer the following questions about the article.

1 The writer uses the word 'guitar' sixteen times in this text. What two other words does he use instead of 'guitar'?

....

2 In paragraph 1 the writer uses the phrase 'pop stars' to refer to people who play guitars. What word/words does he use before that to refer to pop stars?

....

3 Paragraphs 4 and 5 are about materials used to make guitars. What materials are mentioned?

a) ....
b) ....
c) ....
d) ....
e) ....
f) ....

Guitar Legends

1 Whether it's the melodic sound of an Eric Clapton solo or the growl of a heavy metal band, the electric guitar has influenced popular music and culture more than any other instrument. Rock's greatest musicians have always been closely identified with their guitars. But the instruments being designed for tomorrow's pop
10 stars may look and sound rather different from today's familiar electric and acoustic guitars.

It is only sixty years since the electric guitar was invented. Since then there have been incredible changes to the technical design of the instrument. From what was once a rounded wooden box with a hole in the front, the guitar has evolved into
20 the smooth solid body of the rock guitarist's 'axe'. The most modern guitars are really computer-controlled synthesisers.

Adolph Rickenbacker's Electro String Company produced the world's first electric guitar. It was made of wood and played on the user's lap. The first real breakthrough in design came in 1950 when Leo Fender, a
30 Californian radio repairman, made the first solid-bodied electric guitar, the Fender Telecaster. Soon after the inventor Les Paul made the famous Gibson Les Paul. Fender launched its stylish Stratocaster two years later. These guitars became standard instruments against which newer guitar designs are measured.

All sorts of different materials have
40 been used to make guitars. Acoustic guitars are made from wood, which gives a soft tone. Wood is also a popular material in electric guitar manufacture, but more modern materials such as glass and carbon fibre are also used. There have also been guitars with metal bodies and necks though these were never popular with players, who claim metal
50 feels cold in the hand.

Plastics, on the other hand, have been more used in guitar bodies. A company that makes parts for the aerospace industry has begun to use a kind of fibreglass that was originally used in helicopter blades to make the bodies for its electric-acoustic instruments. Other makers have begun to experiment with graphite, a
60 material that is ten times stiffer than wood but much lighter. It doesn't expand or contract as the temperature or humidity changes either. This makes it particularly suitable for guitar necks and for tennis rackets, for which it is also used.

As long as scientists and musicians work together
70 harmoniously, the electric guitar will continue to benefit from technological innovations. But for all the efforts of the guitar companies' design engineers, production managers and quality controllers, it's the musicians who finally make the instruments sing – and not necessarily in the way the guitar maker intended.

from *Focus* magazine

3 Choose the correct alternative to answer the following questions.

1 What is likely to change in the future?

   A the influence of the guitar on popular culture
   B styles of guitar music
   C the guitars themselves
   D how musicians feel about their guitars

2 The first electric guitar was

   A computer-controlled.
   B played sitting down.
   C not hollow inside.
   D designed by Leo Fender.

3 The guitars that were designed in the fifties

   A were unsuccessful.
   B are often compared to guitars designed today.
   C were made of wood.
   D were played sitting down.

4 Which material was disliked by musicians?

   A metal
   B wood
   C plastic
   D carbon fibre

5 Why is graphite a good material for guitar necks?

   A It has been used for tennis rackets.
   B It is heavier than wood.
   C It is more flexible than wood.
   D It is not affected by atmospheric conditions.

6 Recent technological innovations

   A have not really improved the electric guitar.
   B have been ignored by musicians.
   C cannot determine the way the guitar will be played.
   D are not what musicians hoped for.

Speaking: opinion exchange

Paper 5, Part 4

About the exam
In the last part of Paper 5 the examiner will ask your opinion about something.

Strategy
Make sure you know how to:
● ask someone else what their opinion is.
● express your opinion.
● agree/disagree politely with someone else's opinion.
● ask for/give advice.

1 Listen to two candidates doing Paper 5, Part 4 and fill in the gaps in the following extracts.

1 .... it depends on the instrument.

2 .... if you only want to enjoy playing, ... if you want to have a good time, you can start to learn when you are quite old and it doesn't matter.

3 Well, ... a good teacher ... like me. .... a clarinet at the beginning. .... to see if you like it. .... every day.

4 Well, ... a small drum kit and practise while you listen to albums by your favourite groups. When you are a little bit better, ... a group. Oh, and .... to lots of rock concerts and watch the drummers. That's the best way to learn.

2 In which extract or extracts is the candidate:

a) giving advice.   ....

b) giving an opinion.   ....

c) disagreeing politely.   ....

3 Listen to the following sentences/phrases on the cassette and mark the word on which the main stress falls. Then practise saying the sentences yourself.

EXAMPLE: I don't really agree.

1 As far as I'm concerned ...
2 I completely agree.
3 That's right.
4 From my point of view ...
5 I couldn't agree more.

8 Looking good

Listening: multiple matching

Paper 4, Part 3

About the exam
You may hear other sounds such as traffic noise, noise from machinery or people talking in the background on the recording. This is to make it more realistic. There are no sounds once the actors start speaking.

1 You are going to hear five women talking about clothes. Listen and match each extract to a situation below where it is taking place. There is one extra situation which you do not need to use. Write the number of the appropriate extract in the gaps.

A outside   ....
B in a shop   ....
C at home   ....
D in an airport   ....
E at college   ....
F at a party   ....

2 Now listen to the extracts again and match them to the following statements. There is one extra statement which you do not need to use. Write the number of the appropriate extract in the gaps.

A She thinks it looks silly.   ....

B She doesn't want to leave the house.   ....

C She thought about what he would need.   ....

D She didn't know what caused the problem.   ....

E Her mother hadn't seen the clothes before. ....

F She is very pleased with them.   ....

Vocabulary: clothes

1 Write words for the following items of clothing.

2 Read the following descriptions of the models in the pictures below. There are two mistakes of meaning in each sentence. Find the mistakes and write the descriptions out again correctly in your notebooks.

1 Claudia is wearing a high-heeled evening dress and long shoes.

2 Nick is wearing checked trousers and a grey skirt.

3 Paul is wearing a striped blouse, jeans and wellington boots.

4 Kate is wearing a spotted dress and striped tights.

5 Tim is wearing a scarf and dungarees with a plain, leather bow-tie.

3 Mark where the main stress falls in the following words:

EXAMPLE: 'cardigan

1 sandals   6 sweatshirt

2 pullover   7 raincoat

3 bracelet   8 earrings

4 pyjamas   9 waistcoat

5 dungarees   10 T-shirt

Grammar: *used to/would*

1 Match the first parts of the sentences in Column A with the second parts in Column B. Write the appropriate letter in the gaps.

Column A		**Column B**
1 Did you	....	a) to getting up so early.
2 Are you	....	b) walk along the river holding hands.
3 They used	....	
4 We would	....	c) use to smoke?
5 I'm not used	....	d) to live near here.
6 We didn't	....	e) getting used to the food?
		f) use to watch so much TV.

2 In which of the following sentences can you use both *would* and *used to*? Mark them with a tick (✔). In which sentences is there only one possibility? Cross out the one you cannot use.

1 When I was younger, we *used to/would* go into town on Saturday night.

2 We *would/used to* spend most of Saturday afternoon getting ready.

3 My friend Diana *would/used to* live only a few minutes walk from my house.

4 She *used to/would* come over to my house after lunch.

5 We *used to/would* wash our hair and decide what to wear.

6 We *used to/would* think we looked really glamorous in our flared trousers, platform shoes and little tops.

7 My older brother *would/used to* give us a lift into town and arrange to pick us up later.

3 Complete the following sentences in your own words.

1 When I was younger, I used to ....

....

2 My friends and I would ....

....

3 One thing I don't think older people will ever get used to is ....

....

57

Writing: description

Paper 2, Part 2

About the exam
You may be asked to write a description of a person in Paper 2, Part 2.

1 Read the following task and the answers that two students wrote. Which one is more interesting, Description A or Description B?

Write a description of your favourite relative.

Description A

My favourite relative is my grandfather.

The first thing you notice about him is his huge moustache. He has had it since he was eighteen and takes very good care of it. Then you notice his eyes. They are very dark, almost black, but sparkling and lively.

He was very tall when he was younger and he's still quite tall even at eighty-five. He walks with a stick that he has had for years now and he always wears an old black cap when he goes out. My grandmother bought him a new one last year, but he won't wear it.

But the most characteristic thing about my grandfather is his voice. He has the most wonderful deep voice. You appreciate this most when he laughs his big booming laugh. He laughs a lot and always has a funny story or a joke to tell to cheer you up.

Description B

My favourite relative is my Aunt Lucy.

She is my mother's older sister. She is forty years old, but she looks younger than that. She has dark hair and is slim with green eyes. She wears glasses.

She likes fashionable clothes. Her favourite colours are green and blue. She has a nice green jacket that she wears. It suits her. She does not wear very much jewellery apart from a silver ring.

She has a nice voice. She sings in a folk group in the town where she lives. She is a teacher at a high school there and her students like her.

I think she is a very good person.

2 Read the following comments a teacher wrote on Description B. Then write a description of a relative following the teacher's advice and using the outline on page 59.

Your description is very accurate, but you need to make your writing more interesting.

For example, you say your aunt 'looks younger'. How much younger? A bit? A lot? Years? You tell me she 'has 'dark hair', but you don't say whether it is curly or straight, thick or shiny. Is it long or short? And what else can you say about her eyes? Are they soft and gentle or bright and sparkling? Are they more or less striking because of her glasses?

You talk about the jacket she wears and tell me that it's green. What else can you say about it? Is it new? What is it made of? Why does it suit her? And what about the ring? Why does she always wear it? Because it was a gift?

You comment on her voice, good, but don't use 'nice'. Is it deep or soft and gentle?

And finally why do her students like her? What do they say about her?

Outline

I suppose the first thing anyone notices about my ... is her/his ... . S/he's got ... and ... . S/he's not very ..., but ... .

What I like most about her/him is the way s/he ... . Once you get to know her/him better you realise s/he ... .

S/he always wears ... . S/he's also got ... .

But the most distinctive thing about her/him is ... . S/he is ... . I suppose that's why s/he is my favourite relative.

3 Now write a description of another person you like and admire in 120–180 words.

1 Decide which person to write about.

2 Think about this person's
   - physical features (hair, beard/moustache, nose, eyes, mouth, hands).
   - general build.
   - unusual habits and/or hobbies.
   - favourite items of clothing.
   - voice or laugh.

3 Write a plan including the points you thought of.

4 Write your description.

5 As always, check your work carefully.

┌ **Hot tip!** ◀ ─ ─ ─ ─ ─ ─ ─ ─ ┐
DON'T just write a list of details about the person you are describing! Think of general characteristics and how they relate to the person's character.
└ ─ ─ ─ ─ ─ ─ ─ ─ ─ ─ ─ ─ ─ ─ ─ ┘

4 Write a description of a famous person but do not say who it is. When you have finished show it to another student and see if s/he can guess who it is.

Vocabulary and grammar:
open cloze

▸ **Paper 3, Part 2**

About the exam
Paper 3, Part 2 tests your knowledge of grammar and vocabulary. Sometimes there is more than one possible word for vocabulary gaps.

Strategy
If more than one word seems possible, choose the one which fits the context best.

For example:

We have to .... for the play we're putting on.

In this sentence *practise* and *rehearse* would both be possible, but *rehearse* is specific to the context of theatre and plays.

Two different students have completed the following sentences from gap fill exercises. Circle the best answer in each case.

1 When we got to the cinema there were very few tickets left so we couldn't sit ***down*/*together***.

2 The common cold has been called the single most expensive ***illness*/*problem*** in the world.

3 Runners suffer more injuries than many other ***people*/*athletes***.

4 All kinds of ***things*/*materials*** have been used to make guitars: wood, fibre glass, plastic and metal.

5 He is very secretive. He never tells anyone ***anything*/*everything*** about his personal life.

6 She was wearing sandals ***although*/*because*** it was cold and wet outside.

7 He decided to ***be*/*become*** a professional football player and gave up his job at the bank.

8 Do you like to wear a particular ***brand*/*kind*** of trainers such as Nike or Reeboks?

┌ **Hot tip!** ◀ ─ ─ ─ ─ ─ ─ ─ ─ ┐
Even if you can't think of a word that fits the context exactly, use a general word that is the right part of speech. You may get some marks for this. If you leave a gap unfilled, you get no marks.
└ ─ ─ ─ ─ ─ ─ ─ ─ ─ ─ ─ ─ ─ ─ ─ ┘

Reading: gapped text

Paper 1, Part 3

About the exam
In this part of Paper 1 you decide where to put sentences or paragraphs that have been removed from the text.

Strategy
The sentences that have been removed often express the main idea of the paragraph. As you read, write down what the main idea of each paragraph is.

1 Read the following article about the invention of the safety razor, answering the questions at the end of each paragraph as you read.

A Hairy Problem Solved

(1___) Cave drawings show that the earliest razors were sharks' teeth and clam shells. Sharpened flint was used where it could be found. The Egyptians 6000 years ago made razors from solid gold. By the eighteenth century they had developed into elaborate steel devices. Nevertheless one painful problem remained: men continued to cut themselves.

1 Is this paragraph mainly about
   A the history of the razor?
   B expensive materials used for razors?

In 1762, a Frenchman named Jean-Jacques Perret found a way of protecting the shaver's skin by attaching a safety guard to the steel blade. Perret even wrote a book about shaving called *Pogotonomy or the Art of Learning to Shave*. (2___) As a result, millions of male chins still suffered the consequences daily.

2 Is the main idea that Perret
   A invented a safe way of shaving?
   B wrote a book about shaving?

One such chin belonged to King Camp Gillette, a travelling salesman from Wisconsin, in the United States. One of Gillette's bosses was William Painter, the inventor of the disposable bottle-cap. Painter told Gillette that he would become rich if only he invented 'something which will be used once and thrown away'. (3___)

3 Is the main idea that
   A Gillette got some useful advice?
   B Gillette had a boss called Painter?

The answer came to Gillette in front of his shaving mirror in 1895. (4___) Why not substitute a thin steel blade that could be held in a clamp and thrown away? 'I stood before the mirror in a trance of joy,' he wrote to his wife. 'Our future is made.'

4 Is the main idea that
   A Gillette suddenly had an idea?
   B he wrote to his wife?

(5___) Finally things began to change when he met William Nickerson. Together they formed the American Safety Razor Company. They took out a patent in Boston in 1901. In 1903 they sold just 51 razors and 168 blades. They persevered and by the end of 1904 they had parted with 90,000 razors and 124,000,000 blades.

5 Is the main idea that
   A Gillette formed the company with someone else?
   B the razor was not immediately successful?

2 The following sentences have been removed from the text. Decide in which numbered gap each sentence should go and write in the appropriate letter. Be careful! There is one extra sentence that you do not need to use.

A He realised that only the straight edge of his old-fashioned razor was doing any work.

B However, his invention remained relatively unknown.

C The customer would have to come back and buy another.

D Men have always searched for the perfect close shave.

E Gillette realized he needed to work with someone else.

F But for six years, Gillette failed to convince people.

Word formation

> ### Strategy
> Check your spelling. In the word you form, you may need to:
> - decide if you need to double a consonant.
> - decide if you need to drop an 'e'.
> - decide if the word ends in -ence or -ance.
> - decide if the word ends in -sion or -tion.
> - decide if the word ends in -able or -ible.

1 Fill in the gaps in the following sentences with the correct form of the word in capitals. Use your dictionary if you are uncertain about spelling.

1 We have all got used to .... products such as razors and nappies. (DISPOSE)

2 The telephone is a wonderful .... (INVENT)

3 The .... of the safety razor revolutionised shaving. (PRODUCE)

4 Attacks on young people wearing expensive clothing are a common .... (OCCUR)

5 Nevertheless many young people show a marked .... for particular labels. (PREFER)

6 We visited Stratford-on-Avon and saw a .... of Shakespeare's Romeo and Juliet. (PERFORM)

7 In the .... of her composition she said she did not think co-education was a good idea. (CONCLUDE)

8 When she was offered the part in the film, she accepted without a moment's .... (HESITATE)

> ### Learner training
> Use your dictionary to check spelling and word stress as well as meaning.

2 Mark where the main stress falls in each of the words you formed above.

EXAMPLE: di'sposable

Speaking: problem solving

> ### About the exam
> In Paper 5, Part 3 the examiner may ask you and the other candidate to find a solution to a problem. This is so that he or she can hear you both speak spontaneously.

> ### Hot tip!
> There is no 'right' or 'wrong' solution, so don't worry if the examiner stops you before you have solved the problem.

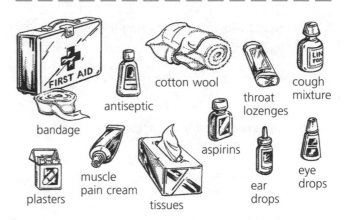

cotton wool

cough mixture

throat lozenges

antiseptic

bandage

aspirins

muscle pain cream

plasters

tissues

ear drops

eye drops

Listen to an examiner giving two candidates instructions for Part 3 of Paper 5 and look at the pictures. Then decide if the following statements are true or false. Mark them **T** (true) or **F** (false).

1 They have to put the items in order of importance. ....

2 They have to choose a limited number of items. ....

3 They can add other items that are not in the picture. ....

4 They should each decide on their own answer. ....

> ### Strategy
> If you do not understand what you are supposed to do, ask the examiner to explain again. Say: 'I'm sorry. Could you repeat that?' or 'Could you explain again? I'm not sure what we have to do.' You may lose marks if you do not do what the examiner has asked you to do.

Grammar: *can/could/may/might*

1 Rewrite the following sentences using *can,
could, may* or *might*.

1 It is possible that he is Italian.

....

2 Do you know how to play the piano?

....

3 You are not allowed to speak during the exam.

....

4 It is not possible that they are still on holiday.

....

5 You are not allowed to smoke on the plane.

....

6 It is possible that it will be a nice day tomorrow.

....

7 He didn't know how to spell 'conscious'.

....

8 Am I allowed to leave the room?

....

2 There are mistakes in all of the following
sentences. Find the mistakes and write the sentences
out again correctly in your notebooks.

1 That mustn't be the postman. He never comes this
early.

2 I might not to come to class on Wednesday. I've
got to go to the dentist.

3 Could you riding a bicycle when you were seven?

4 You couldn't borrow my new blouse. I want to
wear it myself.

5 I don't think we should buy him a shirt. He could
not like the colour.

6 You ought to take a raincoat. It might rained.

Grammar: key word transformations

> **Paper 3, Part 3**

Strategy
In Paper 3, Part 3 there are often questions testing:

a) *-ing/-ed* adjectives. d) comparatives.
b) structures with *like*. e) reported speech.
c) gerunds and infinitives. f) modal verbs.

Try to recognise what the question is testing.

Decide which of the above the following items test.
Write the appropriate letter a) – f) in the box. Then
complete the second sentence so that it has a similar
meaning to the first sentence using the word in **bold**
and other words.

1 I will not lend you my jacket.
   refuse
   I .... my jacket. ☐

2 Claudia isn't as thin as Kate.
   than
   Kate is .... Claudia. ☐

3 Psychology interests me.
   am
   I .... psychology. ☐

4 I want a cup of coffee.
   would
   I .... a cup of coffee. ☐

5 'Do you enjoy football?', she asked him.
   if
   She asked.................................... football. ☐

6 He hates travelling by bus.
   stand
   He .... by bus. ☐

7 My advice is to buy a computer.
   ought
   You .... a computer. ☐

8 Tom is a faster worker than Mike.
   works
   Tom .... Mike. ☐

9 You can't smoke here.
   allowed
   You .... here. ☐

9 Too much of a good thing

Vocabulary: multiple choice cloze

Paper 3, Part 1

About the exam
In this part of Paper 3 you are tested mainly on your knowledge of vocabulary.

Learner training
Instructions for machines are often in English. Practise reading the instructions as you use the machine.

Read the following text and choose the correct alternative to fill each gap.

1 **A** dish **B** meal **C** food **D** plate
2 **A** depending **B** relying **C** according **D** corresponding
3 **A** receipt **B** menu **C** prescription **D** recipe
4 **A** made **B** served **C** cooked **D** prepared
5 **A** peeled **B** skinned **C** grated **D** cracked
6 **A** butter **B** salt **C** peas **D** eggs
7 **A** frying **B** roasting **C** cooking **D** boiling
8 **A** boil **B** roast **C** fry **D** scramble
9 **A** ladle **B** knife **C** saucepan **D** spatula
10 **A** stir **B** mix **C** sprinkle **D** whisk
11 **A** saucepan **B** plate **C** bowl **D** dish
12 **A** drop **B** pour **C** put **D** mix
13 **A** course **B** bowl **C** plate **D** pan
14 **A** heat **B** hot **C** heating **D** warmth
15 **A** hard **B** stiff **C** rigid **D** crisp

Spanish Omelette

The traditional Spanish omelette is a full (1).............. in itself. Each Spanish family produces its own individual version of it (2).............. to the season and the availability of vegetables. The following (3).............., however, is the most familiar, often also containing strips of red and green peppers. It can be (4).............. hot or at room temperature.

450 g potatoes, (5).............., washed and finely sliced
Salt
150 ml vegetable oil
1 large onion, peeled and finely chopped
6 eggs
4–5 tablespoons olive oil

Sprinkle the potatoes with (6).............. . In a large (7).............. pan, heat the vegetable oil. Add the potatoes and onions and (8).............. them over a medium heat for 15 minutes, turning them occasionally until they are properly cooked and soft. Remove from the pan with a (9).............. and drain off most of the excess oil.

(10).............. the eggs in a (11).............. with a little salt, add the potato mixture and mix well. In a smaller non-stick frying pan, heat the olive oil and (12).............. in the egg mixture, rotating the pan in order to spread it evenly. Cook over a medium heat until it starts to solidify, then turn down the heat. While cooking, shape the omelette into a round, pressing the edges away from the sides of the frying pan.

Place a large (13).............. over the pan and quickly invert the omelette on to it. Slide the omelette back into the frying pan and return it to the (14).............. for a further 5–6 minutes, shaping it into a neat circle. Serve with a (15).............. green salad.

Grammar: countables / uncountables

Circle the one alternative in the following sentences which is **not** possible.

1 Would you like *some/a little/a few* more chicken?

2 Can I have another *piece/lump/bit* of that delicious chocolate?

3 I had *some/a bit of/a* good news the other day.

4 I tried on *a/some/a pair of* jeans, but they didn't suit me.

5 I don't usually have *much/many/a great deal of* spare time during the week.

6 She gave me *some/a piece of/many* good advice about the exam.

7 *Many/Few/Much* local people came to the meeting.

8 Why not come and stay with us for *a couple of/a pair of/a few* days?

9 Would you like *another/some/more* toast?

10 *The/Some/A* police arrived straight away.

11 We usually have *a lot of/a/some* very nice weather at this time of year.

12 How many *lumps/teaspoons/slices* of sugar do you usually have in your coffee?

13 Could you give me another *piece/sheet/slice* of paper, please?

14 You haven't brought *much/many/a lot of* luggage with you.

15 I would like *some/a bit of/a few* information about your courses.

▣ Listening: note taking

Paper 4, Part 2

About the exam
You hear each recording twice. There is a pause before you hear the recording for the second time and another pause before the next recording begins.

Strategy
Make good use of your time during the test.
- The first time you listen, answer as many questions as you can. Write in note form (e.g. *Mon* for *Monday*) and don't worry about spelling.
- Check your answers, especially spelling, in the first pause.
- When you hear the cassette the second time, listen for the information you need to answer the other questions.
- Check your answers to these questions during the second pause.
- You have five minutes before the end of the test to transfer your answers from the question paper to the answer sheet. Check your answers again.

◄ **Hot tip!** ◄
DON'T answer on the answer sheet while you are listening to the recordings!

Listen to a doctor talking about foods and how they affect our moods and complete the following notes.

Typical summer foods: (1).................................
Effect: *good mood*
Contain chemicals such as:

Serotonin
Effect: Makes you feel (2).................................
Found in (3)........................., ginger and
(4).................................
Best source: spinach

Folic Acid
Deficiency causes (5).........................,
sleeplessness, forgetfulness, irritability

Selenium
Deficiency causes (6).................................
Found in (7)........................., sunflower seeds,
oysters, cereals, grapes and (8).................................

DMAE
Found in: anchovies and sardines
Effect: Improves (9)......................... and
ability to (10).................................

Speaking: planning

About the exam
In Paper 5, Part 3 you may be asked to plan something, for example a journey or a meal.

Strategy
You should be able to:
- ask for/make suggestions.
- accept/politely reject other people's suggestions.

1 Listen to two candidates doing Paper 5, Part 3 and complete the following extracts.

1 ....!.............................?
They will be very hungry after hiking all morning.

2 It's probably quite cold, ...
.... to start with soup.

3 ....
A fish soup would be good.

4 Mmm ... .
.... serve vegetable soup.

5 OK. We'll serve vegetable soup first. And what shall we have next? ....

6 ....
– with a meat sauce.

7 ....
serve a salad next?

2 In which extract/extracts are the candidates

A asking for suggestions? ....

B making suggestions? ....

C accepting suggestions? ....

D politely rejecting suggestions? ....

Grammar: error correction

Strategy
Look back through the grammar sections in Units 1–9 in the *Exam Maximiser* and the *First Certificate Gold Coursebook*. As you read the following text, look for errors with the language points you have studied.

Read the following text and look carefully at each line. Some of the lines are correct, and some contain an extra incorrect word which should not be there. If a line is correct, put a tick (✔) at the end of the line. If a line has a word which should not be there, circle the word and write it at the end of the line.

Why don't we eat what we should?

1 According to the World Health Organisation almost half our diet
2 should consist of starchy food like such as potatoes and
3 rice and we should eat five portions of a fresh fruit and
4 vegetables every day. Unfortunately, it will to take a long time
5 for the British diet to approach this ideal. People know what
6 they should eat, but they are not quite so good at when it comes
7 to going to the supermarket to buy food. In fact people usually
8 prefer to eating what they want rather than eating what they are
9 told. Perhaps this is why did the proportion of people
10 considered 'obese' or fat doubled between 1980 and 1991.

'It's fast, but I miss the chewing and swallowing'

Vocabulary: phrasal verbs (*put*)

1 Put the words in the following questions in the correct order.

1 put could the to director you through me?

....

2 they wedding have off put their why?

....

3 put money do rainy day you by for a?

....

4 how put could up you with behaviour rude such?

....

5 prices put they up have again the?

....

6 how firemen fire out did put that the?

....

7 vet why have did to the cat your put down?

....

8 put me could London when come I up you to?

....

9 trying you always why put down me are to?

....

2 Write the following sentences again using a phrasal verb with *put* instead of the underlined words. You may have to change the word order in some sentences.

1 They've <u>increased</u> the price of tinned tomatoes.

....

2 Can you <u>provide accommodation for</u> my nephew when he comes to Madrid?

....

3 I'm just trying to <u>connect</u> you, but the line seems to be busy.

....

4 He's always <u>making her look foolish</u> – I don't know why she goes out with him.

....

5 Please <u>extinguish</u> your cigarettes.

....

6 I think we'll have to <u>postpone</u> the match until after the exam.

....

7 They manage to <u>save</u> some money every week.

....

8 Two horses were so badly injured that they had to be <u>killed</u> after the race.

....

9 I don't know why you <u>tolerate</u> her rudeness.

....

Reading: multiple matching

Paper 1, Part 4

About the exam
In Paper 1 you may be asked where a text comes from (for example, a newspaper or magazine) and what its purpose is (for example, to warn or inform).

Strategy
Pay attention to the **structures** used in various kinds of text.

1 Read the texts opposite and mark with a tick (✔) the geographical regions, countries and continents below which are mentioned.

1 Africa 7 Greece
2 Asia 8 India
3 Australia 9 The Middle East
4 Britain 10 Portugal
5 Europe 11 Spain
6 France 12 The West

Text A

Chillies

Chillies are the seed pods of a South American plant. They contain capsaicin, one of the most powerful substances used by a plant to stop predators eating its seeds. The red colour of the seed pod is nature's customary warning that what is inside is harmful. Chillies were first cultivated in South America 800 years ago. The Incas prized the chilli, valuing it in religious rites, even using the pods as a form of currency. Columbus brought the chilli back to Europe in the 15th century. The Portuguese then carried it to trading colonies in India and Africa, where it quickly became a key flavour in local cooking.

Text B

Eating out

Metrocentre offers more than 50 places to eat and drink, including a 650 seater food court. You can try Mexican chilli beans, the best of Italian pastas and pizzas, paella or seafood from Spain, moussaka and delicious pastries from Greece or a spicy Thai stir fry. If you're more of a traditionalist, you might prefer the good old English pub with excellent pub food and a choice of fine beers and soft drinks. Many of these places to eat are open late to allow you to shop first and relax and enjoy a meal afterwards. Some are open on Sunday as well, so bring the kids for a family day out. They'll love our icecream parlour!

Text C

Indians are mango-mad

Could you eat 3 kilos of fruit in four minutes? Or cross a mango with a rose? **Molly Moore** in New Delhi lives and learns.

Slice them, suck them or slurp them – no matter how you cut them, there's not a fruit on earth that produces more passion among Indians than the mango. Sunny Mohar is the living proof. After eating over 3 kilos of the fruit in four minutes flat, the electronics engineer, aged 24, turned to the cameras and declared, 'I'm crazy about mangoes!'. Javed Faridi, aged 55, while no less enthusiastic, is more reserved in his praise. A mango grower like his father before him, he has created 300 hybrids of India's most popular fruit, including a mango crossed with a rose and another the size of a grape.

Text D

Cooking a Chinese meal

The cooking methods the Chinese use are those that are familiar in the West: boiling, deep-frying, steaming and roasting. In addition there is stir frying, which means stirring and tossing the ingredients in very little oil over high heat. It does mean that all the preparation must be done before the cooking starts, and all the ingredients are cut into pieces of even size and shape. The cooking time is often only five minutes from start to finish. Let your guests wait for the food rather than the other way round. If the food has to wait, it will continue cooking in its own heat and the effect will be spoilt.

2 Look at the underlined sentences in each text and match them to the following labels.

1 Direct speech: Text ....
2 Instructions: Text ....
3 A suggestion: Text ....
4 A statement of fact: Text ....

3 Answer the following questions about the texts.

1 Which text comes from
   a) a newspaper article? Text ....
   b) a cookery book? Text ....
   c) an encyclopedia? Text ....
   d) a brochure? Text ....

2 Which text is mainly intended to
   a) teach people how to do something? Text ....
   b) provide factual information? Text ....
   c) entertain and surprise people? Text ....
   d) attract people and persuade them to do something? Text ....

Learner training

We read different types of text for different purposes. When we read for specific information, we **scan** the text until we have found the information we need. When we read something we know we will probably have to read again, we read quickly or **skim** the first time we read to get a general idea.

67

Grammar: future forms

1   There is a mistake in each of the following sentences. Find the mistake and write the sentences out again correctly in your notebook.

1   By the time you read this I am sipping champagne in a café near the Eiffel Tower.

2   Tomorrow there is heavy rain in the north.

3   Bye! I see you next week.

4   We've got to be at the airport two hours before our plane will take off.

5   By the time I'm twenty, I will eat 3,000 bowls of cornflakes.

6   Look out! That wall will collapse.

7   I don't think I am having dinner. I'm not hungry.

8   I'm afraid I can't come to the cinema with you. I will take my nephew to the circus.

9   I'm sure you are doing very well in the exam.

10   I've made up my mind. I buy a new computer.

2   Fill in the gaps in the following letter with an appropriate form of the verb in brackets.

Dear Sir/Madam,

I (1)........................ (write) in reply to your advertisement for tour guides in last Tuesday's Chronicle.

I (2)........................ (study) tourism at the State Tourism School. I (3)........................ (finish) my course next July and (4)........................ (be) available to start work immediately afterwards.

Apart from the tourism course, I (5)........................ (attend) French classes in the evenings for the next six months and I (6)........................ (go) to France for a month as part of a student exchange programme. I am sure my spoken French (7)........................ (improve) as a result. Furthermore, by the time I complete my tourism diploma I (8)........................ (take) the Cambridge First Certificate in English examination. My teacher is certain I (9)........................ (get) at least a pass grade in the exam. I (10)........................ (start) German classes next week as well.

If you require any further information, I can be contacted by telephone on 0171 734 8972. I (11)........................ (be) at home every afternoon this week and in the mornings until 11 for the next month.

I look forward to hearing from you,

Yours faithfully,

Katerina Geraki

Vocabulary: shopping

Fill in the gaps in the following conversation with an appropriate word.

MOTHER: OK. Let me look at my list. First of all we need to go to the (1)........................ because I want to send some flowers to your Aunt Mary. And then we'll go over to the (2)........................ so that I can send these Christmas cards off.

SARAH: Oh Mum, that'll take ages! There are always long (3)........................ on Fridays. You go and post your letters while I go and get the bread from the (4)........................ .

MOTHER: Could you pop into the (5)........................ and get that cough mixture for your father? It's just next door to the (6)........................ . Actually you could pop in there too and get a couple of onions and a cauliflower. No, let's get all the fruit and vegetables with all the other things we need from the (7)........................ .

SARAH: Didn't you say you wanted to go back to that (8)........................ where you bought those sandals that the heel came off?

MOTHER: Yes, but I doubt that they'll give me a (9)........................ . I bought them in the end of season (10)........................ . And I thought they were such a (11)........................ at only £10. Oh no!

SARAH: What's the matter?

MOTHER: I can't find my (12)........................! I must have left it at home and it's got the original (13)........................ for the sandals and all my credit (14)........................ in it.

SARAH: I've got plenty of money so we can still get the things on the list. We could go over to that big shopping mall in Waverly and I could (15)........................ on another pair of those trousers. They didn't have my (16)........................ in when I was there with Sue last week and the pair I tried on were so (17)........................ around the waist I could hardly breathe.

Writing: letter of application

Paper 2, Part 2

About the exam
In Paper 2, Part 2 you may be asked to write a
letter of application.

1 Look at the following job advertisement.

Trading and Commercial Bank
Trainee Managers

We will be recruiting trainee managers to start
work in late June or early July in our branches
all over Europe. Applicants should have a
degree in an appropriate area and a knowledge
of English and/or German. Apply in writing to:

The Personnel Officer,
Trading and Commercial Bank,
134 Collins Street,
Manchester

The sentences in this reply are in the wrong order. Put
them in the correct order. Write the numbers 1–6 in
the gaps.

Dear Sir/Madam,

a) (........) I can be contacted by telephone on 01202
452269 in the mornings or at the above address.

b) (........) I have a working knowledge of German and
have recently passed the University of Cambridge First
Certificate in English examination.

c) (........) I look forward to receiving your reply.

d) (........) I am writing in reply to your advertisement
in last Tuesday's Evening News.

e) (........) I will also complete a degree in Banking
and Finance in June and will be available for work
immediately afterwards.

f) (........) I would like to apply for one of the trainee
manager positions you advertise.

Yours faithfully,

João de Souza

2 Look at the following task.

You see the following advertisement in the
newspaper.

Write **a letter** applying for one of these positions
and asking for more details about the discounts.
Do not write any addresses.

Trainee Travel Agents

We are looking for students who are
interested in training to become travel
agents. To join our training scheme you
must have a knowledge of English and
an interest in travelling. These positions
are unpaid, but you will receive large
discounts on all our organised tours and
holidays.

Write to: Maria Sampras,
Director,
TRAVELWISE,
Via Ardipani,
Rome 04100

---

1 Underline the key words in the instructions.

2 Think about the form of your letter.

   ● Will your letter begin in the same way as the
      letter in Exercise 1?

   ● Will it end in the same way?

3 Plan your letter. Follow the order of the letter in
   Exercise 1.

4 Write your letter in 120–180 words.

5 Check for errors with future forms.

Learner training
You can practise your letter writing skills by writing
to real companies asking for information. Try
writing to banks and embassies. They are often
willing to send you brochures and even posters.

Vocabulary: *do/make*

Fill in the gaps in the following sentences with the correct form of *do* or *make*.

1 Don't .... excuses! You didn't .... your homework and that's that!

2 Could you .... me a favour and lend me your notebook?

3 I want to .... notes while the teacher is explaining.

4 I've lost my wallet. What am I going to ....?

5 My parents expect me to .... things in the house such as .... my bed, helping my brothers .... the washing up and so on.

6 My father .... the ironing and he also .... the best spaghetti sauce in the universe!

7 I didn't realise they were .... fun of me. I suppose I .... a fool of myself.

8 If you want to .... well in the exam, you'll just have to .... more of an effort.

9 I know I always .... a lot of mistakes, but I really am .... my best.

10 .... sure you come to class tomorrow. We're going to .... a test.

11 Take a day off and .... nothing for a change. It won't .... you any harm. In fact it will probably .... you the world of good.

12 I didn't want to .... a fuss, but I really felt I had to .... a formal complaint. They hadn't .... the job properly at all.

13 .... business with you has been a great pleasure. I'm sure both our companies will .... a lot of money out of it.

14 I am afraid that the company has .... a massive loss this financial year.

15 Stop .... so much noise! I've got to .... a very important phone call.

Reading: multiple choice

Paper 1, Part 2

About the exam
In Paper 1 you have **1 hour and 15 minutes** to complete the four parts.

Strategy
Spend an equal amount of time (about 18 minutes) on each of the four parts of Paper 1. Divide each 18 minutes up like this:

- **3 minutes** reading the text and questions once **quickly.**
- **8 minutes** reading the text again and answering the questions.
- **4 minutes** checking your answers and answering any remaining questions.
- **3 minutes** transferring your answers from the question paper to the answer sheet.

1 Read the following text about a woman who has won a lot of competitions and mark with a cross (✗) the things below which are **not** mentioned.

1 a car
2 a TV
3 a fax machine
4 a compact disc system
5 a dog
6 a computer
7 a dishwasher
8 a refrigerator

Enter Mrs Win-a-lot

Introducing the undisputed queen of competitions

Outside Rita Smallburn's home is parked a sparkling blue Renault Clio. Mrs Smallburn won it. It is the fifth car she has won. Inside her sitting room are a video, television, compact disc system, three-piece suite, canteen of cutlery, decanter and glasses, silverware, Trivial Pursuit, Scrabble and an enormous bottle of champagne: all prizes.

In her kitchen are a dishwasher, microwave, French saucepan set, toaster, coffee maker, electric carving knife, kettle, can opener and iron: more prizes.

In fact there is virtually nothing in Mrs Smallburn's entire house, apart from her dog, which she hasn't won. She did not actually win the house she and her family live in, but seven years ago she won another one worth £50,000 which she sold two years later for £100,000. For the last sixteen years she has been the 'Queen of Competitions' or 'compers' as they are known in the trade. Locally she is known as Mrs Win-a-lot.

Since she gave up her job as a geography teacher sixteen years ago, Mrs Smallburn believes she has become much more skilled at winning competitions. 'I expect to win between twenty and forty per cent of the competitions I enter,' she says. 'But my winnings could vary enormously year by year. One year I might win £3,000. The next it could be £100,000.' All her earnings are tax-free.

She enters only about twelve competitions a month now, down from a peak of about fifty when she was younger. Nowadays she is busy running a consultancy in which she shares her competition winning skills with others who would like to achieve success, but the postman's arrival is still a thrill. If her family wants something, she will try to win it. At the moment she is competing for a fax machine. She wouldn't dream of buying anything.

It is an odd life, though Mrs Smallburn denies it is an obsession. 'It's more like an extreme enthusiasm,' she says. To work, the thrill must be in the winning rather than the prizes. The disadvantage is the lack of freedom to buy what you choose. The dog is not allowed to have his favourite brand of pet food. He has to be content with a year's supply of another brand Mrs Smallburn won.

from *The Times* newspaper

2 Choose the correct alternative to answer the following questions. **Time yourself!**

1 Which of the following is something that Mrs Smallburn did not win in competitions?

   A A house.
   B The house where the family live.
   C Money and goods to the value of £3,000.
   D Five cars.

2 Mrs Smallburn used to

   A win more money than she does now.
   B work as a geography teacher.
   C be better at winning competitions than she is now.
   D pay less tax than she does now.

3 How does Mrs Smallburn spend most of her time now?

   A teaching geography
   B entering competitions
   C working in her own company
   D looking after her family

4 Mrs Smallburn does not

   A want to buy a fax machine.
   B want to win a fax machine.
   C look forward to the postman coming.
   D try to win things her family want.

5 What is Mrs Smallburn's attitude to entering competitions?

   A She is obsessed with it.
   B She is very keen on it.
   C She is disappointed with the things she wins.
   D She thinks it is a strange way to earn a living.

6 The writer of the text thinks Mrs Smallburn's 'extreme enthusiasm' is the result of

   A the excellent prizes she has won.
   B the feeling she gets from winning.
   C not being free to buy what she wants.
   D an obsession.

7 The article is intended to

   A shock the reader.
   B annoy the reader.
   C entertain the reader.
   D make the reader feel sad.

Grammar: relative clauses/pronouns

1 Make complete sentences by joining one half in Column A with the other half in Column B using an appropriate relative pronoun. If the pronoun can be left out, write it in brackets. Write the complete sentences out in your notebook.

EXAMPLE: **Mrs Win-a-lot is the name (that) Mrs Smallburn's neighbours call her.**

Column A

1 'Mrs Win-a-lot' is the name ✔
2 The £50,000 house is not the one
3 Mrs Smallburn expects to win between twenty and forty per cent of the competitions
4 That is the compact disc system
5 Mrs Smallburn tries to win the things
6 The blue Renault Clio is the fifth car
7 There is hardly anything in Mrs Smallburn's house
8 The dog has to eat a brand of pet food
9 Mrs Smallburn is one of the rare people

Column B

a) she has won in a competition.
b) she hasn't won in a competition.
c) Mrs Smallburn and her family live.
d) earnings are tax-free.
e) Mrs Smallburn's neighbours call her. ✔
f) was a prize.
g) he doesn't like very much.
h) her family needs.
i) she enters.

2 Do the following sentences contain defining or non-defining relative clauses? Mark the sentences **D** (defining) or **N** (non-defining). Add commas where necessary.

1 She lent me a book. I lost the book that she lent me.   ....

2 Mrs Smallburn has won five cars. A blue Renault Clio which is one of the cars she won is parked outside her house.   ....

3 Pink Floyd who wrote the song 'Money' were performing live in London recently.   ....

4 There are several proverbs about money. I agree with the one which says: 'Money is the root of all evil.'   ....

5 The Central European University which has its headquarters in Prague has a branch in Budapest.   ....

6 My uncle who was very shy when he was a child is now a multimillionaire.   ....

7 My uncle who does not show off his wealth by wearing expensive clothes and accessories gives a lot of money to charities.   ....

8 Several groups played at the festival. The first group who played were Dire Straits.   ....

3 There are mistakes in six of the following sentences. Find the mistakes and write the sentences out again correctly in your notebook.

1 The Spanish omelette she cooked was delicious.

2 The house where we used to live in was bigger than this one.

3 My boyfriend, who used to be a brilliant athlete, has put on five kilos in the last two months.

4 The single object what I treasure most is an old coin my grandfather gave me.

5 The woman I spoke to told me I could have a refund if I brought the original receipt.

6 The waiter, to who I gave a very generous tip, didn't even thank me.

7 The insurance on the house, that was very expensive, didn't cover the cost of the repairs.

8 The loan I took out to pay for my studies has been very useful.

9 Inflation, which has risen to 200 per cent, is crippling the economy.

10 He inherited a lot of money from his grandfather, who he was extremely well-off.

11 The salesman who he sold me this T-shirt didn't tell me I couldn't return it.

12 The town where I was born has changed a lot in the last ten years.

Vocabulary: money

1 Complete this crossword.

Across

4 to take out money you have put in the bank
6 to use money to make a profit out of something that will increase in value
7 to give someone the use of something, such as money, for a limited period of time
9 to get money by working

Down

1 to have enough money to do or buy something without difficulty
2 to have to pay money to someone because they lent it to you
3 to risk your money or property on horse races, in card games or in business
5 to receive money, goods or property from someone who has died or moved on
8 something that you owe to someone else

2 Now fill in the gaps in the following sentences with an appropriate word. The first two letters of each word have been given to help you.

1 The cashier would not let me take any more money out of my cu.............. account as I was already £50 ov.............. .

2 Excuse me. Would you have ch.............. for a £20 no..............?

3 Would you like to pay ca.............. or by ch.............. or credit card?

4 I wouldn't buy sh.............. in that company if I were you. They made a lo.............. last year.

5 The waiters in that restaurant get low wa.............., but they make a fortune in ti.............. .

6 You can withdraw money and order a bank st.............. from ca.............. machines.

7 If you want to buy a house, go to a building society for your mo.............. .

8 The problems with the ec.............. in my country have affected the ex.............. ra.............. badly.

9 I'm a bit ha.............. up at the moment. Do you think you could le.............. me £10?

10 By donating money to ch.............. you can often get substantial ta.............. deductions.

Writing: discursive

Paper 2, Part 2

About the exam
In Paper 2, Part 2 you choose **one** of four alternative questions. These may include a report, a story, a description, an article or another letter. You also have the option of writing about one of the set texts.

Strategy
Make sure your answer is appropriate for the instructions and covers all the points mentioned.

1 Read the following answer a student wrote to a question in Paper 2, Part 2. What kind of answer is this student trying to write?

A a report
B a story
C an article giving an opinion

2 Now look at the answer again. It is very well-structured, but there are five mistakes with verb tenses. Find the mistakes and write the sentences out again correctly in your notebook.

3 There are also two mistakes with vocabulary. Find the mistakes and write the sentences out again correctly in your notebook.

4 What grade would you give this candidate: Excellent, Good, Satisfactory or Unsatisfactory?

In my opinion students should do some paid work while they are studying. There are three main reasons why I am thinking this.

First of all I believe it is important to have work experience. If you had never worked before, it is very difficult to get used to work when you finished your studies. I have a part-time work in my mother's office and I am sure this helps me in the future.

Secondly I think young people must to learn to appreciate the value of money and they can only do this if they earn some themselves. If your parents just gave you money for everything you want, you can never understand about saving for things. My parents give me some money each week, but I also save money from my work.

Finally, by working students can know other people who are not at school. This is good because you can learn new things about the world. At my mother's office I knew a girl who has taught me many things about the environment and pollution.

For these reasons I think it is important for young people to work. Of course they should not work too much. They have to have time to study too!

5 Write your answer to the following question.

> A local English language newspaper has asked students to write articles expressing their opinions about this question:
>
> *Should students do part-time work?*
>
> Write your **article** for the newspaper.

1 Pay attention to the key words in the instructions:
article   English language newspaper   opinion

2 Think of at least three arguments to support your opinion.

3 Write a plan putting your arguments in order.

4 Write your answer in 120–180 words. Use these linkers:
  ● First of all/Firstly/In the first place   ● Finally
  ● Secondly/In the second place

5 Check your work very carefully for mistakes with verb tenses, vocabulary and relative clauses.

Listening: multiple choice

Paper 4, Part 1

About the exam
There are always eight extracts in Paper 4, Part 1. Each extract is about **30 seconds** long. You choose between three alternatives to answer each question.

Strategy
Study the questions carefully. Are you asked:
a) what they are talking about?
b) who they are talking to?
c) what they want someone to do?

1 Look at the following questions and write a), b) or c) *(see Strategy box above)* in the gaps according to what you are asked.

1 You hear this man talking on a public phone. The man is arranging
  A to hold a meeting.
  B to give a party.
  C to play sport.   ....

2 You are in a community centre. You hear this man talking in a meeting room. The man wants
  A to persuade the audience to buy something.
  B the audience to tell him what they think about something.
  C to get the audience to answer some questions.   ....

3 You walk past a classroom and hear this exchange. The teacher wants Adela to
  A show the others how she found the answer.
  B tell the others the answer.
  C explain why she didn't do the homework. ....

4 You hear a girl talking on the telephone. She is talking to
  A a friend who has started a new job.
  B someone who might give her a job.
  C a teacher at the school she attends.   ....

5 You hear this man talking on the radio. The person he is talking about
  A is going to make a record.
  B has recently made a record.
  C has just been on tour.   ....

6 You hear two people talking in a bank. What is the woman doing?
  A enquiring about bank procedures
  B applying for a loan
  C arguing about bank rules   ....

7 You hear this man talking about a newspaper article he has read. What was the article about?
  A crime
  B health
  C economics   ....

8 You hear this man talking on the telephone. How does the other speaker react to what the man says?
  A He refuses to accept a reservation for such a small group.
  B He asks the man to call back the next day.
  C He offers various additional services.   ....

2 Now listen and choose the correct alternative in each case.

Vocabulary: numbers

📟 **1** Listen to the cassette and write the numbers that you hear.

a) ....

b) ....

c) ....

d) ....

e) ....

f) ....

g) ....

h) ....

i) ....

2 What kind of numbers are they? Match the numbers that you wrote above to one of the following categories. Write the appropriate letter in the gaps.

1 a temperature   ....
2 a telephone number   ....
3 a football score   ....
4 the population of a
   town   ....
5 a speed   ....
6 a weight   ....
7 a decimal   ....
8 a fraction   ....
9 a price   ....

📟 **3** Practise saying the following numbers. Then listen to the cassette and check.

a) 0121 730 654   f) 16
b) 13   g) £3.50
c) 50   h) $19.99
d) 1½   i) 647,958
e) 4.75   j) 5,340,414

Speaking: prioritising

> **Paper 5, Part 3**

About the exam
This part of the test lasts for about three minutes.

Hot tip! ◀--------------------------

DON'T worry if you do not finish putting all the things in order. The examiner will stop you when you have been speaking for three minutes.

Strategy
Don't try to dominate the other candidate. You may also get marks for **interaction**. Encourage the other person to speak by:
● asking her/him questions.
● making suggestions.
● saying a word if s/he hesitates or pauses for too long.
Don't interrupt the other person. Wait until s/he has finished speaking.

📟 Below are some pictures of things which young people like to spend money on. Listen to two pairs of candidates doing Part 3 of Paper 5. They must put the things in order of priority according to how important they think they are. Which candidates do you think got good marks for interaction?

Interview 1: Loukas   Julie   *Interview 2*: Olivier   Dominique

Writing: transactional letter

About the exam
Part 1 of Paper 2 is **compulsory**. There is only one question. You always have to write either a formal or informal letter.

1 Look at the instructions below and the letter a candidate wrote in reply. Then decide which of the following examiner's comments were made about the letter. Mark them with a tick (✔).

1 The letter is very accurate.

2 The letter is not well-structured.

3 The letter is in an inappropriate style.

4 The writer has followed the instructions.

5 The letter provides all the necessary information.

You were travelling by train recently and left something that belongs to you on the train. Write a letter to the lost property officer enquiring about the thing you lost. Use these notes in your letter. Do not write any addresses.

– *date of journey*
– *destination and departure time*
– *description of object*

How are you? I'm fine. But I lost something on one of your trains and I'm going to tell you about it. OK?

Well, I got a train to Bristol a couple of weeks ago. Anyway, the train left Paddington station a bit late. It was supposed to leave at eleven, but in the end it left around twelve.

I left my favourite basketball cap on the train. It's bright red with black lettering saying Chicago Bulls. You've got it, haven't you? Let me know if you haven't.

I don't really feel like coming all the way to London to get it. You can send it to me, can't you? Here's my address:

11 St John's Road
Bracknell

Bye for now and thanks.
All the best,

Alex

Strategy
If asked to write to an official or a company, you should not use:
- question tags.
- contractions (e.g. *aren't, it'll, you've*).
- linkers like *well, anyway, by the way*.
- *All the best* or *Love* at the end of your letter.

You should:
- begin your letter with either *Dear Sir/Madam* or *Mr/Ms/Dr* + the person's surname.
- use formal language (e.g. *I look forward to receiving your reply*).
- end your letter with *Yours sincerely/Yours faithfully*.
- sign your letter with your full name.

2 Write a letter in answer to the question in Exercise 1.

1 Write a plan. You should follow this structure.

- Explain why you are writing.
- Say what you lost and when; describe it.
- Ask how you can get it back.
- Thank them in advance

2 Write your letter in the appropriate style in 120–180 words. Check your letter carefully.

Reading: gapped text

Paper 1, Part 3

About the exam

In Part 3 of Paper 1 you read a text from which various paragraphs (or sentences) have been removed. These paragraphs are in a different order on another page. You decide where to put each paragraph. There is always an extra paragraph that does not belong.

Strategy

- Read the text through once.
- Read the extracted paragraphs.
- When you think you know which paragraph goes in each gap, check that there is a relationship in meaning between this paragraph and the paragraphs that go before and after it.

LIGHTNING STRIKE

It is not surprising that people in the past were afraid of lightning and thought that it was a sign of anger from their gods. In fact we still find lightning thrilling and fascinating. It is now also an important area of research for scientists, who are trying to uncover its secrets and are looking for ways to predict storms and protect people against lightning strikes.

(1____)

In England and Wales things are not quite as bad as they were in Italy, but about a dozen people are struck by lightning every year and a quarter of those are killed as a result. Men are six times more likely to be struck by lightning than women.

(2____)

The experience of Roy Sullivan just goes to show how dangerous it can be to work outside. Roy, a former park ranger in Virginia, USA, held the world record for being struck by lightning. He was first hit in 1942, losing just the nail from his big toe. He was struck again in 1969, 1970, 1972 and 1973. In 1976 a strike hurt his ankle and in 1977 he suffered chest and stomach burns. After surviving all this, he killed himself in 1983!

(3____)

But even the most advanced forecasting systems can sometimes be caught out when the weather springs one of its surprises. In March 1993, Florida and other states of America were struck by driving blizzards – and severe lightning storms. At the peak the 'Sunshine State' was hit by an astonishing 5,000 strikes an hour. The cause of the storm and the reason it suddenly died out as it travelled north, is yet another mystery of the lightning phenomenon.

A

Predicting when and where lightning is likely to strike is one of the ways we have made it less of a danger. Forecasting lightning is taken most seriously in America, where scientists keep a constant lookout for weather patterns that could lead to violent storms using weather satellites and ground-based stations. Once the storms appear, teams of observers in the areas at risk report back on where the storm is and where it is going.

B

Things used to be much worse. According to research by Dr Derek Elsom the number of fatalities has dropped by 80 per cent since the mid-1850s. This isn't because lightning is less common, but because fewer people now work in the open.

C

Before scientists started this vital work people could not do very much to protect themselves or their buildings from lightning. In fact up until the eighteenth century people were given dramatic proof that lightning really can strike the same place twice. Between 1388 and 1762, the famous bell tower of San Marco in Venice was severely damaged or completely destroyed nine times.

D

Many people – including scientists – claim to have seen ball lightning and are in no doubt about its existence. The experiences of a certain William Morris during a thunderstorm in 1936 are typical: 'I saw a red-hot ball come down from the sky. It struck our house, cut the telephone wire, burnt the window frame and then buried itself in a tub of hot water. The water boiled for some time afterwards, but when it was cool enough for me to search I could find nothing there.'

Vocabulary: weather

Choose the correct alternative to fill each gap in the following sentences.

1 It's absolutely .... outside, so wear your gloves.

   A cold   **B** chilly   **C** freezing

2 We had to postpone the match because it started to really ....

   A drizzle   **B** pour   **C** shower

3 Tomorrow will be mild with the possibility of a few .... in the evening.

   A rain   **B** showers   **C** sleet

4 It's only a bit of light .... You won't need an umbrella.

   A sleet   **B** drizzle   **C** hail

5 Close to the Equator the weather is hot and .... and there are often electrical storms.

   A damp   **B** mild   **C** humid

6 The old house was very cold and .... in winter.

   A humid   **B** damp
   C freezing

7 Open the window. There's a lovely cool ....
   outside .

   A breeze   **B** gale   **C** gust

8 There was such a .... that my umbrella blew inside out.

   A rain   **B** breeze   **C** gale

9 The ground was completely white. I thought it was snow at first, but it was just a heavy ....

   A hail   **B** frost   **C** sleet

Grammar: the article

1 Fill in the gaps in the following dialogue with *a, an, the* or *(-)* if no article is needed.

The ghastly guest guide

A: Working as a hotel manager, you must have some interesting stories to tell about guests.

B: Yes, indeed. Although we have (1).......... many very charming clients, some of our guests do incredible things.

A: Such as?

B: Well, (2).......... people will steal anything. All kinds of things go from (3).......... hotels, including (4).......... dinner plates. One couple stole (5).......... sheets and blankets from their bed, but one of the maids saw them do it. So (6).......... hall porter who carried their luggage down, took (7).......... sheets and blankets out and replaced them with (8).......... set of telephone directories.

   We also get some very unreasonable requests. I worked at (9).......... hotel in (10).......... London where (11).......... couple wanted to have (12).......... dinner all on their own in (13).......... hotel ballroom, with (14).......... gypsy violinists and (15).......... palm tree. And they also wanted to be able to see (16).......... moon!

   Some people completely destroy their rooms. One couple managed to spill (17).......... coffee over an area nine metres square. And they didn't even tell us about it. It was everywhere – on (18).......... TV, across (19).......... floor and on (20).......... bedclothes!

---

2 Read the following text and look carefully at each line. Some of the lines are correct, and some have an extra incorrect word which should not be there. If a line is correct, put a tick (✔) at the end of the line. If a line has a word which should not be there, circle the word. In this case, all of the extra incorrect words are articles.

What is jet lag?

0   When you fly from the Europe to the Middle East, America or
1   Asia the flight will be longer than the four hours and
2   will involve crossing several time zones. The time difference
3   between your point of departure and final destination can
4   be as much as the twelve hours. It can also mean flying from
5   winter to summer or spring to autumn. You leave the Athens
6   at seven o'clock on a winter's morning and arrive in Melbourne,
7   which is seven hours ahead, more than a twenty hours later on
8   a hot summer's day. Naturally your body still thinks you are
9   in Athens. Because of this you will almost inevitably
10 suffer from a mild or even quite severe jet lag.

Strategy
Sometimes the extra words in this kind of exercise will be articles. Check each line carefully. Are all the articles necessary?

Vocabulary and grammar: open cloze

About the exam
There are fifteen gaps in the text. The gaps test your knowledge of **vocabulary and grammar**.

Strategy
These are the most common grammatical words that are removed from the text:
- prepositions (e.g. *on, in, to*).
- quantifiers (e.g. *little, few*).
- auxiliary verbs (e.g. *do, are, have*).
- determiners (e.g. *the, most, another*).
- relative pronouns (e.g. *whom, who, where*).
- possessive adjectives (e.g. *my, his, their*).

Check for these when you fill in the gaps.

Read the following text through once quickly and then fill in the gaps with an appropriate word.

Where are the rainforests?

Rainforests once occupied almost all the land around the Equator, (1)..................... there is hot sun and rainfall almost every day. In these hot, wet areas, trees and (2)..................... kinds of vegetation grow fast, feeding massive numbers (3)..................... insects and animals.

Until recently, the rainforests filled river valleys in warmer countries (4)..................... Australia. They climbed hillsides of great (5)..................... chains such as the South American Andes, and covered islands (6)..................... Borneo to the West Indies.

In West Africa, the rainforests cover (7)..................... wide strip of the coast from Sierra Leone to Gabon. In the last century these forests (8)..................... mostly uninhabited. The Europeans arrived and soon began chopping (9)..................... the trees for timber and to make way for massive plantations of cocoa, peanuts and cotton.

Today, two thirds of the West African forests (10)..................... gone. But elsewhere in Central Africa it (11)..................... still possible to find huge undisturbed forests. Nineteenth century explorers along (12)..................... river Zaire called Africa the 'dark continent'. Even today (13)..................... are no roads in some places. The inhabitants include pygmies, (14)..................... are trying to lead (15)..................... lives in harmony with the forest.

Grammar: modals of deduction/criticism (past)

1 Match a sentence in Column A with a sentence in Column B. Write the appropriate letter in the gaps.

Column A

1 You must have had a terrible fright. ....

2 I might be able to come. ....

3 That can't be Mary. ....

4 You should take a coat. ....

5 He can't have forgotten again. ....

6 That must be Michael. ....

7 You should have told me. ....

8 She might not know. ....

9 You can't have spent it all. ....

10 They might have seen it. ....

Column B

a) He always gets home from work at about this time.

b) I only gave it to you yesterday.

c) It's been on for a couple of weeks.

d) I reminded him about fifty times.

e) I would have got you a present.

f) It's going to get cold later.

g) You're still trembling.

h) I certainly haven't told her.

i) She is supposed to be at school.

j) I'll have to ask my parents though.

2 There are mistakes in five of the following sentences. Find the mistakes and write the sentences out again correctly in your notebook.

1 Would you mind buying me a coffee? I must leave my money in my other coat.

2 They can't have left already. We're only five minutes late.

3 You'd better phone him about the match. He might have forgotten.

4 Don't wait for me. I might have been late.

5 It mustn't have been Mary who stole the money. She was with me all evening.

6 She might be offended. She is very sensitive you know.

7 It can't be snowing! It's the middle of July.

8 I might have stayed at home this Saturday night. I've got a test on Monday.

9 That can't be the answer. You must have made a mistake somewhere.

10 You should tell me. I didn't know you were coming.

'You're not thinking of putting me back in there are you?'

Grammar: key word transformations

Paper 3, Part 3

About the exam
There are ten key word transformation questions. They test your knowledge of grammar and vocabulary, such as collocation and idioms, as well as phrasal verbs.

Strategy
Before you complete the sentences try to work out what the question is testing.

1 Look at the following questions. Are they testing grammar, vocabulary or phrasal verbs? Mark them **G** (grammar), **V** (vocabulary) or **PV** (phrasal verbs).

1 Could I stay with you for the weekend?
put
Could you .... for the weekend? ....

2 It is not possible that Tim was angry.
can't
Tim .... angry. ....

3 What is the price of this bag?
much
How .... cost? ....

4 I don't like this wet, windy weather at all.
stand
I .... this wet, windy weather. ....

5 You should stop smoking.
give
You should .... smoking. ....

6 You are not allowed to speak during the examination.
may
You .... during the examination. ....

7 She was imitating a teacher when the headmaster walked in.
taking
She was .... a teacher when the headmaster walked in. ....

2 Now complete each sentence so that it has a similar meaning to the first sentence. Use the word in **bold** and other words. You must use between two and five words.

Speaking: picture prompts

Paper 5, Part 2

About the exam
Sometimes the photographs in Paper 5, Part 2 will be designed to make you speculate.

Strategy
Make sure that you can use modals of deduction accurately.

Hot tip! ◀
You may get better marks in this part of Paper 5 if you say how you feel about the photograph and give a personal comment.

Listen to a candidate doing Part 2 of Paper 5, look at the photos and write down:

1 three examples of deductions about the past.

a) ....
....

b) ....
....

c) ....
....

2 three examples of deductions about the present.

a) ....
....

b) ....
....

c) ....
....

3 two examples of Eleni making personal comments about the photos.

a) ....
....

b) ....
....

Vocabulary: problems/disasters

1   Complete this crossword puzzle.

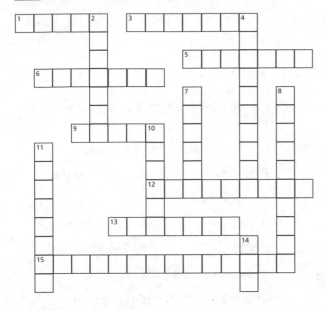

Across

1 a great overflow of water onto a place that is usually dry
3 an illness caused by an infection or disorder in the body or mind, not by accident
5 an organisation that gives money and help to people who are poor, sick or in difficulty
6 a person who has been forced to leave their country for political or religious reasons
9 bad weather conditions with strong wind and often rain, lightning and thunder
12 an unexpected and dangerous situation that must be dealt with quickly
13 a very violent wind that spins at great speed
15 the situation in which there are too many people living in one place

Down

2 a long period of dry weather when there is not enough water
4 a sudden, violent shaking of the Earth's surface
7 a very serious lack of food
8 the killing or death of the last remaining animals of a certain kind
10 a small piece of rock or metal that burns brightly when it falls into the air round the Earth
11 the noun from *solve*
14 money, food and services given to people who need them

Listening: selecting

Paper 4, Part 4

About the exam
In this part of Paper 4 you may have to answer True/False or Yes/No questions about a conversation or an interview.

Strategy
Listen for details that make the statements true or false or provide a 'yes' or 'no' answer to the questions.

┌─ Hot tip! ◄
You have a fifty per cent chance of being right, so **never** leave a question unanswered.

You are going to hear an interview with Dr Goodman, a scientist who works with UNESCO's biosphere programme. Listen and answer 'Yes' or 'No' to the following questions.

1   Did the project start recently? ....

2   Are there biosphere reserves in a lot of different countries? ....

3   Is the new Brazilian reserve far from the capital city? ....

4   Are there animals and plants that are threatened with extinction on this reserve? ....

5   Do UNESCO scientists work on their own on the reserves? ....

6   Does Brazil have more than one reserve? ....

7   Are all the reserves the same size? ....

8   Are all the reserves in warmer parts of the world? ....

9   Do scientists working on the reserves ever get to meet? ....

10   Do some reserves share very similar circumstances and experiences? ....

Speaking: opinion

Paper 5, Part 4

About the exam
The examiner asks you to express your opinion about questions related to the task in Part 3.

Strategy
You are asked for your opinion. There is no 'right' answer. For example, if the examiner asks you: 'What is the best age to start learning a foreign language?', pause for a moment to work out what you think. Use expressions like:
- *Well, it depends ...*
- *I'm not sure, but I think ...*
- *I suppose ...*

If the examiner says something like: 'Do you think so?', it is because s/he wants you to say a bit more or give reasons for your opinion, not because you are wrong.

Listen to two candidates doing Part 4 of Paper 5 and make notes of all the words/phrases they use to express their opinions and to agree/disagree.

....

....

....

....

....

Writing: linking expressions

Read the text below and circle the alternative which is **not** possible in each case.

1	**A** On the other hand	**B** Furthermore	**C** However
2	**A** therefore	**B** however	**C** as well as these
3	**A** Furthermore	**B** However	**C** In addition
4	**A** Despite	**B** However	**C** Nevertheless
5	**A** So	**B** Although	**C** Therefore
6	**A** on the other hand	**B** as well as this	**C** however
7	**A** Although	**B** Despite	**C** In spite of
8	**A** In addition to this	**B** Furthermore	**C** Although
9	**A** because	**B** because of	**C** as
10	**A** Because	**B** Therefore	**C** So

A lot of people think that television in my country has improved over the last few years. (1)........., there are people who think it has got worse.

Only ten years ago the only television channels were the two state-owned stations. Nowadays, (2)........., in almost every part of the country you can receive as many as four more channels with your normal TV set. (3).......... you can buy a satellite dish or pay to receive cable television.

(4)........., does this mean the quality of what is shown has improved? There are a lot more movies, game shows, sports programmes and the so-called reality shows in which real people talk about dramatic things that have happened to them. (5)....... if you like a lot of choice and want to be entertained more than anything else, you would probably say that television has improved.

If, (6)........., you thought of television as an educational aid, you are probably very disappointed with what is on offer. (7).......... the large number of channels, there are definitely fewer documentary programmes. (8)........., the documentaries that are shown are of poorer quality than they were a few years ago. There are also fewer programmes about art and music (9).......... advertisers have found that these programmes attract only a small audience.

(10).......... television has improved in terms of the number of channels and the choice of programmes, but, in my opinion, it does not provide as much information as it used to, which is its main purpose.

Writing: discursive

About the exam
In Paper 2, Part 2 you may have the option of writing an article in which you talk about the advantages and disadvantages of something, the arguments for and against something or in which you write your opinion about a subject.

1 The article on page 84 was written in answer to the following task.

You have been asked to write an article for a student newspaper on the following topic:

Has television improved in your country over the last ten years?

Write your **article** saying what most people think and giving your own point of view.

Read these two plans and decide which one the writer followed.

Plan A

Introduction:	my opinion about the statement (television *has* improved).
Paragraph 1:	describe a situation.
Paragraph 2:	first reason for my opinion (more channels = more programmes = more choice).
Examples:	movies, game shows, sports programmes, reality shows.
Paragraph 3:	second reason for my opinion (no more boring educational programmes).
Examples:	documentaries, programmes about art and culture.
Conclusion:	state my opinion again: television has improved because it's more entertaining.

Plan B

Introduction:	question as a statement; two points of view;
Paragraph 1:	describe a situation – more channels than before.
Paragraph 2:	more choice; entertainment mainly.
Paragraph 3:	not educational; fewer documentaries; fewer cultural programmes.
Conclusion:	what most people think; what I think.

Did the writer of the text on page 84 follow the right plan for the task?

2 Write your answer to the question in Exercise 1.

1 Underline key words in the instructions.

2 Think of arguments for and against.

3 Write a plan using Plan B above as a basis.

4 Write your article in 120–180 words using appropriate linking expressions from page 84.

5 Check your work carefully.
   • Does it answer the question?
   • Have you used linking expressions correctly?
   • Is your answer grammatically correct?

┌ **Hot tip!** ◄ ─ ─ ─ ─ ─ ─ ─ ─ ┐
From now until the exam write at least one extra composition a week. Spend 45 minutes (no more, no less) planning, writing and checking your answer. Give it to your teacher. If your teacher is too busy, exchange answers with a friend.
└ ─ ─ ─ ─ ─ ─ ─ ─ ─ ─ ─ ─ ─ ─ ┘

Grammar: modifiers/intensifiers

Circle the correct alternative in the following sentences.

1 Thanks. The party was *very/really* fantastic.

2 I thought the film was *absolutely/very* terrible, but Mary quite enjoyed it.

3 Their house is *really/very* enormous. Even the bathroom is *absolutely/very* big.

4 My boss is *really/absolutely* good-looking.

5 See you soon! Have a *terrific/terrifying* time.

6 I'd certainly go there again. The staff were *very/absolutely* helpful.

7 The amount of rubbish along the side of the road was *quite/very* incredible.

8 She cooked a(n) *absolutely/quite* terrible meal.

9 I haven't seen such a *delicious/superb* match for a long time.

10 Their new secretary is *very/absolutely* efficient.

Vocabulary: phrasal verbs (*get*)

There are mistakes with word order or the particle in all of the following sentences. Find the mistakes and write the sentences out again correctly in your notebook.

1 I've been trying to get him through to on the telephone all afternoon, but the line is engaged.

2 You really must get up to some work. The exam is in a few weeks' time.

3 I know how to get over our Mum. She always lets me do what I want.

4 I don't get Mary on with very well. She's not my kind of person.

5 I hope you won't get anything up to while we're out. The babysitter will tell me if you do.

6 She doesn't earn a lot – just enough to get down.

7 I'd never do anything dishonest because I'm sure I'd never get away it with.

Grammar: *have to/don't have to/ must/need*

1 Put the words in the following sentences in the correct order.

1 have how we to do many write compositions?

....

2 with you help needn't the shopping.

....

3 needn't you gone much to so have trouble.

....

4 to just I've got pass.

....

5 to you often have do weekend study at the?

....

6 are how words write we to many supposed?

....

7 mustn't ink use you.

....

8 draft to we need do write a?

....

2 Now match each of the sentences above to an appropriate response below. Write the number of the sentence in the gap.

a) Between 120 and 180.   ....

b) I know, but I'd like to.   ....

c) What am I supposed to write with then?   ....

d) Don't worry. I'm sure you will.   ....

e) The letter from Part 1 and another question from Part 2.   ....

f) Yes, I'm afraid I do.   ....

g) It was a pleasure.   ....

h) No, but you should always plan your work before you start to write.   ....

3 Choose the correct alternative to fill in the gaps in the following sentences.

1 I .... go to the supermarket. My Mum asked me to get some things for lunch.

  A have to   **B** needn't

2 I .... go to the dentist. I haven't been for more than two years.

  A don't have to   **B** must

3 She said she .... go to the supermarket.

  A must   **B** had to

4 You .... drive me to the airport. I can get the bus.

  A don't need to   **B** must

5 How wonderful! Tomorrow's Saturday and we .... get up at 6·45.

  A mustn't   **B** don't have to

6 You .... tell anybody. It's a secret.

  A needn't   **B** mustn't

7 She .... retake any of her examinations. She passed them all in June.

  A didn't need   **B** needn't

8 You .... get a good night's sleep before the exam.

  A must   **B** have to

Grammar: error correction

> **Paper 3, Part 4**

About the exam
The texts used for error correction are always at least seventeen lines long. The first two lines are examples and you have to check another fifteen lines. You write your answers on the separate answer sheet.

Strategy
Answer in the question booklet first. When you are sure, transfer your answers to the answer sheet.

Look at each line of the following text. Some of the lines are correct and some have a word which should not be there. If a line is correct, put a tick (✔) by the number **on the separate answer sheet.** If a line has a word which should **not** be there, write the word **on the separate answer sheet.** There are two examples at the beginning (**0** and **00**).

How TV helped me learn a language

0	When I first came to live in Spain, I could not (to)
00	speak any Spanish. I had to learn to speak quickly ✔
1	because of my job. Some friends suggested to buying a
2	television and this turned out to be a really good advice.
3	At the first, I did not really understand anything at
4	all, but little by little I began to pick up the main ideas.
5	I would been read an English newspaper the same day
6	so I knew that what was happening around the world
7	anyway and I could understand the news. But the best of
8	programmes for learning Spanish were the game shows.
9	I must have watched hundreds of them in the first few
10	months after I came to live here. Because of the same
11	patterns are repeated again and again, you learn the rules
12	of the language almost automatically. Despite of the fact
13	that they were not the kinds of programmes I would normally
14	have watched, I began to quite enjoy of them. Although I
15	speak Spanish well now, I still watch them sometimes.

Part 4			
0	*to*	8	
00	✔	9	
1		10	
2		11	
3		12	
4		13	
5		14	
6		15	
7			

Reading: multiple matching

Strategy
- Read the statements you have to match to the texts once very quickly.
- Underline key words.
- Read the text(s) very quickly.
- Underline key words.
- Match the statements to the text.

You are going to read about four modern companies. For questions 1–13 choose from the companies A–D.

A	FUBU
B	Reef Brazil
C	Diesel
D	Gap

Its founder started by making something he couldn't buy at the time. `1 ☐`

It has an international design staff. `2 ☐`

It doesn't work with people who don't live up to its standards. `3 ☐`

It was started by a group of people who all lived in the same place. `4 ☐`

Its approach has attracted a lot of interest. `5 ☐`

It originally sold two kinds of goods. `6 ☐`

The people who work for the company have a lot of independence. `7 ☐`

It has gained the support of some famous people. `8 ☐`

It was founded in one country but now carries the name of another country. `9 ☐`

Though their headquarters are in one place, they are international companies. `10 ☐  11 ☐`

They don't make such a wide range of goods as the other companies. `12 ☐`

It is closely connected with a particular leisure activity. `13 ☐`

Not just a business, but a way of life

How a company presents itself can have an important influence on how much investment they attract. Here is what four clothing companies have to say about themselves

A

FUBU is about pride and respect in what you wear and who you are!
FUBU started in 1992 when Daymond John decided to try and make some money by designing and selling the kind of hats he wanted to wear himself but could never find. Daymond turned half of his home in Queens, New York into a factory and the other half into a living space for the 'Team'. The 'Team' consisted of a group of neighbourhood friends, all of whom are an integral part of the company. By 1995 FUBU were making T-shirts, rugby shirts, sweatshirts, denim, underwear, outerwear, boots and shoes with raw materials from around the world. Today FUBU make women's and children's clothes as well. The collection is also sold internationally in France, Japan, Germany and Australia. Top musical artists such as Mariah Carey and Snoop Doggy Dog have given FUBU their stamp of approval.

B

Reef Brazil is a company based on a commitment to a particular lifestyle that includes travelling and boarding sports.
The story of Reef started in 1977 when two brothers, Fernando and Santiago Aguerre, formed the 'Asociación Argentina de Surf', which eventually convinced the government to lift a ban on surfing. In 1979, Fernando and Santiago opened a surf shop in Mar del Plata, Argentina and started promoting a series of surf contests. Santiago and Fernando travelled all over the world on surf trips. In Brazil they met a sandal manufacturer, and began importing the sandals to their surf shop. Soon the brothers decided to move on from selling to designing what became one of the most innovative beach sandals ever made. Today, Reef Brazil makes not only sandals, but shoes, socks, and a whole line of girls' footwear. But, although you can find Reef Brazil products in over 90 countries worldwide, the brothers have not forgotten why they started the business: to live and nurture the lifestyle they love.

C

Diesel is the 'Haute Couture' of Casual.
Diesel was born 20 years ago and is today an innovative design company, manufacturing jeans and casual clothing as well as accessories. It is present in over 80 countries with 11,000 points of sale and 20 company-owned stores. When Renzo Rosso founded the company in 1978, he surrounded himself with creative, talented people – innovators who, like him, rejected the conventions of the fashion industry. He gave his open-minded new designers broad stylistic freedom. The Diesel staff is made up of a wide variety of people and personalities from all parts of the globe. Diesel people and their working methods are so unconventional that they have been the subject of countless magazine and newspaper

articles as well as documentary television programmes. They have also been studied by consulting organisations, international conglomerates, universities and business schools. The headquarters are located in Molvena, in the north-eastern part of Italy, where the company manages 15 subsidiaries across Europe, Asia and the Americas. Diesel employs over 1,000 people worldwide.

D

For every generation there's a Gap.

Gap founder Don Fisher opened the first Gap store in 1969, on Ocean Avenue in San Francisco. The store, which sold jeans and records, was named after a cultural phenomenon that was the talk of the times: 'the generation gap'. In 1991 Gap again focused on that earlier era with its instantly recognizable campaign, 'For every generation there's a Gap'. The company has world headquarters in the San Francisco Bay Area in California, in addition to a product development office in New York. It also operates offices in each of the countries in which Gap sells jeans, casual clothing, accessories and toiletries for children and adults – the United Kingdom, Canada, France, Japan and Germany. Gap Inc. maintains a 'Code of Conduct' which is designed to ensure that business partners operate ethically and that merchandise is produced under appropriate conditions in the United States and around the world. Gap will not do business with people who refuse to abide by the Code, and make it clear that compromising the letter or spirit of the Code will result in serious consequences – up to and including the termination of orders and any future business dealings.

Vocabulary: media

1 Find words in this word search grid to match the following definitions.

J	H	E	A	D	L	I	N	E	T
C	O	Y	E	S	L	G	R	G	R
R	F	U	D	M	K	R	F	O	S
O	C	A	R	T	O	O	N	S	L
S	A	K	N	N	X	V	U	S	T
S	P	O	C	H	A	H	E	I	Q
W	G	B	A	W	K	L	Z	P	S
O	E	D	I	T	O	R	I	A	L
R	Q	P	B	I	L	V	W	S	X
D	C	D	X	J	U	X	P	O	T

1 humorous drawing often dealing with something in the news in an amusing way ....

2 the part of the newspaper giving the opinion of the person in charge of the newspaper on a problem or event ....

3 the title printed in large letters above a story in a newspaper ....

4 informal talk or writing about other people's private lives ....

5 a person whose job consists of collecting information and writing things for newspapers and magazines ....

6 a printed word game which you do by fitting words guessed from questions and information into a pattern of numbered squares going down and across ....

2 Fill in the gaps in the following dialogue with an appropriate word. The first letter of each word has been given to help you.

A: I can't seem to find the BBC World Service on this radio. Perhaps the (1) f.................... has changed.

B: It might just be that the (2) b.................... are getting low. Shall I get some when I go out to the newsagent's?

A: Could you? I want to listen to the news (3) h.................... at eight.

B: I'll go just as soon as this has finished. These (4) s.................... are absolute rubbish, but once you've seen a couple of episodes you're hooked.

A: You don't seem to be getting very good reception. Perhaps you should move the (5) a.................... .

B: Oh, we never get Channel 5 very clearly. Pass me the (6) r................... c...................., will you? I just want to change over to see if the match has started.

A: I thought you said you were going to the shops as soon as 'Days of Our Lives' had finished.

B: Couldn't you go instead?

🔊 Listening: multiple matching

Paper 4, Part 3

About the exam
There are always five different speakers who talk about a theme such as travel, the media or health.

Strategy
* Read the instructions and ask any questions before the cassette starts.
* Listen for clues to match each speaker to the prompts.
* Check your answers when you hear the cassette again.
* Don't leave any questions unanswered on the answer sheet – guess if necessary!

You will hear five different men talking about experiences they have had with the media. For questions **1–5** look at the statements **A–F** and match them to the speakers. There is one extra statement which you do not need to use. Use the letters once only.

Speaker 1 ....   Speaker 4 ....

Speaker 2 ....   Speaker 5 ....

Speaker 3 ....

A He was taken in by an advertisement.

B He was interviewed on the radio.

C He was in a television advertisement.

D Something he wrote was in a newspaper.

E He was rejected because he didn't seem natural.

F He was worried that people would notice something.

Word formation

Paper 3, Part 5

About the exam
There are ten gaps in each word formation text. You write the words you form on a separate answer sheet.

Strategy
* Read the text through once to get a general idea of what it is about.
* Decide what part of speech is missing for each gap.
* Form words to fill each gap and write them above the gaps.
* Read the completed text to check that it makes sense.
* Check that the words are spelt correctly.
* Transfer your answers to the answer sheet.
* Be careful to follow the right numbering.

Read the following text and use the word given in capitals at the end of each line to form a word that fits in the gap in the same line. There is an example at the beginning (**0**). Write your answers on the answer sheet.

EXAMPLE: (**0**) *variety*

Media career opportunities

Nowadays there is a (0)...*variety*... of career opportunities   **VARY**
in the media. It is possible to study (1)...............   **JOURNALIST**
at most universities, many of which offer (2)...............   **OPTION**
courses in reporting on sports and (3)............... . Newer   **ENTERTAIN**
degrees in media studies, which were (4)...............   **AVAILABLE**
as recently as ten years ago, attract (5)...............   **ENTHUSIASM**
students from all over the country.

Some graduates prefer to work in (6)...............   **ADVERTISE**
as it allows them to use their (7)............... in the   **CREATE**
(8)............... of increasingly sophisticated TV and   **PRODUCE**
press advertisements.

(9)............... not all graduates find work easily as   **FORTUNATE**
there is still a lot of (10)............... in the media   **EMPLOY**
industry, but things are improving.

Part 5			
1		6	
2		7	
3		8	
4		9	
5		10	

It's a mad world

Vocabulary: animals

1 Match the sentences in Column A to a response in Column B. Write the appropriate letter in the gaps.

Column A

1 Are you sure it's true that they're getting married? ....

2 I'll never meet a girl as beautiful as Helen. ....

3 It was meant to have been a surprise party, but it was obvious he knew about it all along. ....

4 What did your Dad say when you told him you'd decided not to sit for your exams? ....

5 She'll be furious when she finds out I broke her favourite vase. ....

6 I've got to go into town to the doctor tomorrow morning. ....

7 She told him she thought he was a really terrible manager. ....

Column B

a) Why don't you kill two birds with one stone and go to the bank as well?

b) That must have really put the cat among the pigeons.

c) He nearly had kittens at first, but then he calmed down and was quite nice about it.

d) Wouldn't it be better to take the bull by the horns and tell her?

e) What nonsense! There are plenty more fish in the sea.

f) So who do you think let the cat out of the bag?

g) Well, I heard it straight from the horse's mouth.

2 Label the features on these animals and then write the name of one real animal which has each feature.

1 .... 7 ....
2 .... 8 ....
3 .... 9 ....
4 .... 10 ....
5 .... 11 ....
6 ....

3 What animal is being talked about in the following sentences?

1 He always barks at the postman. ....

2 I can hear them mooing from over the hill. ....

3 He gave a mighty roar. ....

4 It raised its head and hissed. ....

5 She neighed as I came into the field. ....

6 If you stroke her, she purrs loudly. ....

Speaking: problem solving

Paper 5, Part 3

About the exam

In Paper 5 you are given marks for use of grammar and vocabulary, pronunciation, fluency, and ability to communicate. The examiner may also assess you on task achievement (how well you do each of the things you are asked to do in Paper 5).

Strategy

When you do a problem solving task:
- make sure you understand what to do.
- cover all the points you are asked to talk about.
- ask for the other candidate's opinion.

1   Listen to the interlocutor giving two candidates instructions for a task and study the map below. Mark the following statements **T** (true) or **F** (false).

1   Each candidate has to talk for three minutes.   ....

2   The candidates should decide together which animals they want to see.   ....

3   The problem is that the zoo is going to close soon.   ....

4   The candidates will need to know the words for various kinds of animals.   ....

2   Listen to Dimitra and Giorgos doing the task. Who got good marks for interactive communication?

Grammar: conditionals

1   Fill in the gaps in the following sentences with the most likely form of the verbs in brackets.

1   If you .... (be) happy, your immune system .... (work) well.

2   What .... (you/buy) if you .... (win) the lottery?

3   I .... (be) home by six thirty unless my plane .... (be) late.

4   If I .... (have) time tomorrow evening, I .... (sew) those green buttons on your jacket.

5   No matter how hard you .... (try), you .... (not/convince) me you're right.

6   We .... (not/drive) all the way to the airport if we .... (know) their plane had been delayed.

7   If you .... (divide) two thousand five hundred and ninety-six by fifty-four, you .... (get) forty-eight point oh seven.

8   They .... (meet) three years earlier if she .... (come) to my eighteenth birthday party.

9   I .... (lend) you my new shirt to wear to the party, so long as you .... (promise) to give it back.

10   If I .... (be) you, I .... (tell) him.

11   If you .... (mix) an alkali with a fat, you .... (make) soap.

12   I .... (let) you stay up and watch TV tonight provided that you .... (finish) your homework first.

13   If he .... (not/stand) under that tree during the thunderstorm last week, he .... (not/get) struck by lightning.

14   What .... (you/do) if you .... (be) Prime Minister?

2 Complete the following sentences in an appropriate way.

1 If I do well in my exams, my parents ....
....

2 I might not have met my best friend if ....
....

3 If I could change one thing about myself, I ....
....

4 The world would be a better place if ....
....

5 If I stay out in the sun in the summer, I ....
....

6 If I had to choose two records (or CDs or cassettes) to take to a desert island, I ....
....

7 I wouldn't live anywhere else in the world unless
....

Vocabulary and grammar:
open cloze

Paper 3, Part 2

About the exam
You have 1 hour and 15 minutes to do the five tasks in Paper 3 and transfer your answers to the answer sheet.

Strategy
- Read the text once quickly to find out what it is about.
- Read it again, paying attention to the words around the gap.
- Decide what part of speech is missing.
- Fill in the gaps on the question paper.
- Read the text again to make sure it makes sense.
- Make guesses for any gaps you cannot fill.
- Transfer your answers to the answer sheet.
- All of this should take you **no more than** fifteen minutes.

Spend a maximum of fifteen minutes filling in the gaps in the following text and copying them on to the answer sheet.

Life of a tiger

The tiger can live in almost (0)......*any*...... natural environment from hot, steamy jungles to snowfields with sub-zero temperatures. A female tiger has her first cubs when she is less (1)................... four years old. About half usually die before they (2)................... a year old. They kill their first small animals when they are about one and leave their mother a year (3)................... .

Tigers are good swimmers, can climb trees (4)................... eat 23 kilos of meat in a night. They can jump nearly nine metres, (5)................... is about the length of a double-decker bus. A tiger depends (6)................... its sharp eyes and keen ears. It waits in cover and rushes at the animals it hunts, jumping on (7)................... . If it fails, it often (8)................... up because it gets tired very easily. It can go for more than a week (9)................... catching anything.

Tigers communicate by many sounds, including a roar that can be (10)................... over several miles. Adult tigers usually live alone, (11)................... they are quite friendly with each other. They mostly hunt (12)................... night. They often meet while they (13)................... out hunting, rub heads together and then part.

They have similar bodies (14)................... lions. Nevertheless, (15)................... never mate together in the wild. Occasionally they do in zoos and their offspring are called 'tiglons' or 'tigons'.

Part 2		Do not write here
1		1
2		2
3		3
4		4
5		5
6		6
7		7
8		8
9		9
10		10
11		11
12		12
13		13
14		14
15		15

Vocabulary: places

1 Label these pictures.

1 .... 4 .... 7 ....

2 .... 5 .... 8 ....

3 .... 6 ....

2 Fill in the gaps in the following sentences with an appropriate word. The first letter of each word has been given to help you.

1 My father expects me to help mow the l................... at the weekends.

2 He keeps all the gardening tools in a s................... in the corner of the garden.

3 There's no room for those suitcases down here. Put them up in the a................... .

4 The burglars got in by climbing up a d................... and through the bathroom window.

5 They got on so well with their neighbours they decided to take down the f................... between their gardens.

6 There must be someone home. I can see smoke coming out of their c................... .

7 We keep all the wine in the c................... because it's so much cooler down there.

8 I couldn't see over the h..................., but I could hear children playing in the front garden.

Writing: describing places

Paper 2, Part 2

About the exam
Another option you may have to choose from in Paper 2 is describing a place or building.

Hot tip!
You will get better marks if your description is interesting to read.

1 Circle the best alternative in the following sentences.

1 If you like water sports, your visit to Lake Eildon will certainly be *spectacular/enjoyable*.

2 The new campsite and sports centre are located just outside the town in *colourful/glorious* countryside.

3 One thing that makes the cathedral different is its *exotic/unusual* spire.

4 Vienna is the place to visit for music-lovers and its cafés are famous for their *charming/delicious* cakes and pastries.

5 The landscape is varied, offering *spectacular/colourful* views of the valleys.

6 The market is very *colourful/delicious* with stall-holders in traditional costume selling *exotic/glorious* fruit and vegetables.

7 If you visit the mountain villages, have lunch in one of the *charming/enjoyable* taverns where the local wine is served.

2 Look at the following task and the answers two candidates wrote. Then match the candidates' answers to the examiner's comments.

Describe your ideal home, saying where it would be and how you would decorate one of the rooms.

Candidate A

My ideal home would be a bungalow in the country not far from where I live.

I would build my bungalow on a hill just outside the village of Saint Andrew. It would have spectacular views of the village, which is very charming, and the sea. There would be a large garden around the house, full of colourful flowering plants and exotic fruit trees.

The living room would have huge windows so that I could sit and watch the small fishing boats coming into the harbour. I would build a large terrace outside the living room so that we could go out there on summer evenings and look at the stars. Inside I would build a big chimney so that we could be warm in winter. There would be huge sofas and comfortable armchairs covered in skin.

My house would also have lots of spare bedrooms so that all my family and friends could come and visit me. Maybe you would like to come and visit too.

Candidate B

I live in the city in a appartment. I like very much. It is very nice. It have four bedrooms, a kitchen, a bathroom and a living room.

In the my bedroom there are a bed, a desk, a chair and other furnitures. All is paint in pink. I have on the wall a poster of Johnny Depp. He is my favourite actor. In the desk there is a lamp and a computter. I like play computter game.

I have one brother. My brother like her bedroom too. We are all very contents living in the centre of the city, because of we can to go out to the street which is very excited.

---

1 Comments on Candidate........'s answer

Grade: Unsatisfactory

There is little attempt to structure the answer in terms of the instructions.

The vocabulary used is very simple and not entirely appropriate to the task.

There are basic errors with verb forms and word order.

The use of the Present Simple would confuse the reader, making it difficult to tell if the writer was describing an ideal or simply his actual home.

2 Comments on Candidate........'s answer

Grade: Very good

A well-organised piece of writing which meets the requirements of the instructions.

A range of ideas is communicated with a good range of vocabulary and structures, though there are two minor errors with vocabulary.

The use of the conditional (*would*) makes it clear that the writer is talking about an ideal, though the last sentence is inappropriate in a description of this kind.

3 Find the two vocabulary mistakes the examiner mentions in the good composition. Write the sentences with these mistakes out again correctly in your notebook.

4 Now write your answer to the task in Exercise 2.

1 Underline key words in the instructions.

2 Think of ideas: What kind of house or flat would you choose? Would you build it in the country or in a city, town or village? What would you be able to see/do there? Which room will you describe?

3 Write a plan of your composition following Candidate A's answer.

4 Write your description in 120–180 words making sure that you use some of the vocabulary you studied in this unit and appropriate conditional forms.

5 Check carefully for spelling errors and mistakes with verbs.

Grammar: key word transformations

Paper 3, Part 3

Strategy
- Complete the sentences on the question paper **without** changing the form of the word given.
- Check for spelling and verb form mistakes.
- Write only the missing words in the space on your answer sheet.
- Check that you have copied your answers accurately.

Complete the second sentence so that it has a similar meaning to the first sentence. Use the word in **bold** and other words to complete each sentence.

1 She said she would lend me her notes.
   promised
   She .... me her notes.

2 Although she studied very hard, she didn't do very well in the exam.
   despite
   She didn't do very well in the exam
   .... very hard.

3 My father often played the piano while we sang.
   used
   My father .... while we sang.

4 If I don't feel better tomorrow, I'll go to the doctor.
   unless
   I'll go to the doctor tomorrow
   .... better.

5 You mustn't talk during the test.
   supposed
   You .... during the test.

6 I couldn't tolerate her bad behaviour any longer.
   put
   I couldn't .... her bad behaviour any longer.

7 I have a degree and also extensive sales experience.
   addition
   I have extensive sales experience
   .... a degree.

8 She lost her job because her work was careless.
   carefully
   If she ...., she would not have lost her job.

🎧 Listening: gap fill

Paper 4, Part 2

Strategy
- Listen for the general idea and specific information.
- Answer as many questions as you can the first time you hear the recording.
- Fill in the other answers the second time you listen.
- In the pause check spelling and grammar.

You will hear a man being interviewed about ghosts and haunted buildings in Europe. Listen and complete the gaps in these notes which summarise what the speaker says. After you have heard the recording for the second time, transfer your answers to the answer sheet. Spend only **one minute** doing this.

Number of sites visited in Britain:
(1).........................

Marks of violent past events released by
(2)......................... and particularly sensitive people.

Dracula: real person: ruled part of Romania in
(3).........................
Tirgoviste: (4)......................... of Dracula's kingdom and where he had his palace.
Said to have killed more than (5)......................... people.

Location of Ecclescrieg House, the castle that inspired Bram Stoker: Aberdeenshire,
(6).........................
One member of the family who lived there was the commander (7).........................
Died in mysterious circumstances. Body
(8).........................

Dunnottar castle: used to imprison rebels after Royalist rebellion in (9).........................

More than (10)......................... people kept in dungeon.

Part 2			
1		6	
2		7	
3		8	
4		9	
5		10	

Reading: multiple matching

Strategy
- Read the paragraph headings and the text once quickly to get a general idea.
- Pay attention to the structure of the text.
- Find the main idea in each paragraph.
- Write the paragraph headings in the spaces on the question paper.
- Read the text through with the headings.
- Transfer your answers to the answer sheet.
- Do not spend more than **eighteen minutes** on this part of the test.

Read this magazine article about a pet bear. Choose the most suitable heading from the list **A–H** for each part of the article **1–7**. There is one extra heading which you do not need to use. Transfer your answers to the answer sheet below.

A A mystery resident with a big appetite.
B Make yourself at home.
C Specially designed.
D A nasty temper.
E A bit of luxury.
F Too gentle for his own good.
G An understanding wife.
H Keep out!

Bear necessities

(1 _H_)
The solidly built house of wood and stone is set amid fifty acres of Scottish forest in the hills above Gleneagles. A sign by the gates warns that this is private property. A custom-built coach parked in front cost £120,000, but as we all know stars are very fussy about these things.

(2___)
There's a forty-five foot swimming pool in the garden – but when this particular star was working in Hollywood he had his own jacuzzi too. Beside the pool is a little log cabin with a pile of rubber tyres inside. Go into the house itself and you notice that everything is big — up to and including the meals.

(3___)
In the kitchen most of the food is firmly locked away, but on the breakfast bar in the morning you'll find a healthy portion of baked beans with bread and eggs, plus coffee with lots of sugar and cream. And at teatime, a dish cooked with tomato soup, potatoes and fifteen pounds of fresh meat. It makes you wonder who on earth lives here.
The solution is provided by a sign outside Andy and Maggie Robins' home. It reads: 'Warning – Hercules the bear walks free beyond this gate.'

(4___)
It all started back in the days when Andy was still a professional wrestler.

He went to the USA and met an Indian who kept a bear. When Andy got married, he confessed to his wife that he wanted a bear as part of the family. Most women would probably have begun divorce proceedings, but not Maggie, a farmer's daughter and keen horse-rider. Hercules was bought almost fifteen years ago from the wildlife park in Scotland where he was born. He was four feet tall, but very wild then. Today it's eight feet from the ground to the tip of his nose.

(5___)
Commercials and films have made him famous, and when he was lost a few years ago it was headline news. But there was nothing for the public to worry about. Hercules is a very friendly bear. His owners say this has stood in his way professionally when he has gone for roles that need a big bad bear. 'He's tried to get serious parts in films – but he's got an awfully soft face,' says Maggie.

(6___)
At home, three children up the road often come round to tea. This is Hercules' house as much as it is the Robins' so he goes where he likes. He'll watch TV when there's something good and loud on, like a Tom and Jerry cartoon. And he appreciates an occasional curry or perhaps something Italian for supper for a change.

(7___)
He sleeps in the log cabin by the pool, but he loves the pretty four-poster bed in the Robins' bedroom. To some degree this house has been made 'Hercules-proof' with bare walls and corridors that have been made wider than usual. 'It's true there aren't that many ornaments about,' says Maggie, 'but that's really more because of Andy than Hercules.'

from TV Quick

1	A	B	C	D	E	F	G	**H**
2	A	B	C	D	E	F	G	H
3	A	B	C	D	E	F	G	H
4	A	B	C	D	E	F	G	H
5	A	B	C	D	E	F	G	H
6	A	B	C	D	E	F	G	H
7	A	B	C	D	E	F	G	H

Guilty or not guilty?

Vocabulary: crime

Choose the best alternative to fill the gaps in the following sentences.

1 She was .... by a man who threatened to tell her employer about her past.

   A hijacked **B** blackmailed

2 The .... had a knife so she gave him her bag.

   A smuggler **B** mugger

3 Department stores lose millions from ....

   A pickpocketing **B** shoplifting

4 The police think a/an .... lit the fire.

   A arsonist **B** forger

5 He .... his father's signature on £20,000 worth of cheques.

   A forged **B** smuggled

6 When you travel on public transport, always keep your bag carefully closed in case of ....

   A hijackers **B** pickpockets

7 The .... said she was sure he was the man she had seen running away from the bank.

   A witness **B** judge

8 It took the .... twenty-four hours to decide.

   A accused **B** jury

9 Eventually they managed to reach a ....

   A plea **B** verdict

10 The judge gave him a suspended ....

   A punishment **B** sentence

11 .... exists in some parts of the USA.

   A Probation **B** Capital punishment

12 The police have .... a woman in connection with last Tuesday's robbery.

   A arrested **B** accused

13 The judge agreed to .... her on bail.

   A acquit **B** release

Reading: multiple choice

Paper 1, Part 2

About the exam

There are four types of questions you may be asked in this part of the exam.

1 Questions about what the text means.

2 Questions about the meaning of pronouns (e.g. *it, them*) and demonstratives (e.g. *this, that, those*).

3 Questions about the individual words.

4 Questions about where the text comes from or what its purpose is.

Strategy

For questions which ask you about what the text means you should:

- answer without looking at the alternatives.
- find evidence for your answer in the text.
- find the alternative closest to your answer.
- make sure the other answers are wrong. Do they say the opposite of what the text says? Do they say something that may be true but which is not in the text? Do they say something similar but not exactly the same as the text?

Spend **eighteen minutes only** reading the text opposite, answering the questions and transferring your answers to the answer sheet.

1 What did the court decide about Mr Howarth?

   A That he should never be allowed to drive again.
   B That he should pay a fine and be prohibited from driving for a year.
   C That he should take another driving test at once.
   D That he should not be punished.

2 How did the police learn about Mr Howarth?

   A Men carrying out roadworks reported him.
   B Other drivers reported him.
   C A police car had to swerve to avoid him.
   D Another driver telephoned them.

3 Why did Mr Howarth stop in the end?

   A Some policemen managed to stop him.
   B Another driver stopped him.
   C He realised they would catch him eventually.
   D There were road works on the road and he had
      to stop.

4 Mr Howarth did not realise his mistake at first
   because

   A there were other cars travelling in the same
      direction.
   B the incident happened at night.
   C there were not many cars and he couldn't see
      the other side of the road clearly.
   D he was not wearing his glasses.

5 Mr Howarth realised he was on the wrong side of
   the road

   A when the police stopped him.
   B after driving seventeen miles.
   C when he saw other cars swerving to avoid him.
   D before he had driven a whole mile.

6 Why did Mr Howarth plead guilty?

   A Because he thought he had done a terrible
      thing.
   B Because he was dazed and confused.
   C Because he had driven off when the policeman
      stopped him.
   D Because he had not stopped as soon as he could
      have done.

7 How did Mr Howarth feel about the incident?

   A Terrified and upset.
   B Angry and frustrated.
   C He did not think he had done anything wrong.
   D He was glad it was over.

8 Mr Howarth's lawyer claimed that

   A he had done a very wicked thing.
   B this was not typical of his normal behaviour.
   C he was not to blame for what happened.
   D he was too old to be driving.

An 82-year-old chartered accountant who has had a perfect driving record since passing his test before the Second World War was banned for a year yesterday for travelling seventeen miles in the wrong direction on a dual carriage way.

William Howarth became confused as he tried to avoid roadworks and set off on a road between Oxford and Newbury in the wrong direction, magistrates at Abingdon were told.

Howarth, who uses a hearing aid and wears glasses, was driving in the fast lane of the northbound carriageway as he travelled south causing several drivers to swerve on a dark January afternoon. A police car in the correct lane drove alongside Howarth's car and stopped him, but as the policeman climbed over the central barrier Howarth set off again. He continued for another ten miles until a police road block forced him to stop.

Howarth pleaded guilty to dangerous driving and was also fined £175. He was ordered to re-take his test if he wants to drive again after the year in which he is banned from driving is over.

He leaned forward as he strained to hear yesterday as Mr John Horn, prosecuting, said police received a number of 999 calls saying a car was travelling in the wrong direction.

Mr Robert Hawes, defending said Howarth still worked five days a week as an accountant, sometimes until eight at night, and had a 'perfect' 60-year driving record. He had driven on to the road as he tried to avoid roadworks and had not at first realised he was in the wrong lane because traffic was light and trees blocked his view of the opposite carriageway.

'Within a mile, he realised he was on the wrong carriageway and his intention was to get off as quickly as possible and get back on to the right road.

'There were in fact eight lay-bys along the route where he could have stopped and for that reason he accepts that he is guilty.

'This was not a wicked piece of driving. Mr Howarth was disorientated. It was a nightmare journey for him and he was dazed, confused and in obvious shock.'

from *The Daily Telegraph* newspaper

1	A	B	C	D
2	A	B	C	D
3	A	B	C	D
4	A	B	C	D
5	A	B	C	D
6	A	B	C	D
7	A	B	C	D
8	A	B	C	D

Grammar: *make/let/allow*

1 There are mistakes in seven of the following sentences. Find the mistakes and write the sentences out again correctly.

1 The police made him to stop.

2 The judge decided not to allow him to drive.

3 Are you allow to stay out after ten o'clock?

4 Do your parents make you studying English?

5 Will the teacher let us go home early?

6 They allowed us going to the party.

7 Does she let you stay up late on Fridays?

8 My parents make me wear clothes I didn't like.

9 When I was younger, I didn't allowed to go swimming unless my parents were with me.

10 They wouldn't let me to go.

2 Complete the following paragraphs in your own words.

<u>Children of your own</u>
I wouldn't let my sons or daughters ....
.... I probably wouldn't allow them .... either.
And I think I would probably make them ....
....

<u>The society we live in</u>
I don't think people should be allowed ....
.... In fact I think they should be made ....
.... What's more we shouldn't let our politicians ....

<u>Crime</u>
I don't think the police should be allowed ....
.... I think people who commit violent crimes should be made ....
.... And I don't think we should let ....

Vocabulary: phrasal verbs (*make*)

1 Match the following phrasal verbs with *make to* a definition below. One of the verbs goes with two of the definitions. Write the numbers 1–5 in the gaps.

1 make up
2 make out
3 make for
4 make out (that)
5 make up for

a) to see, hear or understand something with difficulty ....

b) to prepare something by putting different parts together e.g. a bed ....

c) to reduce the bad effect of something ....

d) to pretend ....

e) to move towards something ....

f) to invent a story or piece of information in order to deceive people ....

2 There is a mistake with word order in each of the following sentences. Find the mistakes and write the sentences out again correctly in your notebooks.

1 You won't make for lost time up by working all night. You'll be too tired to work tomorrow.

2 What he told me wasn't true. He just made up it.

3 When the police asked him where he had been that night, he made that he had been with me out, but I was in France that week.

4 The escaped prisoners tried to make the mountains for where they thought they would be able to hide.

5 She muttered something under her breath, but I couldn't make exactly out what she said.

6 If your friend wants to spend a couple of days here, we could make a bed for her in the spare room up.

7 They had a terrible row and didn't speak to each other for a couple of days, but they've made up it and are the best of friends again.

Writing: narrative

About the exam

Most of the questions in Paper 2, Part 2 involve writing for a particular situation and audience.

Strategy

● Pay attention to the situation described in the instructions.
● Decide how the situation will affect the style of your answer.

Hot tip!

NEVER memorise a composition to use in the exam! It may not be an appropriate answer to the question.

Choose between the alternatives in Column A to find a word that matches a definition from Column B. Write the words in the gaps.

Column A

a) fidget/writhe/wriggle
b) wonder/consider/reckon
c) exclaim/mutter/insist
d) lob/hurl/toss
e) inform/insist/order
f) stagger/tiptoe/wander
g) chuckle/giggle/snigger
h) munch/nibble/swallow
i) grasp/clutch/hug

Column B

1 to speak (usually angry and complaining words) in a low voice   ....

2 to laugh quietly   ....

3 to think about, especially in order to make a decision   ....

4 to eat with small repeated bites   ....

5 to take and keep a firm hold of   ....

6 to walk on one's toes with the rest of the feet raised above the ground   ....

7 to hit or throw in a slow high curve   ....

8 to move one's body around restlessly, so that one annoys other people   ....

9 to command   ....

2 Use as many of the words in groups a)–i) as you can to make the paragraph below a more interesting piece of writing. Write it out again in your notebook.

He walked along the corridor quietly, thinking about what he would do if the gang were still there. When he was about to climb the stairs, he heard someone laughing in one of the rooms on the second floor. He held the gun and continued to climb the stairs. Suddenly he felt someone hit him very hard from behind and he walked a few steps further and then fell and moved on the ground in pain, telling himself that he had been a fool to try this on his own. The man who had hit him told him to give him the gun and with what little energy he had left he threw it to him. The man laughed and said, 'Now you're really in trouble, Mason.' He took a bottle from his jacket and drank half the contents in one go. Mason thought he would be lucky to get out of there alive.

3 Here are two questions which ask you to write a narrative. Answer both of them. Spend **45 minutes** on each.

You work as a journalist for a local English language newspaper. Write a news story for the following headline:

Local girls home after cycling journey across the USA.

You have entered a detective story competition. Write a story that begins with the following words:

He woke quite suddenly to the sound of someone opening the back door of the house.

1 Study the instructions carefully and underline key words.

2 Think of ideas and write them down in any order. Ask yourself questions about the situation if you have difficulty thinking of original ideas.

3 Write a plan, putting your ideas in order in paragraphs.

4 Write your answer in 120–180 words. Use narrative tenses (Unit 5) carefully and make your writing interesting.

5 Check your work carefully. Exchange answers with a classmate and check their work, too.

Vocabulary: multiple choice cloze

Paper 3, Part 1

Strategy
- Read the text all the way through to find out what it is about.
- Read the text again and choose the best alternative.
- Check that you have not made mistakes with commonly confused words or 'false friends'.
- Mark your answers on the answer sheet.

For questions **1–15** read the text and decide which answer **A**, **B**, **C** or **D** best fits each space. There is an example at the beginning (**0**). Mark your answers on **the separate answer sheet**.

EXAMPLE:

0 A hurt   **B** damage   **C** illness   **D** injury

0	A	B	C	D

1 **A** discovered   **B** invented   **C** done   **D** manufactured
2 **A** extremely   **B** scarcely   **C** slightly   **D** hardly
3 **A** Despite   **B** However   **C** Although   **D** Otherwise
4 **A** does   **B** has   **C** is   **D** makes
5 **A** controlling   **B** preventing   **C** dealing   **D** stopping
6 **A** along   **B** around   **C** at   **D** over
7 **A** under   **B** less   **C** more   **D** below
8 **A** extends   **B** shrinks   **C** reduces   **D** expands
9 **A** suspect   **B** guilty   **C** accused   **D** arrested
10 **A** Few   **B** The   **C** Several   **D** These
11 **A** include   **B** are   **C** create   **D** involve
12 **A** because   **B** because of   **C** as   **D** therefore
13 **A** thought   **B** reckoned   **C** considered **D** wondered
14 **A** approved   **B** granted   **C** allowed   **D** let
15 **A** expect   **B** hope   **C** anticipate **D** wait

Foam gun will prevent escapes

DEALING with prison escapes and riots without serious (0).......... to prisoners or guards would still be a major problem without the invention of a new range of non-lethal weapons.

A sticky-foam gun has been (1).......... by scientists at the Sandia National Laboratories in New Mexico. The gun sprays you with (2).......... sticky spaghetti-like material which makes movement absolutely impossible.

(3).......... it sounds like something from a cartoon, the sticky foam has a serious purpose. It (4).......... it impossible for anyone hit to reach for a gun or run away. This means that the guns could be an ideal way of (5).......... with escaping prisoners or criminals. They may also be used with rioting prisoners or violent criminals who have to be moved (6).......... the country.

In (7).......... two seconds, the gun can squirt half a litre of foam. This then (8).......... to fifty times its original size. 'If the foam is sprayed at arms and legs, the (9).......... would stick to himself and anything he touches, including the floor,' says Tom Goolby, one of the researchers working on the gun.

(10).......... other non-lethal weapons have also been developed. These (11).......... instruments that make low-frequency sounds that make you feel as if you are going to be sick and non-toxic chemicals called 'stickums' or 'slickums'. These make roads sticky or slippery and (12).......... impossible to drive on.

All these weapons are being (13).......... by the Department of Justice. It is expected that the foam guns will be (14).......... for use in prisons later this year. The other weapons will have to (15).......... a little longer.

from *Focus* magazine

Part 1				
1	A	B	C	D
2	A	B	C	D
3	A	B	C	D
4	A	B	C	D
5	A	B	C	D

6	A	B	C	D
7	A	B	C	D
8	A	B	C	D
9	A	B	C	D
10	A	B	C	D

11	A	B	C	D
12	A	B	C	D
13	A	B	C	D
14	A	B	C	D
15	A	B	C	D

Listening: multiple choice

About the exam
The eight extracts you hear in this part of the exam are completely unrelated.

Strategy
Listen for clues to help you decide:
● what they are talking about.
● where they are.
● what the relationship between the speakers is.

You will hear people talking in eight different situations. For questions **1–8**, choose the best answer **A**, **B** or **C**.

1 You are on a plane. You hear this woman speaking. She is speaking to

A her husband.
B another passenger.
C a flight attendant.

2 You are visiting a friend. You hear his two younger brothers talking in another room. They are

A doing their homework.
B arguing about a computer game.
C watching television.

3 You are waiting to use a public telephone. You hear this woman talking. She is talking about

A a problem with an electrical appliance.
B a problem with a dentist's appointment.
C a problem with one of her customers.

4 You hear this man speaking on a TV set in another room. What kind of programme is it?

A the news
B a film
C a quiz programme

5 You hear these two women talking on a bus. The first woman

A is criticising the second woman.
B is giving the second woman some advice.
C is agreeing with the second woman.

6 You hear this man talking to another man. He is talking about

A taking a cat to the vet.
B taking a dog to the vet.
C taking a baby to the doctor.

7 You hear this man talking on the telephone. He is talking to

A a business associate.
B someone he hasn't met before.
C his wife.

8 You are in another room. You hear this woman talking on the TV. What is she doing?

A demonstrating how to cook something
B describing a meal she prepared recently
C explaining how she normally prepares her favourite dish

Speaking: opinion

About the exam
The examiner will assess you on the following categories:
● use of grammar
● use of vocabulary
● pronunciation
● fluency
● ability to communicate

Strategy
If you do the exam with another candidate, remember you are not competing against this person. Ask their opinion as well as giving your own.

Listen to two candidates doing Paper 5, Part 4 and assess them on the categories listed below. Was their performance: poor/satisfactory/good/excellent? Write **P** (poor), **S** (satisfactory), **G** (good) or **E** (excellent) in the gaps.

	Nicole	Diego
1 use of grammar/vocabulary	....	....
2 pronunciation	....	....
3 ability to communicate	....	....

Grammar: passives

1   Rewrite the following sentences using the correct passive form of the verbs in *italics*.

1   They're *making* a film about Indian tigers.
A film about Indian tigers ....
....

2   No one has *painted* this house for ten years.
This house ....
....

3   They *provide* over one hundred scholarships for students every year.
Over one hundred scholarships for students ....
....

4   I realised someone had *stolen* my wallet.
I realised my wallet ....
....

5   Someone has to *guard* this prisoner day and night.
This prisoner ....
....

6   Water might *affect* the Joker badly.
The Joker ....
....

7   The police *were interviewing* people in the neighbourhood last night.
People in the neighbourhood ....
....

8   A police roadblock finally *forced* Mr Howarth to stop.
Mr Howarth ....
....

2   Rewrite the following sentences using an appropriate passive form so that they sound more formal.

1   You have made some kind of a mistake.
Some kind of a mistake ....
....

2   We remind you not to put bottles in the overhead lockers.
Passengers ....
....

3   We will refund your money in full if you are not satisfied.
Your money ....
....

4   Our customer relations office is dealing with your complaint.
Your complaint ....
....

5   We will send successful candidates a letter inviting them to attend a second interview.
Successful candidates ....
....

6   We sent the goods on 15th April.
The goods ....
....

7   If no one has delivered the equipment by 15th May, please contact us again.
If the equipment ....
....

8   We will replace furniture that our employees damage in transit.
Furniture damaged in transit ....
....

9   Perhaps you would like another cup of coffee while we are preparing your bill.
Perhaps you would like another cup of coffee while your bill ....
....

10   We apologise for the delay. Technicians were checking the plane.
We apologise for the delay. The plane ....
....

15 The power of words

Grammar: hypothetical meaning

1 Fill in the gaps in the following sentences with a correct form of the verbs in brackets. In some of the sentences there is more than one possibility.

1 I wish I .... (*study*) harder. The exam is tomorrow and I've only revised half the course.

2 We wish you .... (*come*) for Christmas. The rest of the family will all be here.

3 I wish I .... (*can/drive*) a car.

4 I wish I .... (*have*) a computer.

5 I wish you .... (*do*) that. It drives me crazy!

6 I wish you .... (*be*) here. You'd love it!

7 I wish you .... (*tell*) me the answer. I'll never guess.

8 I wish I .... (*know*) more vocabulary. I keep forgetting the words for things.

9 If only I .... (*not/do*) that. I'll regret it for the rest of my life.

10 If only I .... (*can/afford*) that dress. It really suits me.

11 I'd rather we .... (*we/stay*) at home tonight. I'm a bit tired.

12 I'd rather you .... (*not/lend*) him that book. It was a present from my grandfather.

13 It's time you .... (*leave*) for the airport. You have to check in two hours before the time on your ticket.

14 Just suppose someone .... (*recognise*) you. They'll probably have reported you to the police.

15 Suppose we .... (*arrive*) a bit earlier. Then we'll be able to help Mary with the food.

2 Complete the second sentence so that it has a similar meaning to the first sentence. Use the word in **bold** and other words.

1 I'm sorry I didn't phone him.
   wish
   I .... him.

2 How about buying her a CD?
   suppose
   Just .... her a CD.

3 I regret saying that to her.
   only
   If .... that to her.

4 You should go to bed now.
   time
   It's .... to bed.

5 I would prefer to have a light lunch.
   rather
   I .... a light lunch.

6 I'd prefer you not to tell him.
   rather
   I .... him.

7 It really annoys me the way you click your fingers.
   wish
   I .... click your fingers.

8 I am really sorry he isn't here.
   only
   If .... here.

9 Shouldn't you start revising for your exams now?
   time
   It's .... for your exams.

Speaking

Paper 5 all parts

Strategy

Relax! Many candidates actually enjoy Paper 5.

Part 1 (interview)

Before
- Revise vocabulary for education, family and free time activities.

During
- If you do the exam with another candidate, listen to what s/he says and show that you are interested.

Part 2 (individual long turn)

Before
- Revise modal verbs.

During:
- If you don't know a word for something, use another word or describe the thing.
- Relate the photograph to your own experience.

Part 3 (collaborative task)

Before
- Revise language for agreeing/disagreeing and asking for/making/accepting/rejecting suggestions.

During
- Make sure you understand what you have to do.
- Make sure you do **all** the things the examiner asks you to do.
- Remember there is no 'right' answer.
- If you do Paper 5 with another candidate, ask for and respond to the other person's suggestions.

Part 4 (discussion)

Before
- Revise the language for expressing/asking for opinions.

During
- Remember! There is no 'correct' opinion.
- Ask the other person what s/he thinks and respond to what s/he says.
- Don't say: 'I don't know.'

Remember:
- DON'T prepare a speech!
- DON'T try to dominate!
- DON'T treat it as a competition!

1 Listen to two candidates doing Paper 5 and look at the photos and map they refer to. Assess each candidate on the categories listed below. Was their performance: poor/satisfactory/good/excellent? Write **P** (poor), **S** (satisfactory), **G** (good) or **E** (excellent) in the gaps.

	Anna	Francisco
1 use of grammar/vocabulary	....	....
2 pronunciation	....	....
3 ability to communicate	....	....

1

2

3   4

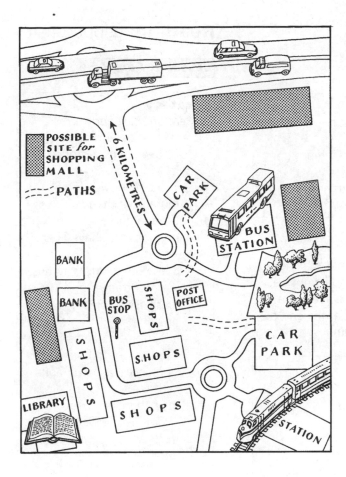

6 KILOMETRES

CAR PARK

BUS STATION

BANK

BANK

BUS STOP

SHOPS

POST OFFICE

S H O P S

S.HOPS

CAR PARK

LIBRARY

S H O P S

STATION

📟 **2** The candidates pronounced the following words incorrectly.

1) saucepans   2) fruit
3) comfortable   4) convenient

How should they be pronounced? Listen to the cassette and check your answers.

📟 **3** How do you pronounce the following words ?

1) bear   4) clothes   7) wallet
2) stir   5) money   8) occasion
3) weapons   6) scientist

Listen to the cassette and check your answers.

Grammar: *to have something done*

Rewrite the following sentences using the correct form of *have* + an object + the past participle of an appropriate verb.

1 The hairdresser cut my hair last week.

I ....

....

2 Some painters are painting the Wilson's house.

The Wilsons ....

....

3 The tailor has turned my trousers up.

I ....

....

4 A pickpocket stole my friend's wallet.

My friend ....

....

5 A photographer took a photo of us.

We ....

....

6 An optician tested my eyes.

I ....

....

7 The dry-cleaner is cleaning my new jacket.

I ....

....

8 A repairman has fixed our refrigerator.

We ....

....

9 The man from the supermarket delivers their groceries.

They ....

....

10 There's something wrong with my car. The mechanic is going to service it next week.

I ....

....

Grammar: error correction

Strategy
- Read the text very quickly to get a general idea of what it is about.
- Read it again and 'say' the words in your mind.
- Look for errors with: articles, auxiliaries, comparatives, prepositions and pronouns.
- Write your answers in the question booklet first. Then transfer them to the answer sheet.

For questions **1–15**, read the text below and look carefully at each line. Some of the lines are correct and some have a word that should not be there. If a line is correct, put a (✔) at the end of the line. If a line has a word that should **not** be there, circle the word and write it at the end of the line. There are two examples at the beginning (**0** and **00**).

	Speed in handwriting	
0	The speed of your handwriting can be estimated by the	✔
00	fluency and continuity of your script; (the) disconnected	*the*
1	writing is usually slower than connected is writing,	
2	which is made in a continuous motion. A very fast script	
3	shows of intelligence and an ability to get down to	
4	essentials quickly. Very large handwriting is rarely as fast,	
5	as the writer tends to waste the time and effort. It is a	
6	fact that the more articulate you are the faster than you	
7	will write it, so fast writing is a clear indication of your	
8	ability to speak in fluently as well as your mental	
9	capacity. In the same way, the more is simplified your	
10	writing, the quicker you will write, and the more elaborate	
11	your writing, the more time you do take over it. Intelligent	
12	writers often depart from the writing style they were	
13	taught at school because of they find it too slow. They	
14	adopt to an original and economical form of writing. Many	
15	executives have small, fast writing, but a large signatures.	

Reading: gapped text

Strategy
- Read the text and the sentences/paragraphs that have been removed once quickly.
- Find the main idea in each paragraph of the text.
- In the sentences or paragraphs that have been removed:
  – work out what pronouns, demonstratives and possessive adjectives refer to.
  – look for a meaning/ relationship between the sentences or paragraphs and the text.
  – pay attention to linking words like *however, furthermore, therefore,* etc.

Read the magazine article opposite about writing. Seven paragraphs have been removed from the article. Choose from the paragraphs **A–H** the one which fits each gap (**1–6**). There is one extra paragraph which you do not need to use. There is an example at the beginning (**0**). Mark your answers on the answer sheet.

WHO INVENTED WRITING?

Our ability to communicate through the written word is something we all accept. Yet the invention of writing was extremely important for modern civilisation.

(0 _H_)
Over the past 3,500 years different civilisations and cultures across the world have created at least 700 different forms of writing. To our eyes most of these scripts look quite distinct, and people who can read only one script cannot understand another.

(1 ___)
All European and Arab scripts originally come from Egyptian hieroglyphs. Most Asian scripts do too, even if the link is less direct. Modern Korean and Vietnamese, however, come from Chinese.

(2 ___)
The first forms of writing were pictograms, simple pictures of objects. Gradually, the direct line between the picture and the object it represented disappeared. In the next phase the pictograms were replaced by symbols which represented objects or 'logograms'.

(3 ___)
A later stage of development which successfully overcame the problem of Egyptian hieroglyphs was the alphabetic system. In this system words are made up of combinations of characters or letters representing different sounds. Early versions of the alphabet system are the basis of the Cyrillic and Roman scripts still used in Europe today.

(4 ___)
The traditional view was that writing was invented in Mesopotamia and then spread to Egypt. It was thought that Chinese script developed independently a thousand years later.

(5 ___)
A second discovery is even more controversial. It has always been accepted that the Sumerians invented the first fully developed writing system. New evidence demonstrates that they only did this after the Mesopotamians had been using a script for at least 200 years.

(6 ___)
So if China developed the first writing, did the idea spread from East to West, and not the other way round? It will take time and more evidence to convince all archaeologists that this is true, but, as they say, the writing is probably on the wall.

A So, the complicated way the world's writing systems developed is well understood. There is, however, still a lot of controversy about which of the four ancient scripts came first.

B Chinese script, unlike Egyptian hieroglyphs, is still used today. Its 50,000 characters have barely changed at all over a period of at least 4,000 years. But how did these ancient scripts develop?

C The first task for writing specialists is to discover the number, frequency and position of individual symbols. They then have to look for groups of symbols that occur repeatedly and for anything that could represent a number.

D The third discovery is perhaps the most controversial of all. It suggests the Chinese were writing before the Egyptians. The evidence points to the development of some Chinese characters as early as nearly 7,500 years ago.

E However, if the evolution of the world's writing systems is traced back through time it becomes clear that nearly all of them originated from just four sources: the ancient scripts of Egypt, Mesopotamia, China and Mexico.

F But a series of new archaeological discoveries is making many people question this theory. Firstly, it now seems that the Egyptians were using a script before the Mesopotamians.

G Ancient Egyptian hieroglyphs in fact combined pictograms with logograms. Because of this a new symbol is required for each new word, making the system very complicated and perhaps accounting for the fact that it hasn't survived in the same way as Chinese characters.

H With it came the ability to keep administrative records and pass messages over long distances. This made it possible for central governments to organise large populations and economies. And, of course, it was also a means of passing on knowledge and literature between generations.

	A	B	C	D	E	F	G	H
1	A	B	C	D	E	F	G	H
2	A	B	C	D	E	F	G	H
3	A	B	C	D	E	F	G	H
4	A	B	C	D	E	F	G	H
5	A	B	C	D	E	F	G	H
6	A	B	C	D	E	F	G	H

Vocabulary: spoken and written language

Complete this crossword.

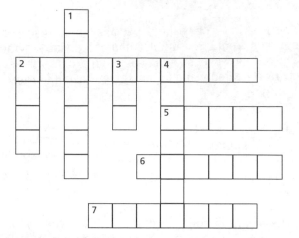

Across

2 correct something which someone has said which you believe is wrong
5 say something very loudly or speak very loudly
6 speak in a low voice, often expressing irritation
7 speak very quietly so only someone nearby hears

Down

1 say or write about something in a few words
2 talk in a friendly and informal way
3 quarrel noisily
4 talk about the details of something with someone

⌨ Listening: selecting

Paper 4, Part 4

Strategy

- Listen carefully to the instructions the supervisor gives.
- Look through the questions before you listen to the cassette.
- The first time you hear the cassette, answer as many questions as you can.
- Answer the other questions the second time you listen.
- Transfer your answers to the answer sheet in the five minutes at the end of the test.

Remember: you only have time to **transfer** your answers, not to think about them and work them out.

You will hear a teacher talking about reading. Choose the best alternatives **A**, **B** or **C** to answer questions **1–7**. Mark your answers on the answer sheet.

1 The speaker says reading and driving are similar because
   A they are both very difficult to learn.
   B you have to practise a lot to be good at them.
   C you have to pass reading and driving tests.

2 The speaker says young people
   A can often only read very slowly.
   B often don't learn to read at all.
   C should read while travelling by car.

3 The problem, according to the speaker, is that
   A they are not given interesting things to read.
   B they don't do what their teachers tell them to do.
   C they are unable to become involved in what they read.

4 One reason some young people read very slowly is
   A they say the words aloud or in their heads.
   B they watch too much TV.
   C they don't recognise all the words.

5 The speaker thinks saying the words aloud
   A is the best way to read.
   B should not be allowed.
   C is a necessary stage children go through.

6 The speaker blames adults because
   A they give children the wrong messages.
   B they complain about children not reading.
   C they make reading seem difficult.

7 The speaker says that
   A we should have learnt to read by the time we leave school.
   B we have to keep practising reading.
   C we should do regular exercise.

Writing: discursive

Paper 2, Part 2

Strategy

- Remember you **must** answer Part 1. You choose **one** of the alternatives in Part 2.
- If you choose to write a discursive composition, read the instructions **very** carefully and underline key words.
- Think of as many ideas as you can. Ask yourself questions. Think about what people you know would think.
- Plan your answer.
- Write your answer. Use interesting vocabulary and use linking expressions.
- Check your work for your 'typical mistakes'.

Remember in Paper 2:

DON'T write a composition you have memorised!
DON'T spend more than **45 minutes** on each answer!
DON'T answer the set texts question if you have not studied at least one of the books!
DON'T write your answer out again unless it is absolutely necessary!

1 Look at the following task.

> You have been asked to write an article for a local paper on the following theme:
>
> *There should be only one international language.*
>
> Write the **article**, giving arguments for and against this question.

Now look at this answer a candidate wrote. Grade the answer from 0–8 (8 is the top mark) in the following categories.

a) Range of vocabulary and structures. ....

b) Accuracy of vocabulary and structures. ....

c) Spelling and punctuation. ....

d) Appropriacy of style (formal/informal). ....

e) Organisation and cohesion (structure and making links between ideas). ....

f) Task achievement. ....

Should there be one international language? There are points for and against this statment.

To begin with if people used only one language, comunication would be cheaper. There would be no need for translattors because everyone would know a language. On the other hand, perhaps people would stop to use their languages and this is a shame, because all the languages of the world are like a beautiful treasure.

Another point is that there would be less misunderstanding. If everyone spoke the same language, we would all get along well. However, I do not think this is true. Probably many people would not speak the language very well, and they would not always understand everything either. In addition to this the people who are nattive speaker would have a unfair advantage.

As far as I am concerned one international language is not a good thing, because we do not want to loose our languages. It is worth remembering that Esperanto was not so sucessful.

2 The writer has made six spelling mistakes, one mistake with the use of gerunds and infinitives and one mistake with the use of articles. Find the mistakes and write the sentences out again correctly in your notebook.

3 Now write your answer to the question in Exercise 1. Use some of these linking words/phrases:

- *to begin with*
- *on the other hand*
- *another point is that*
- *to sum up*
- *however*
- *in addition to this*
- *it is worth remembering that*
- *as far as I'm concerned*

Practice exam

PAPER 1 – READING

PART 1

You are going to read part of a leaflet about Hearing Dogs for Deaf People. Choose the most suitable heading **A–I** for each part (**1–7**) of the leaflet. There is one extra heading which you do not need to use. There is an example at the beginning (**0**).

In the actual exam you will mark your answers **on the separate answer sheet**.

A It's not just the dog that needs to learn.

B Will any dog do?

C Becoming someone's ears

D Understanding deafness

E A fair exchange

F Many benefits

G An expression of gratitude

H Learning to live with others

I What do hearing dogs do?

Hearing Dogs for Deaf People

(0 _I_)

Dogs acting as guides for the blind are now a familiar sight in most cities. Less familiar are 'Hearing Dogs for Deaf People', but in Britain more than 600 such animals exist. In 1982 an innovative programme was established to provide deaf adults with dogs to alert them to sounds in the home such as the doorbell, alarm clock, telephone or smoke alarm. Instead of barking, they use a paw to gain attention and then lead the deaf person to the sound source.

(1 ____)

Small and medium-sized dogs make the best hearing dogs. They don't have to be pure bred, though guard dogs and fighting breeds are considered unsuitable. The dogs must be between the ages of seven weeks and three years. They are selected for their high intelligence and friendly disposition, keen responses to sound and willingness to please.

(2 ____)

Dogs come from many sources, including rescue centres. In this way unwanted and abandoned dogs can be trained to lead active and useful lives in return for good appreciative homes. Even those dogs that do not pass the initial assessment or are later considered to be unsuitable are found good homes as family pets.

(3 ____)

Immediately after selection, they spend several months with a Puppy Socialiser. These are volunteers who take the dogs into their homes for anything up to six months. In this time, the dog learns to obey simple commands and becomes acquainted with all aspects of everyday life, particularly how to get on with other animals and children.

(4 ____)

Once the dogs have got through this initial stage, their training in earnest begins. Kindness and reward are used to teach them. Sounds training, which lasts sixteen weeks, takes place in purpose-built training houses. These houses are designed to simulate the home of the dog's future owner (after all, not all telephones or doorbells sound the same).

(5 ____)

The deaf person also needs time to adapt to the dog with the help of the trainers. For this reason one week before the sounds training is completed, the owners are invited to stay in a flat at the training centre. This is then followed by three months living with the dog in their own home before the final assessment which, if passed, qualifies the dog as a hearing dog for a deaf person.

(6 ____)

The practical value of a hearing dog is immediately obvious but the therapeutic value should not be underestimated. Many people who have hearing dogs find their confidence and independence increases and as a result they go out more and participate in activities which they have previously avoided. The hearing dog, with its yellow coat, instantly tells people that the person they are talking to has a hearing loss. They should then know to face the person and speak clearly, and not too fast, allowing the deaf person to read their lips.

(7 ____)

Although the programme is expensive to run, it has clearly made an enormous difference. One owner, Paul Bullock, has the following to say about his dog: 'Popeye has given me confidence, saved my life, made new friends for us, made others more aware of deafness and broken down some of the barriers that deafness causes. He is my friend and confidant and I talk to him all the time, but above all, he is my ears. I owe Popeye far, far more than he owes me.'

You are going to read an interview with the daughter of a famous film director. For questions **8–14**, choose the correct answer (**A**, **B**, **C** or **D**).

In the actual exam you will mark your answers **on the separate answer sheet**.

My father, the Master of Suspense

1 Patricia Hitchcock is small like her father, Britain's most famous and commercially successful film director, Alfred Hitchcock. She also has something of the intense gaze recognisable from photographs of her mother, Alma. This genetic fusion is entirely apt, for, like his only child, Hitchcock's films were very much a collaborative effort with his wife, who was older than him by just a day and outlived him by only two years.

10 In the early years of their relationship, Hitchcock was actually the junior partner. The couple met at one of the London film studios. It was still the silent era, and Hitchcock, who had become obsessed with film-making, pestered the studio until they gave him a job designing title cards. Alma was a film editor and at first would have little to do with him. They finally fell in love after he was given his first directing break, on a never completed film called *Number 13*. From their marriage to his death in 1980, theirs was as much a creative as an emotional partnership.

20 Alma's role was to oversee scripts through development to post-production. 'I don't think she ever got the credit she deserved,' says her daughter. 'In part it was because she was a woman in a man's world, but she was also a very quiet person who liked to lead a very quiet life.'

Patricia Hitchcock was born in London in 1928, three years after her father made his directing debut in *The Pleasure Garden*. A year later Hitchcock's *Blackmail* was released. His growing reputation made a move to
30 America inevitable. The family arrived in New York on the eve of the Second World War, never to return to London, except for Patricia who went to the Royal Academy of Dramatic Arts when she was 16. After

graduating, she was quickly assimilated into the family 'firm', appearing in several of Hitchcock's films including *Psycho*.

Real life with the Hitchcocks, though, rarely matched the thrills and unexpected twists of their films. There were no unpleasant secrets or murderous neighbours. Rather, the opposite was the case. According to their 40 daughter, the couple thrived on mundanity. Hitchcock's favourite meal was steak and chips. He also abhorred violence. 'The thought of it appalled him. He was an extremely kind and gentle man,' says Patricia.

Perhaps because of his fame, Hitchcock enjoyed remarkable control over the film-making process, which would typically include hours spent on framing individual shots. In a career that lasted over half a century, his daughter recalls only one occasion where there was a major disagreement with the studio over a 50 script.

He was, anyway, says Patricia, above all a commercial director, who made films he believed his audiences wanted to see. 'You must remember that when *Psycho* first came out it was not well reviewed by the critics, especially because he made them go and see it at a cinema instead of the private showings they were used to. And he wouldn't let anyone go in after it had started. But it was instantly a huge success at the box office.' 60

Is there anyone working today who has inherited the Hitchcock mantle? She thinks probably not. But her father would, she believes, have admired Steven Spielberg. 'It's not the sort of film he would have made, but he would have loved *ET*. It was pure entertainment, and that was what he was always about.'

8 Alfred Hitchcock's wife Alma:

A was two years older than her husband.
B was two years younger than her husband.
C was a day younger than her husband.
D died two years after her husband.

9 Alfred and Alma Hitchcock first met:

A when he was directing his first film.
B when he was given a job in a film studio.
C when they became partners in a film studio.
D when he gave her a job as a film editor.

10 Why does Patricia Hitchcock believe her mother never became famous?

A Because Alfred Hitchcock never gave her credit for the work she did.
B Because she was not interested in becoming famous.
C Because she did not have a lot to do with the production stage of film-making.
D Because she didn't get on well with men.

11 What was the name of Alfred Hitchcock's first completed film?

A *Number 13*
B *Blackmail*
C *Psycho*
D *The Pleasure Garden*

12 When Patricia Hitchcock turned 16:

A she began working in her father's films.
B she went to live in New York.
C she went back to London to study.
D she visited England for the first time.

13 Patricia Hitchcock remembers her father as:

A a man with a violent temper who dominated her mother.
B a typical celebrity who was often difficult to work with.
C an unpleasant and secretive person who often had problems with the neighbours.
D a rather conventional man who wanted to make films people would enjoy.

14 What does 'that' in line 66 refer to?

A pure entertainment
B the sort of films Alfred Hitchcock would have made
C Steven Spielberg's film, *ET*
D the director who is most like Alfred Hitchcock

PART 3

You are going to read a newspaper article about tulips. Seven sentences have been removed from the article. Choose from the sentences **A–H** the one which best fits each gap (**15–21**). There is one extra sentence which you do not need to use. There is an example at the beginning (**0**).

In the actual exam you will mark your answers **on the separate answer sheet**.

Tulipmania

Greed, desire, anguish and devotion all played a part in the development of the tulip from a wild flower of Central Asia and the Caucasus to the worldwide phenomenon it is today. When merchants first brought it to the flower markets of Europe, it caused a sensation. Only the rise of football as a spectator sport could draw people's interest away from the thousands of intensely competitive tulip growers' societies that existed in England in the nineteenth century. (**0** _H_)

Holland was the setting for perhaps the most mysterious of these events. What might be called 'Tulipmania' engulfed the country in the 1630s and has puzzled historians and economists ever since. Before tulipmania took hold, a bulb sold for 46 guilders. Within a month, the price had risen from 60 guilders to 1,800 guilders. At the height of the fever, one bulb could sell for the equivalent of 15 years' wages for the average Amsterdam bricklayer. (**15** ____)

It was partly a matter of timing. The Dutch East India Company had been set up in 1602 and this, combined with Amsterdam's increasing importance as a port, marked the beginning of an era of great prosperity for the Dutch. Merchants got rich and so did lawyers, doctors, pharmacists and jewellers. (**16** ____)

And the flower itself had a unique trick that added dangerously to its other attractions. (**17** ____) A plain red tulip might emerge the following spring looking completely different with its petals feathered and flamed in intricate patterns of white and deep red. Though tulip lovers of the time did not know it, these 'breaks' were caused by a virus spread by insects. It was not until the 1920s and the invention of the electron microscope that the mystery was solved.

(**18** ____) Some, taking the advice of contemporary alchemists, laid powdered paint on their tulip beds, expecting the colours miraculously to affect the flowers. It was no stranger than the alchemists' own attempts to turn base metal into gold. In fact, it was rather better, for while the alchemists consistently failed, the tulip growers occasionally succeeded. They just did not know why.

Connoisseurs had always rated 'broken' flowers more highly than plain-coloured ones. For that reason, the broken flowers were the ones that commanded outrageous prices. But the virus was the joker in the tulip bed. (**19** ____) Virus-weakened tulips did not reproduce as freely and vigorously as virus-free bulbs and that, too, increased their value.

Though other European countries experienced similar bouts of tulipmania, the Dutch soon came to lead the world in tulip cultivation. (**20** ____) The Dutchman Carolus Clusius created a tulip collection so fine that he couldn't bring himself to sell it. Inevitably the fame of his collection spread and it was eventually stolen. As soon as the thieves had the tulips, they planted seeds to produce more.

(**21** ____) People who were unable to afford tulip bulbs commissioned paintings by masters whose works were considered cheap substitutes for the real flowers. Jan van Huysum, the great master of Dutch flower painting, could rarely charge more than 5,000 guilders for a canvas, but at an auction in 1637, at the height of Dutch tulipmania, a trader paid 4,000 guilders (the equivalent of a year's wages) for a single bulb.

A Because its cause was not known, its effects could not be controlled.

B In seventeenth-century Holland, books were often illustrated with engravings of garden flowers and were purchased at a cost far less than that of bulbs.

C How had this bizarre situation come about?

D It could change colour.

E One possible explanation for this domination rests on a famous theft.

F The tulip, which had only recently been introduced, became the ultimate status symbol in much the same way as a fast sports car might be today.

G Early growers had a thousand theories on the best way to bring about the magic break.

H There is no denying that the flower has had an eventful history full of mystery and drama.

I Tulipmania is supposed to have ended when the state finally intervened to bring an end to the three years of frenzied trading in the flower.

PART 4

You are going to read descriptions of four board games. For questions **22–35**, choose from the games (**A–D**). Some of the games may be chosen more than once. When more than one answer is required, these may be given in any order. There is an example at the beginning (**0**).

In the actual exam you will mark your answers **on the separate answer sheet**.

Of which of the games **A–D** are the following true:

| A Quarto |
| B La-Tre |
| C Monopoly |
| D Scrabble |

It was originally created by a woman.

| 0 | C |

It uses the same board as another famous game.

| 22 | |

It can be played at two levels of difficulty.

| 23 | |

It has pieces which are all different from one another.

| 24 | |

It is not played skilfully by most people.

| 25 | |

It has been produced and sold by individuals rather than companies.

| 26 | | 27 | |
| 28 | |

It has won prizes.

It requires good players to use their communication skills.

| 29 | |

It will soon look a little different.

| 30 | |

It lets you make some choices for your opponent.

| 31 | |

It exists in many different versions.

| 32 | |

It involves taking your opponent's pieces.

| 33 | |

It was invented by someone who enjoyed doing word puzzles.

| 34 | |

It is owned by more people than any other game.

| 35 | |

Board games

Game A
Quarto has already collected a clutch of awards around the world. The playing board has 16 circles arranged in a square, and there are the same number of playing pieces made of polished wood. Each piece possesses four of eight different characteristics: light or dark; short or tall; solid or hollow; round or square. No two pieces are identical. The idea is to form a line of four pieces, all containing one single characteristic – all dark, or all hollow, for example. You take turns to select any one of the pieces and pass it to your opponent, who places it in a circle of his choice on the board. Being the one that selects your opponent's pieces, you have only yourself to blame if you lose.

Game B
La-Tre was invented by Richard Morgan, who has taken the brave step of manufacturing and marketing his game himself. The playing board is as for chess. Each player has two types of pieces – attackers and defenders. The winner is the player who captures all the opponent's attacking pieces. These are mainly captured by jumping over your opponent's piece on a clear path, and landing on the empty square beyond. The same piece can then zoom off in another direction for further captures, all in one turn. Should you become a La-Tre addict, you may well wish to progress to the advanced game.

Game C
Monopoly, the world's biggest selling game, was actually invented by Elizabeth Magie, though it was Charles Darrow who started marketing it as his own creation in 1933. Despite its popularity, few of us really know how to play it well. Although it is played with a dice, winning is not solely a question of luck. More important are an understanding of economics and an ability to tempt other players into doing deals. A serious Monopoly session starts with everyone going around the board buying properties. Soon people realise that progress can only be made if deals are done. To be successful you need to persuade others that the deal will benefit them even though you are actually only interested in winning.

Game D
The second most popular game, **Scrabble**, was invented by an American crossword fan, in 1948. This famous word game, which can be played by up to four players, is available in 30 languages in 121 countries. Despite this success, it is soon to be redesigned in a bid to attract more players. Designers are expected to consider changing the typeface of the letters and reverting to the use of wood for the tiles. The essential characteristic of the good Scrabble player is flexible, lateral thinking and such individuals should be comfortable with modifications and not particularly concerned about how the board or tiles look. As long as the basic rules and values of the tiles stay the same then fans will be happy.

PAPER 2 – WRITING

PART 1

You **must** answer this question.

1 A youth orchestra from abroad will be visiting your area next month. You have offered to help the tour manager organise their stay.

Read the e-mail message the tour manager has sent you and the notes you have made below. Then write a letter to the tour manager, covering the points in the notes and adding any relevant information about your area.

Write a **letter** of between **120–180** words in an appropriate style.

Do not include addresses.

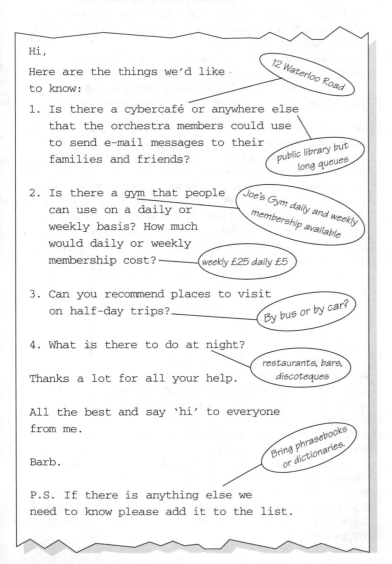

Hi,

Here are the things we'd like to know:

12 Waterloo Road

1. Is there a cybercafé or anywhere else that the orchestra members could use to send e-mail messages to their families and friends?

public library but long queues

2. Is there a gym that people can use on a daily or weekly basis? How much would daily or weekly membership cost?

Joe's Gym daily and weekly membership available

weekly £25 daily £5

3. Can you recommend places to visit on half-day trips?

By bus or by car?

4. What is there to do at night?

Thanks a lot for all your help.

restaurants, bars, discoteques

All the best and say 'hi' to everyone from me.

Barb.

Bring phrasebooks or dictionaries.

P.S. If there is anything else we need to know please add it to the list.

PART 2

Write an answer to **one** of the questions **2–5** in this part. Write your answer in **120–180** words in an appropriate style, putting the question number at the top.

2 An international young people's magazine is investigating the question: Do young people know how to create their own entertainment?

Write a short **article** for this magazine, based on your own experience.

3 You have decided to enter a short-story competition. The competition rules say that the story must begin or end with the following words:

Alice woke to the sound of something … or someone … tapping on the window.

Write your **story** for the competition.

4 You recently started to work for the local council and you had to visit a new sports facility (for example, a football stadium, a swimming pool or tennis centre) in your area. Now you must write a **report** for your boss.

Write your **report** commenting on its good and bad points.

5 **Background reading texts**
Answer **one** of the following questions based on your reading of **one** of the set books.

Either

(a) Could a film be made of the book? Give a brief account of the story and say whether or not you think it could be made into a successful film.

Write your **account** giving enough details for someone who may not have read the book.

Or

(b) A local magazine is holding a competition called 'A letter from …'. The competition rules are as follows:
  • All entries must be in the form of a letter to a friend.
  • The letter must be written as if it were from a character in a book writing to another character.
  • It should explain something about the writer's actions or behaviour in the book.

Write your **letter** for the competition.

PAPER 3 – USE OF ENGLISH

PART 1

For questions **1–15**, read the text below and decide which word **A**, **B**, **C** or **D** best fits each space. There is an example at the beginning (**0**).

In the actual exam you will mark your answers **on the separate answer sheet**.

Example:

(**0**) **A** equal   **B** even   **C** careful   **D** balanced

An orange a day keeps the doctor away

Most people today know how important it is to have a (**0**) .... diet. If for some (**1**) .... this is not possible we have available to us a wide (**2**) .... of dietary supplements including vitamins and minerals. One of the earliest researchers to recognise the role dietary deficiencies (**3**) .... in disease was the Scottish surgeon, James Lind. Lind analysed the diets of thousands of British sailors who had taken long sea voyages and discovered that they ate (**4**) .... or no fresh fruit such as lemons or oranges. He (**5**) .... to the conclusion that a lack of these fruits led to the disease (**6**) .... as 'scurvy'. Scurvy had occurred (**7**) .... human history during times of warfare and famine when people could not get fresh foods like fruit, vegetables and meat. However, when Europeans began to make long voyages of exploration in the fifteenth and sixteenth centuries the problem (**8**) .... more acute. By the eighteenth century, more sailors were dying of scurvy on British ships than as a result of warfare. Lind proved his theory by (**9**) .... the crew of one ship with a supply of fresh lemon juice and comparing the health of the sailors at the end of a long voyage with a second crew that had had only conventional meals. Many of this second group of sailors developed scurvy while the crew who had had (**10**) .... to the lemon juice were healthy. Lind published his findings in 1753. Although he tried (**11**) .... again to get the authorities to follow his (**12**) .... it was not until 1794 that the first Royal Navy squadron set sail with enough lemon juice to (**13**) .... a 23-week voyage. The experiment was such a success that the Admiralty (**14**) .... it compulsory for all British navy ships to carry a supply of citrus fruit or fruit juice. From that point on hardly a

1	**A** motive	**B** cause	**C** reason	**D** defect
2	**A** range	**B** collection	**C** set	**D** series
3	**A** do	**B** make	**C** play	**D** affect
4	**A** little	**B** few	**C** scarce	**D** less
5	**A** reached	**B** came	**C** arrived	**D** got
6	**A** called	**B** named	**C** known	**D** well-known
7	**A** along	**B** over	**C** in	**D** throughout
8	**A** turned	**B** turned out	**C** came	**D** became
9	**A** providing	**B** giving	**C** delivering	**D** bringing
10	**A** access	**B** right	**C** permission	**D** admission
11	**A** more than once	**B** repeatedly	**C** over and over	**D** constantly
12	**A** warnings	**B** advice	**C** suggestion	**D** ideas
13	**A** last	**B** endure	**C** take	**D** support
14	**A** had	**B** got	**C** did	**D** made
15	**A** had	**B** caught	**C** contracted	**D** suffered

PART 2

For questions **16–30**, read the text below and think of the word which best fits each space. Use only **one** word in each space. There is an example at the beginning (**0**).

In the actual exam you will write your answer **on the separate answer sheet**.

WHAT'S IN A NAME?

How do people choose names (**0**) ...*for*.. their babies? In the past, many names were chosen for (**16**) .... religious associations or because of national or family tradition. If a boy's great-grandfather, his grandfather and father were all called Patrick, then (**17**) .... was very likely that the new-born baby would be called Patrick as (**18**) .... Sometimes parents wanted to please a wealthy or much loved relative (**19**) .... naming the baby after him or her and in countries (**20**) .... as Spain a child was often given the name of the saint whose feast day coincided (**21**) .... the birth. Mostly names (**22**) .... good connotations, though there are exceptions. Parents in some parts of the world gave their babies names like 'Ugly' or 'Disagreeable' so as to (**23**) .... the child unattractive to demons.

Nowadays the main consideration in most English-speaking countries seems to be fashion combined with (**24**) .... the name sounds. New names are sometimes invented simply (**25**) .... they sound pleasant. In Britain the influence of television soaps, pop music and Hollywood is clear as is the increasing appeal (**26**) .... less common names. In the United States current naming trends include naming children after places, using traditional last names as first names and borrowing (**27**) .... other languages and cultures.

There are hundreds of books and even web sites devoted (**28**) .... listing names for anxious parents who still can't make (**29**) .... their minds. Despite the almost bewildering range of choices plenty of children still end up in classrooms where three, four or even more of their classmates have the (**30**) .... name.

PART 3

For questions **31–40**, complete the second sentence so that it has a similar meaning to the first sentence using the word given. **Do not change the word given.** You must use between two and five words.

31 It's too late to phone Tom.
if
We could phone Tom .... late.

32 The others were on the point of leaving when we got to the station.
about
The others .... when we got to the station.

33 I expect you were tired after going to bed so late.
must
You .... after going to bed so late.

34 I find it really annoying the way people talk in the cinema.
wish
I .... in the cinema.

35 Travelling by bus is not as convenient as travelling by car.
less
Travelling by bus .... travelling by car.

36 Would you prefer me to come back later?
rather
Would you .... later?

37 'Is the museum open tomorrow?' asked the tourist.
asked
The tourist .... open the following day.

38 Cases of the disease have occurred very rarely since the eighteenth century.
ever
Since the eighteenth century cases of the disease .... occurred.

39 I couldn't sleep last night because of the heat.
impossible
The heat .... me to sleep last night.

40 'Congratulations! You've passed all your exams!' said her teacher.
on
Her teacher .... all her exams.

PART 4

For questions **41–55**, read the text below and look carefully at each line. Some of the lines are correct, and some have a word which should not be there. If a line is correct put a (✔) at the end of it. If a line has a word which should **not** be there, circle the word and write it at the end of the line. There are two examples at the beginning (**0** and **00**).

In the actual exam you will transfer your answers to the **separate answer sheet**.

TIME TO LEARN TO RIDE A BIKE

0	In my opinion, encouraging people to ride bicycles would do a lot towards	✔
00	reducing the huge number of cars (that) on our roads. The trouble is I can't	*that*
41	actually ride one myself. When I was a baby one of my older brothers he fell	
42	off his bicycle and broke his arm. My parents were so upset as by this incident	
43	that they decided to sell his bicycle. They also decided that my sisters and I would	
44	be better than off without them. As a result none of us learnt to ride as children and	
45	although various friends have done of their best to teach us over the years no one	
46	has succeeded so far. When I was younger this often caused me the embarrassment.	
47	When my friends went off on cycling trips I would have to invent excuses for not	
48	going with them or I confess to being unable to ride a bike. Later, as a student in	
49	Cambridge, I felt strange because of there were only a few people who didn't cycle to	
50	and from classes and the library. Once I went on for holiday to a small island where	
51	the only means of the transport was bicycles and my friend had to ride everywhere with	
52	me on the back of his bike. Now that I'm working it wouldn't have matter so much	
53	if I didn't firmly believe that cycling to be the answer to our cities' growing traffic	
54	and environmental problems. I suppose I'll just have to learn it even if it does mean	
55	a few bumps and bruises and a lot of wounded pride.	

PART 5

For questions **56–65**, read the text below. Use the word given in capitals at the end of each line to form a word that fits in the space in the same line. There is an example at the beginning (**0**).

In the actual exam you will write your words **on the separate answer sheet**.

HOW PLAY HAS CHANGED

The way children play has changed (0) ..*considerably*.. over the last fifty years	**CONSIDER**
In the past, parents did not have to fear for the (56) .... of their children	**SAFE**
if they went out to play. Most (57) .... were communities in which	**NEIGHBOUR**
everyone knew everyone and children could be left to play (58) .... by	**SUPERVISE**
adults. In (59) .... there was hardly any traffic and a street could	**ADD**
be (60) .... transformed into a football pitch or used for a game of tag.	**EASY**
(61) .... things are very different today. Apart from the fact that our	**FORTUNATE**
streets are much more (62) .... than they were in the past, the last fifty	**DANGER**
years have seen the (63) .... of more and more sophisticated games,	**CREATE**
(64) ...., of course, the thousands of computer games on the market.	**INCLUDE**
Too much time spent alone with a computer may damage the child's (65)	**ABLE**
to form friendships with other children.	

PAPER 4 – LISTENING

PART 1

🔊 You'll hear people talking in eight different situations. For questions **1–8**, choose the best answer **A**, **B** or **C**.

1 You hear this woman talking to a shop assistant. Does the woman

  A want to exchange something she bought? _____

  B want her money refunded? _____

  C want to buy another item? _____

2 You hear a man and a woman talking in a restaurant. Is the man

  A giving the woman advice? _____

  B warning her about something? _____

  C promising to do something for her? _____

3 You hear this woman talking on a mobile telephone. Where is the person she is talking to?

  A in an office _____

  B at home _____

  C on a train _____

4 You hear two women talking on a bus. What is the relationship between the two women?

  A They are strangers. _____

  B They are friends. _____

  C They are mother and daughter. _____

5 You hear part of a radio interview. What are the two men discussing?

  A astronomy _____

  B Latin American dancing _____

  C music _____

6 You hear this lecturer talking to some students. What is her attitude to the students?

  A She is trying to motivate them. _____

  B She is angry with them. _____

  C She is frustrated by them. _____

7 You hear a guest talking to a hotel receptionist. What does the receptionist tell him?

  A That it will not be possible for his friend to stay at the hotel until 14th. _____

  B That his friend can stay if he is willing to share a room with another guest. _____

  C That his friend can stay if they put an extra bed in the man's room. _____

8 You hear this radio programme about a recent concert. What is the presenter's opinion of the concert?

  A It was just as bad as he had expected it to be. _____

  B He thought it was surprisingly good. _____

  C He had high expectations but was disappointed. _____

PART 2

🔊 You will hear part of a radio interview about colour-blindness. For questions **9–18**, complete the notes which summarise the information in the interview. You will need to write a word, a number or a short phrase in each box.

Most colour-blind people can't tell the difference between **(9)** ....

There are **(10)** .... types of colour sensor.

If two colour sensors are damaged people see **(11)** ....

The proportion of European men with colour-blindness is **(12)** ....

Distinguishing blue, brown, yellow and green is important for **(13)** ....

Distinguishing red, green and orange is important if you **(14)** ....

Tinted contact lenses fool the brain into **(15)** ....

Wearing one tinted lens is not usually **(16)** .... to other people.

The photographer could not distinguish **(17)** ....

A woman who was treated for colour-blindness could not bear to eat **(18)** ....

PART 3

You will hear five different men talking about summer. For questions **19–23**, choose from the list **A–F** how each man spent the summer. Use the letters only once. There is one letter you don't need to use.

A He was working.
B He spent the summer in a private house.
C He was recovering from an accident.
D He went somewhere he had never been before.
E He took a charter flight to his holiday destination.
F He stayed in a hotel in a foreign country.

19 Speaker 1 ___

20 Speaker 2 ___

21 Speaker 3 ___

22 Speaker 4 ___

23 Speaker 5 ___

PART 4

You will hear a conversation about university accommodation in Britain between a teacher, a student, called Paul Lucas, and his mother, Mrs Lucas.

Answer questions **24–30** by writing

    T (for teacher)
    P (for Paul Lucas)
    M (for Mrs Lucas) in the spaces provided.

24 Who wants some advice? ____

25 Who has already made a decision? ____

26 Who is concerned about cooking? ____

27 Who has read the booklet carefully? ____

28 Who thinks friends can help you study? ____

29 Who lived in a hall of residence in the past? ____

30 Who has been persuaded? ____

PAPER 5 – SPEAKING

PART 1

The interlocutor will ask you and the other candidate about yourselves.

🔲 Listen to the cassette and answer the questions. Pause the cassette after each bleep and give your answer.

1

Candidate A

PART 2

The interlocutor will ask you and the other candidate to talk about some photographs.

🔲 Listen to the cassette and answer the questions. When you hear two bleeps, pause the cassette for 1 minute and answer the question. When you hear one bleep, pause the cassette for 20 seconds and answer the question.

2

Candidate B

3

4

PART 3

The interlocutor will ask you and the other candidate
to discuss something together.

Look at the pictures and follow the interlocutor's
instructions. When you hear the bleep, pause the
cassette for 3 minutes and do the task.

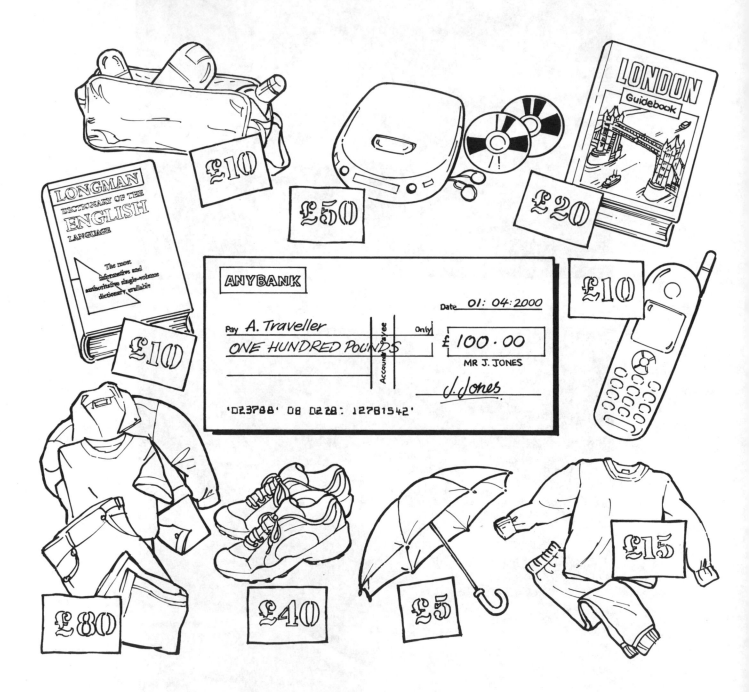

PART 4

The interlocutor will ask you and the other candidate questions related to the theme of Part 3.

 Listen to the cassette and answer the interlocutor's questions. Pause the cassette at the end of each question and discuss it with the other candidate.

Answer key

UNIT 1

Vocabulary p.7

1 1 sail 2 canoe 3 checking in 4 catching
5 maps 6 visit 7 travelling 8 destination 9 trip

2 1 a platform *cars* 2 a flight *ships* 3 a port *trains*
4 a single *planes* 5 an inspector *cars*
6 a steward *buses* 7 a seatbelt *ships*

Reading pp.8–9

2 3 B 4 B 5 D 6 E 7 B

Word formation pp.9–10

1 2 adverb 3 adjective; noun 4 verb 5 adjective
6 noun 7 adjective 8 adjective

Hot tip! negative (*unfortunately*)

2 2 impatient 3 helpful 4 profitable 5 sunny
6 underestimate 7 overcharge 8 likely
9 homeless 10 disappointment

Listening p.10

1 1 F 2 F 3 T 4 ? 5 T

Tapescript

I flew to Malta and then took a ferry to Gozo where I stayed in Sannat – a sleepy town away from the tourist centre. I wanted to explore as much of the island as I could so I decided that hiring a moped was probably the best thing to do.

Victoria, the capital, has a good market and Mgarr, the harbour, is the best place to hire boats to go water-skiing on the lagoon and to visit the nearby island of Comino. But *the* place to go on the island is Marsalforn. It's got the best hotels and the most fantastic disco called *The Rook* – it's an old castle with a dance floor in the battlements. Go swimming at Marsalforn, sandy Ramla bay, the inland sea, or San Blas bay, which is down a steep incline. Tapinu is famous for its church where a scene from the film *Clash of the Titans* was shot.

I really enjoyed my visit. Gozo in the summer is hot and arid, but the beaches are great and the nightlife is fantastic.

2 1 b) 2 e) 3 a) 4 d) 5 c)

Writing p.11

1 1 F 2 I 3 I 4 F 5 F 6 F 7 I 8 F 9 I 10 I
11 F

2 1 informal 2 a) 2 b) 1 c) 4 d) 7 e) 6 f) 5
g) 3

Vocabulary p.12

1 1 e) 2 g) 3 h) 4 d) 5 f) 6 i) 7 c) 8 b)

2 1 ... I'm feeling pretty **pleased**. 2 I was **thrilled** ...
3 My family and I would be **delighted** ...
4 The mountains are really **amazing** ...
5 There are lots of **fascinating** old streets ...
6 The summers can be a bit **exhausting** ...

Grammar pp.12–13

1 1 How do people learn new words? – e)
2 What do we have to do? – f)
3 You don't agree, do you? – i)
4 What do you like doing in your spare time? – d)
5 Where do you want to go this weekend? – g)
6 Why do you get so nervous? – h)
7 Who were you angry with? – b)
8 What does 'miserable' mean? – a)
9 Are you going to translate each word? – j)
10 Did you write a definition of 'cruise'? – c)

2 1 aren't you – e) 2 haven't I – g) 3 isn't he – h)
4 doesn't she – i) 5 didn't you – c)
6 didn't he – d) 7 hadn't he – a) 8 didn't you – f)
9 won't you – j) 10 would you – b)

3 1 down 2 up 3 down 4 up 5 down 6 down
7 up 8 down 9 up 10 up

When Sam's voice goes up, he is not very sure that the information is correct; when his voice goes down, he is fairly sure that the information is correct.

4 2 I wonder why she said that.

     3 I'd like to know how many tourists visit your country each year.

     4 I wonder if this bus goes to Oxford Street.

     5 Could you tell me where the tourist office is?

     6 Do you know if there are any museums near here?

     7 Would you mind telling me what we are supposed to do?

     8 I don't know if she's English or American.

Speaking p.13

SYLVIE: Are you ready to start?

KATRINA: **What do we have to do?**

SYLVIE: Choose holidays for these three families.

KATRINA: OK. **Where do you think the Smith family would like to go?**

SYLVIE: I think the Channel Islands would be good for them because there are safe beaches and they have small children. **Where will we send the Jones family?**

KATRINA: **Do you know when they are taking their holiday?**

SYLVIE: Probably in August like everyone else.

UNIT 2

Vocabulary p.14

1 1 for 2 from 3 on 4 of 5 to 6 of

2 1 terrified 2 responsible 3 proud 4 satisfied 5 keen 6 suspicious 7 ashamed 8 good

3 1 B 2 A 3 B 4 A 5 B 6 B 7 A 8 B

Reading p.15

1 1 *These people* 2 *people who do risk sports* 3 *People* 4 *Risk sports* 5 *executives*

2 1 C 2 A 3 B

Listening p.16

Tapescript

I=interviewer MT=Meregan Turner

I: In today's programme I'll be talking to a woman whose occupation is often thought of as the exclusive province of men. Meregan Turner is one of the very few women who are professional racing drivers. Well, Meregan, I suppose the obvious question is – how does a woman end up in motor racing?

MT: You could say it's in the blood. You see my father was also a racing driver. But I didn't realise how much I wanted to race until some friends took me to Silverstone race track and booked me on to actually drive one day. I just couldn't believe that anything could be so wonderful, that there was anything in the world so super. When I got out of the car, I simply jumped up and down on the spot. And from there on in, I couldn't think about doing anything else at all but motor racing. It's just like falling in love. It's completely taken over my life.

I: How have you found it working in this man's world? Were men protective of you on the track?

MT: No, of course not, and they shouldn't be. But sometimes you get real hostility. One man just wouldn't let me overtake him. When I finally succeeded, he actually turned into my wheels. Then he went straight into the pit and ended up in hospital. But that kind of thing doesn't often happen. Anyway, it's all irrelevant. I didn't go into it thinking, 'I am going to be a female racing driver.' I went into it because I wanted to race. The fact that I was a girl didn't come into it.

I: And ... and what about the men in your life? Do they worry about you?

MT: Well, my father comes to the track and times me. He says he doesn't worry once I start going round. I suppose because he understands what it's actually like he's less likely to think it's dangerous. My boyfriend, Iannis gets terribly worried. He won't watch me because he's terrified I'm going to kill myself.

I: So I don't suppose Iannis ever goes to the track?

MT: No, no. In fact he spends almost a third of the year back in Greece where he comes from. He owns one of the biggest and nicest hotels on Corfu. I applied for a job there once. That's how we met.

I: Don't you miss him when he goes away?

MT: Yes. Terribly. I just don't know what to do with myself. It's like driving backwards down the motorway.

1 racing driver 2 father 3 falling in love 4 men
5 wanted to race 6 understands 7 terribly worried
8 Greece 9 Corfu 10 applied for job

Word formation p.16

1 1 adjective 2 adverb 3 adjective 4 noun 5 adverb; adverb 6 adjective

2 1 complete, final, actual 2 *-ity* 3 *-ive; -ive* 4 danger

3 1 dangerous   2 surprising   3 unpleasant
4 unfair   5 abusive   6 seriously   7 variety

Vocabulary p.17

1 1 f)   2 g)   3 d)   4 a) and j)   5 e)   6 b)   7 i)   8 c)
9 h)

2 1 'debt collector   2 'social worker   3 'traffic
warden   4 private in'vestigator   5 'tax inspector
6 'nightclub bouncer   7 plastic 'surgeon
8 'bus conductor   9 senior li'brarian
10 'newspaper editor

3 1 salary   2 resign   3 strike   4 commission   5 retire
6 bonus   7 sack   8 skill   9 employee   10 earn

C	B	X	H	S	K	I	L	L	C
L	O	N	R	S	A	P	Q	S	O
M	N	M	O	T	P	C	C	D	M
E	U	S	M	R	C	R	K	K	M
A	S	F	T	I	Z	E	C	R	I
R	G	U	B	K	S	T	X	E	S
N	W	H	V	E	Y	I	F	S	S
S	A	L	A	R	Y	R	O	I	I
K	I	J	X	E	D	E	G	G	O
E	M	P	L	O	Y	E	E	N	N

Speaking p.18

Tapescript

I=Interlocutor P=Petra S=Stefan

I: Here are some pictures of various jobs. Could you
work together and put the pictures in order of
priority according to how much you think people
doing each of these different jobs should be paid.
As you decide could you also give reasons for your
decisions?

P: I think you should be paid more if you have to
study for a long time. Umm ... let's see ... nurses
have to study for a long time and nursing is a very
responsible job, so I think they should be paid
more than the other jobs on this list.

S: Umm ... yes ... umm, I agree. It's also a bit
unpleasant ... I mean it can be hard work and
sometimes upsetting or even dirty. I think people
should be paid more for doing dirty and
unpleasant jobs. Shall we put dustmen after
nurses?

P: OK. What shall we put next? I think people who
do jobs that are enjoyable should be paid less. So
perhaps the stockbroker should come last.

S: Ah, no, I don't agree. Being a stockbroker is very
difficult. So I'd put it after dustmen. We ... umm,
should decide which jobs are important.

P: OK. Well, plumbers and traffic wardens are
important. And being a traffic warden is probably
quite difficult.

S: Mmm, mmm ... and ... umm ... what about editors?

P: Oh, I think they should be paid as much as
stockbrokers. It's a very difficult job and it's also
creative. Let's put editors before stockbrokers.

S: Mmm, yes. That's a very good idea. Let's see.
What's left? Referees and bouncers. Do you want
to put them before editors?

P: Yes, because they're not very popular jobs.

2 1 Shall we   2 put next   3 And what about
4 What's left   5 Do you want

3 1 Yes, I agree.   2 OK.   3 That's a very good idea.
4 No, I don't agree.

Grammar p.19

1 1 don't like   2 have   3 sometimes drives; get
4 never get; is always waiting; turn   5 tells; jump
6 are not going   7 are meeting   8 am making; is
bringing; are bringing   9 rings; do we have
10 doesn't listen; gives   11 is always talking; drives
12 rings; always says; are you doing   13 answer;
am talking

2 1 c)   2 e)   3 a)   4 b)   5 d)   6 f)   7 g)   8 j)   9 h)   10 i)

3 1 go   2 are sunbathing   3 are swimming
4 walking   5 don't know   6 is skiing

Writing p.20

1 a formal letter

2 1 F   2 T   3 F   4 T   5 F

UNIT 3

Vocabulary p.21

1 1 d)   2 f)   3 a)   4 g)   5 c)   6 b)   7 i)

2 1 arrogant   2 naughty   3 mean   4 silly
5 generous   6 modest   7 flexible
8 narrow-minded

Listening p.21

Tapescript

Speaker 1

I would describe myself as self-confident. I suppose some people would even say that I can be a bit bossy. Years of looking after my younger brothers has made me like this – I came first after all. I think I would also describe myself as rather ambitious. I like to be the leader and I suppose this is the result of having had to struggle to win back my parents' attention after my brothers and sisters were born. I know that this also means that sometimes I can be a bit aggressive, particularly if people don't do what I say and I know that I'm right. On a more positive note, I'm a good communicator and I think this comes from acting like a kind of link between my parents and the younger children in my family. For example, if one of my sisters wanted something and she didn't think our parents would agree to it, I'd try to persuade them.

Speaker 2

I'm the middle one in my family – I've got two older brothers and two younger sisters. I think this has made me quite independent as the two older ones used to play together and so did the two younger ones, so I was left to play on my own a lot. If I wanted to play with them, I had to fit in with what they wanted and I think this has taught me to be cooperative. Because I had to learn to be flexible I think I'm quite a good parent myself. I've had so much experience with older and younger brothers and sisters that I'm adaptable and I get on with all sorts of different people. One negative thing is that I was a bit overshadowed by my brothers and often felt left out. I think this has left me with a feeling of loneliness and lack of self-confidence.

Speaker 3

I'm the baby in my family and even though I'm in my forties, my older sisters still treat me like a bit of a child. I think I would describe myself as relaxed and open-minded. I wasn't expected to conform like my sisters were, and I was certainly allowed to do all kinds of things they wouldn't have dared even attempt. If I'm honest, I'd have to say that I was a bit spoilt. But I think that having all those people looking after me has made me better at coping with problems in later life than my sisters are. Sometimes I tend to be a bit passive and reluctant to take responsibility for things and I do tend to blame others when things go wrong. I don't want to have any children myself. My husband says this is because I want to be the centre of attention.

Speaker 4

I was an only child and I think this made me responsible, organised and serious. All my parents' hopes and expectations rested on me and I got used to trying to live up to what people think of me. I was always very well organised as a child because I had to fill my own time. My wife says I take life too seriously and I suppose this might come from never having joked with brothers and sisters. I also find it difficult to form friendships or to share my thoughts and feelings with others or let them too close to me. I think I got used to receiving all the attention and that this makes it hard for me to direct my attention to others. Some people would probably say I seem a little selfish.

1 1 Y 2 O 3 M 4 E 5 O 6 E 7 E 8 M 9 Y 10 O

2 a) 4 b) 2 c) 3 d) 1 e) 3 f) 3

Reading p.22–23

1 B

2 1 She was seen performing on TV with her brothers.
  2 She lived in a big house with its own zoo and cinema and her family were famous.
  3 She wanted to be independent.
  4 She feels it has helped her learn.

3 1 A 2 B 3 A 4 A

4 1 Question 4 B 2 Question 3 B 3 Question 2 A

5 1 overshadowed 2 handful 3 understandable

Word formation p.24

1 1 -able 2 -ful 3 over-

2 1 alike 2 appearance(s) 3 tendency 4 overeat
  5 childhood 6 adaptable 7 characteristic
  8 shyness 9 roomful 10 self-conscious
  11 fashionable 12 Unfortunately 13 agreement

Grammar pp.24–25

2 1 T 2 F 3 T 4 T 5 T 6 F 7 T 8 T

Writing pp.26–27

2 Report 1: Candidate B; Report 2: Candidate A

3 1 *writting*: writing 2 *arive*: arrive 3 *bluse*: blouse
  4 *foto*: photo 5 *tipical*: typical

4 1 *I writting inform you ...* : I am writing to inform you ...   2 *She is leave ... and arrive ...* : She is leaving ... and arriving .../She leaves ... and arrives ...   3 *She is studying very hard every day*: She studies very hard every day.   4 *Sometimes she uses glasses, but she will use ...* : Sometimes she wears ..., but she will be wearing ...   5 *Do you want that she bring you a gift?*: Do you want her to bring you a gift?

5 1 *with a blonde hair*: with blonde hair   2 *she is good student*: she is a good student   3 *a blue trouser*: blue trousers   4 *one photo*: a photo   5 *a typical food*: typical food

6 wear

UNIT *4*

Reading p.28

1 Plan A

2 1 F   2 A   3 B   4 E   5 C

3 1 unimaginable   2 dependent   3 traditional   4 catastrophe   5 familiar   6 unacceptable   7 in isolation   8 back up   9 tragedies   10 impending

Grammar p.30

1 1 you like me to help   2 tell me what he looks   3 sounds like   4 plays racket sports like   5 like going to the beach   6 smells like   7 look very like   8 would like to

2 1 **What's** your sister like?   2 She's the same height **as** me ...   3 ... would you like **to go** to the cinema ...?   4 That sounds **like** a good idea.   5 **Would** you like to see anything in particular?   6 I **like** comedies.   7 ..., **if you like**.   8 Are you **like** your brother ...?   9 I**'m like** my mother ...

Vocabulary p.31

1 1 d) – off   2 g) – on   3 c) – up   4 e) – over   5 h) – off   6 b) – up   7 f) – off   8 a) – in

2 1 take up   2 take on   3 take off   4 take up   5 take over

3 1 She **took me off** ...   3 ... I've **taken it up**.   4 ... they only **took them on** a month ago.   5 ... why don't you **take it off**?

Listening p.31

Tapescript

Speaker 1

We went to one of those Virtual Reality places. It was really funny. You go along and put this kind of helmet on your head and there's a plastic thing like a gun that you hold. Anyway, you put some money in the slot, just like in any amusement arcade, put the helmet on and then you really do see all these aliens running towards you and spaceships dive-bombing and this incredible terrain like on Mars or something. It's absolutely fantastic! Much better than an ordinary video game, because it's all around you. You really feel as if you're there. I was so involved that when it finished I went on trying to fire the gun thing. All my friends were laughing at me. I must have looked pretty silly.

Speaker 2

My father gave it to me for Christmas. It was supposed to translate thousands of words and sentences into French, English and German. You just type in a sentence in your language and press a button and a translation appears on a small screen. Well, there must have been something wrong with it because when we were on holiday in France, I typed in a sentence meaning: 'Where is the post office?' and what I thought was the French translation came up on the screen. I went up to this old lady and read out the translation and she burst out laughing. You see, the machine had given me the French for: 'You are the most beautiful woman I have ever seen.' It was really embarrassing.

Speaker 3

It tells you the time all over the world, you can wear it when you're scuba diving, it's solar-powered and it's even got a built-in calculator. But the problem with it is that I can't work out how to stop the alarm. The other day I set the alarm so that I'd remember to look at the time when I was studying. You know, if you're really concentrating, you can forget to look at your watch and miss your favourite show on TV or something. If you don't switch the alarm off, it goes off at the same time every day after that. So the next day in class it started going 'beep beep beep' in the middle of a test and I couldn't work out how to stop it. Eventually it stopped, but the teacher and the other students were a bit annoyed.

Speaker 4

I usually walk up the stairs, but that particular day I'd been up and down all day and I was feeling a bit tired. It was there with the door open so I got in and pressed 3 and nothing happened. Then I pressed 3 again and the 'close doors' button and they did close, but nothing happened. So I pressed 3 again and it sort of jumped up and down a couple of times and then shot up really fast to the third floor. I thought I was going to fly through the roof of the building! Well, the doors opened, fortunately, and I literally fell out shaking like a leaf. I've never taken it again needless to say – it's only two flights of stairs to climb anyway.

Speaker 5

I switched it on and nothing happened. Absolutely nothing. None of the lights that tell you that the battery is low or that the hard disk drive is working went on. It was as if it had died. So I took it to the technician and he flicked the switch on and off a couple of times and got about as much response as I'd done. He checked the battery and the power supply, but there didn't seem to be anything wrong there. Then he flicked the switch again and the screen lit up and everything was running perfectly. 'What did you do?' I said. 'I don't know,' he said. 'No. Come on. Tell me,' I said. 'What did you do?' 'I just frightened it a bit,' he said. Well, quite frankly I could have done that myself.

1 F   2 D   3 C   4 A   5 E

Writing pp.32–33

1 1 b)   2 d)   3 a)   4 c)   5 f)   6 e)   7 i)   8 h)   9 k)   10 j)
11 g)

2 1 The captain **did not believe** ...   2 ... **they had been missing** for only a few hours ...   3 when they **were found** ...   4 ... they all **had** long beards
5 ... as if they **had not shaved** for six months or more.   6 ... when they **disappeared**.

Vocabulary and grammar p.33

1 scientific   2 technological   3 laboratories
4 research   5 problems   6 development
7 revolutionised   8 chemical   9 produce   10 inventor

Speaking p.34

Tapescript

I=interlocutor L=Laura A=Ahmet

I: Now, I'm going to give to each of you two different photographs. I'd like you to show each other your pictures and then talk about them. You each have one minute to do this so don't worry if I interrupt you. Laura, here are your two photos. Please let Ahmet see them. They show technological devices. Ahmet, I'll give you your photos in a minute. Laura, I'd like you to compare and contrast your photos and say how you feel about devices like these.

L: My photographs show a row of houses with ... umm ... I think they are called 'parabolic antenna' or aerials. It's a kind of dish. They are used for receiving satellite TV and you put them on the roof of your house or outside near the roof. We haven't got an antenna like those but I think they would be very useful because you can watch TV programmes in other languages. The other photograph is very different because it is taken inside not outside a house. It shows a girl in her bedroom working ... or maybe she's playing some game on her computer. She looks very concentrated. I think computers are very useful. My mother has one and she use it a lot to write reports and work out how much money she has got to spend. She says she couldn't live without it.

I: Ahmet, could you tell us how you feel about the devices in Laura's photos?

A: Yes ... erm ... I like watch TV so I would like one of those ... how did you call it? ... aerials? I have got a computer at home and I use it a lot to play game. Erm ... that's all.

I: Thank you. Now, Ahmet, here are your two photos. They show two different types of accommodation or housing. Could you please compare and contrast the photos and say how you feel about them.

A: Yes. In the ... err ... first photograph I can see a big building with about twenty or thirty ... I don't know what you call them in English. It's a big city, but I don't know where it is. In the other photo there is a house in the country, the house has a ... err ... I don't know how you say in English ... around it. That's all.

I: Thank you. Now, Laura, could you tell me a little bit about how you feel about the two types of accommodation shown in Ahmet's photographs.

L: Yes, of course. Well, I definitely wouldn't want to live in this block of flats. It looks like it is in the middle of a big city and there is probably a lot of noise and traffic. I like the other picture much better. I would like to visit this house. It looks peaceful and quiet. I would like to sit out on the ... mmm ... balcony ... veranda at night.

1 Laura

2 1 I think they are called ...   2 It's a kind of ...
3 They are used for ...

U N I T **5**

Grammar p.35

1 1 felt fine   2 were worried about her   3 thought she was acting strangely   4 slept well   5 woke up very early   6 she hadn't eaten   7 felt hungry
8 was a new student

2 1 I have to go out to lunch with my parents on Sunday   2 I don't have any special plans
3 I haven't   4 told me he really enjoyed it
5 sounds great   6 I think   7 is usually less crowded

Grammar p.36

1 his name was   2 I had got to know him   3 what year he was in at school   4 how much older he was
5 we had been   6 the movie had finished   7 we had done   8 long we had been in the restaurant   9 we had got home

Grammar p.37

1 promised not to tell   2 advised Laura to try being
3 warned her not to   4 accused her of meeting
5 threatened to tell   6 denied seeing/having seen
7 admitted trying/having tried to phone
8 suggested meeting   9 refused to speak to
10 encouraged Mrs Carter to be   11 decided to ask
12 invited Steve to have   13 agreed (that) Laura was
14 offered to take   15 recommended going out

Grammar p.38

line 1: delete *to*   line 2: delete *more*   line 3: delete *to*
line 6: delete *that*   line 8: delete *for*   line 9: delete *to*
line 10: delete *of*   line 13: delete *at*   line 15: delete *me*

Vocabulary p.38

1 going out   2 infatuated   3 had fallen in love
4 got married   5 got engaged   6 best man   7 aisle
8 vicar   9 choir   10 bouquet   11 have rows
12 was having/had had an affair   13 to get a divorce

Listening p.39

Tapescript

Extract 1

... this is really beautifully written. Towards the end when Maria and Charles meet again after ten years, I was so involved that I literally couldn't put it down. Anybody who enjoys historical novels will love this. I thoroughly recommend *A Second Chance*.

Extract 2

... and that was Gloria Estefan's latest. For those of you who don't speak Spanish she's singing about devoting the rest of her life to her husband. She's certainly got a great voice in any language. And now it's over to the newsroom for a bulletin of world news.

Extract 3

Mmm ... that sounds great. Perhaps some other time. You see, I'm going to my cousin's wedding on Saturday and I ... next Friday? Umm, let me see. Oh, that's right. I have to take my younger brother to see the latest Walt Disney film. ... Thursday? No. I've got volleyball practice until nine thirty and ...

Extract 4

My friend used to say that he was the best-looking boy at university. I never expected him to notice me, though we actually attended the same history lectures for a term. The first time I spoke to him was when I was queueing for tickets to see a film called *Picnic at Hanging Rock*. He just came up to me and said, 'I know this sounds ridiculous, but haven't I seen you somewhere before?'

Extract 5

A: ... so I'm going round to her house to meet her parents.

B: You must be crazy. They'll kill you!

A: No, I don't think so. Her mother sounded really nice on the phone. I think they were just worried when she got home so late. After all, she left the house at about five and we didn't get back till midnight or something. We waited ...

1 C   2 B   3 A   4 A   5 A

Reading p.40

1 1 this feeling inside   2 have much money
3 your song   4 the sun   5 forget

2 A

3 1 B   2 D   3 A   4 C   5 B

4 1 B   2 A   3 B   4 A

5 1 groom   2 bride   3 bridesmaids
4 engagement   5 anniversary

UNIT 6

Grammar p.42

1 1 ... **denied stealing** the necklace.
4 ... **admitted taking** it. 5 ... **refused to say** where she had hidden it, ... 6 ... **were arranging to take** her to the station, she **agreed to return** it. 9 ... **hoped to find** a job there. 10 ... **try to help** her find work. 11 Mary **stopped crying** ...

2 1 wearing 2 to know 3 waking up 4 to make 5 to talk 6 to go 7 smoking 8 to go

Listening p.43

Tapescript

Most of the time we go through life relatively unaware of the fact that deep within the brain is a body clock that works ... well, like clockwork! It's only really when our normal routine is interrupted that we become conscious of our physical and psychological rhythms. But we *do* disrupt them from time to time: by flying from one side of the world to the other and crossing several time zones, falling asleep at the wrong time of day or staying up all night studying for an exam. These rhythms are almost identical from one person to another because they're determined by the Earth's cycle of day into night, night into day. If you are out of step with this cycle, you feel the effects: jet lag, fatigue or poor concentration and memory. If on the other hand you learn to understand your biological rhythms, if you know at what time of day you remember things more easily, when your reactions are fastest, when you are most creative, you can plan your day and always be at your best.

Short term memory works best around midnight because your temperature is lowest and a cool mind genuinely does memorise more effectively. But luckily your memory is still working well at nine o'clock in the morning. Try learning vocabulary or reading texts and answering comprehension questions first thing in the morning or just before you go to sleep at night. But make sure the texts are not too long and don't try to learn more than ten to twelve words at a time. Short term memory only lasts ten minutes or so. After that it won't absorb information efficiently.

Problem solving is easiest mid to late morning, say around eleven o'clock. Unfortunately we are less and less able to solve problems efficiently as the day goes on because we get more and more tired. So mid-morning is the right time to work on your mathematics and to make any important decisions. If you're preparing for FCE, work on your writing at this time of day. Plan and write reports, articles and stories as well.

Long term memory, the sort we use when recalling what happened yesterday or last month, is working most efficiently at around three in the afternoon. If you have to memorise something important, this is the time to do it, whether it's a piece of music or grammar rules. This is the best time of day to study and probably the best time to do the kind of test that requires you to remember things you learnt a while ago. Your reflexes are quickest between about four and six o'clock, so if you play volleyball or basketball, you'll perform best in the late afternoon or early evening.

But what if you have trouble getting out of bed in the first place? To get your body clock running, try combining a splash of cold water on the face with a blast of bright light. The body clock inside your brain is really two tiny structures about the size of two grains of sand. These structures are connected to the eyes so daylight can penetrate the brain and set the clock running to the right time – in much the same way as you set your watch. If you have to travel to the United States or Australia, spend some time in direct sunlight each morning for the first two or three days. You'll recover from jet lag much more quickly.

2 2 the Earth's cycle 3 Short term memory 4 ten minutes 5 eleven o'clock 6 long term memory 7 four and six 8 of bright light 9 the eyes 10 from jet lag

Grammar p.43

1 didn't feel like taking 2 can't afford to buy 3 can't stand studying 4 agreed to accept 5 suggest buying/I buy/I bought 6 refused to lend me 7 pretended to be/that they were 8 expect to pass 9 encouraged me/him/us, etc. to do 10 gave up smoking

Vocabulary p.44

1 A 2 B 3 B 4 C 5 B 6 A 7 C 8 A 9 B 10 C

Vocabulary p.45

1

```
C A P R C H E A T L
L M T G M B A F Z R
A Y E S E C K P K P
S B R M Q W M A R K
S O M T O T X S E L
B H V D I R Z S V E
G F V H Q U I P I S
C N A E D A Y S S S
W J F I X N J N E O
R Y K O L T M Z X N
```

Possible definitions
term: a period of time into which the school year is divided; *cheat*: act dishonestly in order to gain something; *revise*: prepare for a test by studying; *fail*: be unsuccessful in an exam; *class*: a group of students or pupils who are taught together; *mark*: figures given by a teacher to represent how good someone's work is; *lesson*: a period of time in which students are taught; *pass*: be successful in an examination; *memorise*: learn and remember something exactly

2 a) calendar   b) lamp   c) stapler
d) sharpener   e) notebook   f) pencil
g) highlighter   h) paper clips   i) calculator
j) waste-paper bin   k) bookcase

Speaking p.45

1 1 Nilgün   2 Daniel

Writing p.46

1 1 *I am not agree ...* : I do not agree ...   2 *On my opinion ...* : In my opinion ...   3 *I am agree up to a point ...* : I agree up to a point...   4 *This is truth up to a point, ...* : This is true up to a point, ...   5 *As far as I am concerning ...* : As far as I am concerned ...   6 *In my point of view ...* : From my point of view ...

2 1 Dear Mr Lewis,   2 My daughter Helen will not be able to attend school tomorrow morning.
3 She has an appointment with the dentist at nine o'clock.   4 Dr Melrose's surgery is about twenty minutes from the centre of Cambridge.   5 It is unlikely that I can get Helen to school before midday.   6 I would be very grateful if you would excuse her from her English and Mathematics classes.   7 Yours sincerely, Jane Warburton

Reading p.48

2 A   3 D   4 B   5 E   6 F

UNIT 7

Grammar p.49

line 3: delete *for*   line 4: delete *they*   line 6: delete *of*
line 7: delete *have*   line 8: delete *are*   line 9: delete *as*
line 12: delete *that*   line 14: delete *do*

Listening p.49

Tapescript

I=interviewer AD=Alex Dimitriades

I: Well, Alex, it's really great to have you here in the studio. Your very successful film *The Heartbreak Kid*'s just been made into a TV series – *Heartbreak High*. You're almost a household name and I'm sure thousands of girls all over Australia have your photo on their bedroom wall. What's it really like being famous?

AD: I guess when you get invited to all these parties that you never used to get invited to, it is pretty great. But apart from that, it's just like another job really.

I: Do you enjoy it?

AD: Ah, yeah, it's enjoyable, but it has its ups and downs like everything else.

I: Was it hard to adjust to being famous?

AD: Yeah, it was a bit. It was a bit of a shock for me when the movie came out and I got so much attention, but I don't think there'll be such a big fuss when the TV show comes on.

I: How long did it take you to decide to star in the TV version?

AD: The producer had the show in mind for a while and he asked me if I'd be interested. I said I'd think about it and during that time I was doing publicity and promotion for the movie. Once it started quietening down a bit, they came forward and said they were going to make the series. At that stage, I wasn't doing much, so I agreed.

I: Apart from the show, what other plans do you have for the future?

AD: Nothing definite. I'm doing a play at the moment. It's called *The Man Who Became A Dog* and it's showing in Sydney. It's part of an amateur theatre festival and I know a girl who's involved in it. She asked me if I wanted to be in it and I said 'yes' because I've never done live theatre before. I really wanted to experiment.

I: What part do you play?

AD: The dog! It's OK. It's different. It's giving me a bit of variety which is what I like.

I: In the past year you've done film, TV and live theatre. Which do you prefer?

AD: The thing that I'd like to do most is another film, a really good film, a top production.

I: Do you have any idols?

AD: Idols? It's hard to pick someone 'cos I'm not really fanatical about anyone, but I really like Robert De Niro's acting. I like what I've seen him in, but I haven't seen all his films. ·

I: Do you feel comfortable about being a household name?

AD: I am? Yeah, I guess it's alright. What's wrong with that? I mean, of course, there are going to be people who are going to say bad things about you but as long as I don't feel bad, it's OK.

1 F   2 F   3 T   4 T   5 F   6 T

Vocabulary p.50

1 T/F   2 M   3 P/S   4 M   5 F   6 T/F   7 T/F   8 M   9 T
10 M   11 S   12 T/M   13 F   14 M   15 P/S

Vocabulary and grammar p.50

1 1 a film   2 fifteen

2 1 few   2 together   3 row   4 screen   5 cinema
6 going   7 stand/bear   8 had   9 scene/bit
10 such   11 part/role   12 groups/bands
13 comes   14 audience   15 can/should

Grammar p.51

1 1 Have you seen   2 saw   3 did you think   4 liked
5 thought   6 was   7 Have you hurt   8 hit   9 have
been going   10 Have you made   11 made
12 haven't seen   13 Has he gone   14 has been
studying   15 hasn't been going   16 Did you pass
17 failed   18 have taken

2 1 bitten   2 blown   3 built   4 threw; caught
5 bought   6 fallen   7 found   8 spent   9 written
10 sent

Writing pp.52–53

2 1 Candidate B   2 Candidate A

3 1 ... an excursion ...   2 We **left** the school ... and **reached the** museum. 3 so we **had** ...   4 The section I liked **most** was the dolls.   5 **But** Andres and Mehmet really liked the model railway.   6 I **visited** the Science Museum last week to decide if **it would** be good ...   7 However, the museum is very interesting so this makes it **worth the money**. 8 ... although the section on astronomy was closed for **repairs/renovation**.   9 All of the exhibits have short texts in English **explaining** what is shown. 10 Some exhibits had tapes you could **listen to**. 11 ... a bit **difficult** ...

4 1 d) despite/in spite of   2 b) although/even though
3 f) However,   4 a) despite/in spite of
5 e) although/even though   6 c) On the other hand,

Reading pp.54–55

1 D

2 1 'axe'; instruments   2 Rock's greatest musicians
3 a) wood b) glass fibre c) carbon fibre d) metal
e) plastics f) graphite

3 1 C   2 B   3 B   4 A   5 D   6 C

Speaking p.55

Tapescript

I=interlocutor S=Sofia P=Pedro

I: What do you think is the best age to start learning to play a musical instrument?

S: In my opinion it depends on the instrument. But I think if you don't start learning when you are young it is difficult to become really ... umm ... really .... to learn to play really well.

P: Yes, that's true, but if you only want to enjoy playing ... if you want to have a good time, you can start to learn when you are quite old and it doesn't matter.

I: Sofia, you told us before that you play the clarinet. What do you think I should do if I want to learn to play the clarinet well?

S: Well, you should find a good teacher ... like me. If I were you, I wouldn't buy a clarinet at the beginning. You should wait to see if you like it. You should practise every day and ... umm ...

I: And ... umm ... Pedro, you play the drums, don't you? What advice would you give me?

P: Well, you ought to buy a small drum kit and practise while you listen to albums by your favourite groups. When you are a little bit better, it would be a good idea to join a group. Oh, and you really must go to lots of rock concerts and watch the drummers. That's the best way to learn.

I: Thank you very much, I'll certainly think about what you both said. Well, ...

1 1 In my opinion 2 Yes, that's true, but 3 you should find; If I were you, I wouldn't buy; You should wait; You should practise 4 you ought to buy; it would be a good idea to join; you really must go

2 a) 3 and 4 b) 1 c) 2

3 1 As far as I'm concerned ... 2 I completely agree. 3 That's right. 4 From my point of view ... 5 I couldn't agree more.

UNIT *8*

Listening p.56

Tapescript

Extract 1

A: This is 509 5505. I'm sorry but we can't answer your call at the moment, but we'll get back to you as soon as we can if you leave your name and number after the tone.

B: Hello. It's me – Jenny. I won't be able to make the rehearsal tomorrow. I seem to have come out in a dreadful rash all over my arms. I've got bright red spots on my chest as well. I think it could be something to do with that new top I bought. I only wore it once, but it felt very strange and uncomfortable. So you'll just have to make do without me. Perhaps Jackie could read my part. I really can't go out looking like this.

Extract 2

A: So I bought these new trainers and they've made a tremendous difference.

B: Oh, yeah?

A: Yes, they're really good. They've got this air bag in the sole to cushion the impact each time your foot hits the ground. Did you know that a marathon runner hits the ground more than 25,000 times a race?

B: No ... I didn't.

A: Yeah, and the force of each impact is two and a half times the runner's body weight. No wonder my ankles and knees were giving me trouble.

Extract 3

A: I think it looked much smarter round the right way. It looks ridiculous like that and it won't even keep the sun out of your eyes.

B: All the kids are wearing them like this now, Mum. I won't be part of the group if I don't get one.

A: Why can't you just be yourself? You don't have to be the same as everyone else. You're an individual. You ought to be proud of that rather than just doing what all the other boys do. And it's ... what? £20! That's absolutely ridiculous.

B: But, Mum, you promised.

C: So, have we made up our mind yet, young man? Is it to be the Chicago Bulls or ...?

Extract 4

A: The first time I wore them she was away visiting my grandparents and Dad wouldn't notice if I was wearing fluorescent pink Wellington boots and a bikini, he's usually so absorbed in the football on Saturday afternoons. But this time when I put them on to go out on Friday evening, she nearly had a fit! 'You can't go out looking like that! What will the neighbours say?' I even tried showing her some pictures in magazines of some of the top models wearing them, but she flatly refused to let me go out unless I got changed.

B: So what did you wear in the end?

A: Oh, my 501s and a body I got in London. Oh no! I've left my shorts and trainers at home and we've got volleyball this afternoon.

Extract 5

A: What on earth have you got in this suitcase? It weighs a ton!

B: Just clothes.

A: We're only going for two weeks and it's supposed to be boiling hot there so I can't imagine that you'll need all this lot.

B: Well, you never know. When the Widdowsons were there, it was really quite cold. They did a lot of hiking in the mountains though, so I popped my walking boots in and a few novels just in case it turns out to be too wet. Oh, and I noticed that you'd only packed two T-shirts and a pair of shorts for yourself so I've put in a couple of your pullovers and your anorak, too. Oh yes, and your good trousers and jacket just in case we go out. Oh, and I saw that you'd forgotten to put in anything to read so I've packed a couple of your favourite detective stories, too. OK?

1 A 2 B 3 C 1 D 5 E 4

2 A 3 B 1 C 5 E 4 F 2

Vocabulary pp.56–57

1 1 a checked shirt 2 a tie 3 a waistcoat
4 a cardigan 5 a raincoat 6 a pair of Wellington
boots 7 a cap 8 a suit 9 a blouse 10 a belt
11 a brooch 12 a bracelet 13 a dress 14 a pair
of sandals 15 a pair of shorts 16 a T-shirt
17 a pair of trainers

2 1 Claudia is wearing **a long evening dress** and
high-heeled shoes. 2 Nick is wearing **grey
trousers** and a **checked shirt**. 3 Paul is wearing a
striped **T-shirt**, jeans and **trainers**. 4 Kate is
wearing a **plain** dress and **spotted** tights. 5 Tim
is wearing a **cap**, dungarees and a leather **belt**.

3 1 'sandals 2 'pullover 3 'bracelet 4 py'jamas
5 dunga'rees 6 'sweatshirt 7 'raincoat
8 'earrings 9 'waistcoat 10 'T-shirt

Grammar p.57

1 1 c) 2 e) 3 d) 4 b) 5 a) 6 c)

2 Both *would* and *used to* can be used in sentences
1, 2, 4, 5 and 7. In sentences 3 and 6 *used to* is
the only possibility.

Writing pp.58–59

1 Description A

Vocabulary and grammar p.59

1 together 2 illness 3 athletes 4 materials
5 anything 6 although 7 become 8 brand

Reading p.60

1 1 A 2 A 3 A 4 A 5 B

2 1 D 2 B 3 C 4 A 5 F

Word formation p.61

1 1 disposable 2 invention 3 production
4 occurrence 5 preference 6 performance
7 conclusion 8 hesitation

2 1 di'sposable 2 in'vention 3 pro'duction
4 oc'currence 5 'preference 6 per'formance
7 con'clusion 8 hesi'tation

Speaking p.61

Tapescript

Now Efi and Akiko, here is a picture of a first aid kit
and some things that you might put into the kit.

Unfortunately, there is only enough space in the kit for
five of these items. I'd like you to talk together about
this and decide which items you will put into your first
aid kit.

1 F 2 T 3 F 4 F

Grammar p.62

1 1 He could/may/might be Italian. 2 Can you play
the piano? 3 You may not/can't speak during the
exam. 4 They can't still be on holiday. 5 You may
not/can't smoke on the plane. 6 It could/may/might
be a nice day tomorrow. 7 He couldn't spell
'conscious'. 8 May/Can I leave the room?

2 1 That **can't be** the postman. 2 I **might not
come** to class on Wednesday. 3 **Could you ride** a
bicycle when you were seven? 4 You **can't
borrow** my new blouse. 5 He **may/might not
like** the colour. 6 It **might rain**.

Grammar p.62

1 c) refuse to lend you 2 d) thinner than
3 a) am interested in 4 b) would like
5 e) him if he enjoyed 6 c) can't stand travelling
7 f) ought to buy 8 d) works faster than
9 f) are not allowed to smoke

UNIT 9

Vocabulary p.63

1 B 2 C 3 D 4 B 5 A 6 B 7 A 8 C 9 D 10 D
11 C 12 B 13 C 14 A 15 D

Grammar p.64

1 a few 2 lump 3 a 4 a 5 many 6 many
7 Much 8 a pair of 9 another 10 A 11 a
12 slices 13 slice 14 many 15 a few

Listening p.64

Tapescript

We all feel happy to be alive in the summer, but it
may not only be the warmer weather that makes us
feel like this. Although we think we choose what to
eat because it tastes or looks good, in fact we make
unconscious choices based on the way food makes us
feel. Summer foods like seafood and salads are full of
chemicals that put us in a good mood.

One chemical that is found in high protein foods is serotonin. It makes you feel calm and relaxed. It can also be found in coffee and tea, ginger and honey, but the best source is spinach which also contains folic acid in large quantities. A deficiency in folic acid can cause depression, sleeplessness, forgetfulness and irritability.

Fish has traditionally been considered an ideal brain food because it contains high levels of the mineral selenium, which can also affect how you feel. A lack of selenium in your diet can produce tiredness and depression. Apart from fish, sunflower seeds, oysters, cereals, grapes and chicken are good sources.

If you want a food that will cheer you up instantly, then chillies are the answer. They can have a dramatic effect on your mood. When you eat a dish containing chillies, your body reacts because it is encountering something that is almost like a poison. This leads to the release of the body's natural pain killers, giving a sense of well-being. But the experience can become addictive, sometimes causing people to search out stronger and stronger chillies. A slower acting but longer lasting antidepressant called DMAE can be found in anchovies and sardines. DMAE also heightens intelligence and makes it easier to learn. So if you've got an important exam coming up, make sure you eat all these foods that keep you feeling good and thinking clearly.

1 1 seafood and salads 2 calm and relaxed
3 coffee, tea 4 honey 5 depression 6 tiredness and depression 7 fish 8 chicken 9 intelligence
10 learn

Speaking p.65

Tapescript

I=interlocutor M=Marcus B=Birgit

I: Now, Marcus and Birgit, here are some pictures of various foods. I'd like you to talk together to plan a healthy lunch for a group of young people on a hiking trip in the mountains.

M: Well, what do you think? They will be very hungry after hiking all morning.

B: Yes, and they'll need lots of energy for the rest of the day.

M: It's probably quite cold, so I think it would be a good idea ... mmm ... to start with soup.

B: Yes, that sounds fine. Mmm ... a fish soup would be good.

M: Mmm ... I don't know. Maybe it would be better to serve vegetable soup. Some people don't like fish.

B: OK. We'll serve vegetable soup first. And what shall we have next? What about spaghetti?

M: Yes, spaghetti would be good – with a meat sauce.

B: And lots of cheese. Oh, and I think they should have some vegetables.

M: Why don't we serve a salad next?

B: Yes. And what shall we give them for dessert? Perhaps some fruit ... bananas and apples.

M: Mmm ... I'm not sure about that. Perhaps some kind of cake or pie would be better.

B: Yes, but cakes are not very healthy. We could have the fruit and give them a chocolate bar each to eat in the afternoon.

M: Yes, that sounds fine.

1 1 Well, what do you think? 2 so I think it would be a good idea 3 Yes, that sounds fine.
4 I don't know. Maybe it would be better to
5 What about spaghetti? 6 Yes, spaghetti would be good 7 Why don't we

2 A 1 and 5 B 2, 5 and 7 C 3, 5 and 6 D 4

Grammar p.65

line 2: delete *like* line 3: delete *a* line 4: delete *to*
line 6: delete *at* line 8: delete *to* line 9: delete *did*

Vocabulary p.66

1 1 Could you put me through to the director?
2 Why have they put off their wedding/put their wedding off? 3 Do you put money by for a rainy day? 4 How could you put up with such rude behaviour? 5 Have they put up the prices/put the prices up again? 6 How did the firemen put out that fire/put that fire out? 7 Why did the vet have to put down your cat/put your cat down? 8 Could you put me up when I come to London? 9 Why are you always trying to put me down?

2 1 They've **put up** the price of tinned tomatoes/ **put** the price of tinned tomatoes **up**. 2 Can you **put up** my nephew/**put** my nephew **up** when he comes to Madrid? 3 I'm just trying to **put** you **through**, but the line seems to be busy. 4 He's always **putting** her **down**. I don't know why she goes out with him. 5 Please **put out** your cigarettes/**put** your cigarettes **out**. 6 I think we'll have to **put** the match **off/put off** the match until after the exam. 7 They managed to **put** some money **by/put by** some money every week. 8 Two horses were so badly injured that they had to be **put down** after the race. 9 I don't know why you **put up with** her rudeness.

Reading pp.66–67

1 Numbers 1, 5, 7, 8, 10, 11 and 12 are mentioned.

2 1 C   2 D   3 B   4 A

3 1 a) C b) D c) A d) B   2 a) D b) A c) C d) B

Grammar p.68

1 1 By the time you read this **I will be sipping** champagne in a café near the Eiffel Tower.
2 Tomorrow there **will be** heavy rain in the north.
3 Bye! **I'll see** you next week.   4 We've got to be at the airport two hours before our plane **takes off**.   5 By the time I'm twenty, **I will have eaten** 3000 bowls of cornflakes.   6 Look out! That wall **is going to collapse**.   7 I don't think **I'll have** dinner. I'm not hungry.   8 I'm afraid I can't come to the cinema with you. **I'm taking** my nephew to the circus.   9 I'm sure **you'll do** very well in the exam.   10 **I'm going to buy** a new computer.

2 1 am writing   2 am studying/study   3 will finish/will be finishing   4 will be   5 will be attending/am attending   6 am going/will be going
7 will improve   8 will have taken   9 will get
10 am starting/will be starting   11 will be

Vocabulary p.68

1 florist's   2 post office   3 queues   4 baker's
5 chemist's   6 greengrocer's   7 supermarket   8 shoe shop   9 refund   10 sale   11 bargain   12 wallet/purse
13 receipt   14 cards   15 try   16 size   17 tight

Writing p.69

1 d)   2 f)   3 b)   4 e)   5 a)   6 c)

UNIT 10

Vocabulary p.70

1 make; do   2 do   3 make   4 do   5 do; making; do
6 does; makes   7 making; made   8 do; make
9 make; doing   10 Make; do   11 do; do; do
12 make; make; done   13 Doing; make   14 made
15 making; make

Reading pp.70–71

1 Numbers 6 and 8 are not mentioned.

2 1 B   2 B   3 C   4 A   5 B   6 B   7 C

Grammar p.72

1 2 c) where   3 i) (that)   4 f) that   5 h) (that)
6 a) (that)   7 b) (that)   8 g) (that)   9 d) whose

2 1 D   2 N A blue Renault Clio, which is one of the cars she won, is parked outside her house.   3 N Pink Floyd, who wrote the song 'Money', were performing live in London recently.
4 D   5 N The Central European University, which has its headquarters in Prague, has a branch in Budapest.   6 N My uncle, who was very shy when he was a child, is now a multimillionaire.   7 N My uncle, who does not show off his wealth by wearing expensive clothes and accessories, gives a lot of money to charities.   8 D

3 2 The house **where we used to live** was bigger than this one.   4 The single object **(that)** I treasure most is an old coin my grandfather gave me.
6 The waiter, **to whom** I gave a very generous tip, didn't even thank me.   7 The insurance on the house, **which** was very expensive, didn't cover the cost of the repairs.   10 He inherited a lot of money from his grandfather, **who was** extremely well-off.
11 The salesman **who sold** me this T-shirt didn't tell me I couldn't return it.

Vocabulary p.73

1 **Across**   4 withdraw   6 invest   7 lend   9 earn
Down   1 afford   2 owe   3 gamble   5 inherit
8 debt

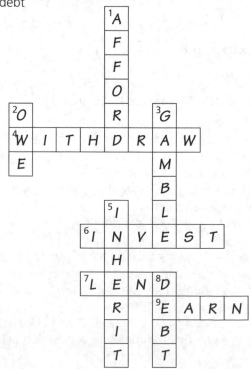

2 1 current; overdrawn   2 change; note   3 cash;
cheque   4 shares; loss   5 wages; tips
6 statement; cash   7 mortgage   8 economy;
exchange rate   9 hard up; lend   10 charity; tax

Writing pp.74–75

1 C

2 1 There are three main reasons why **I think** this.
2 If you **have** never worked before, ...   3 ... when
you **finish** your studies.   4 ... I am sure this **will
help** me in the future.   5 If your parents just **give**
you money ...

3 1 I have a part-time **job** in my mother's office ...
2 At my mother's office I **met** a girl ...

4 Good

Listening p.75

Tapescript

Extract 1

No, I'm not superstitious. I know we'll beat them on
any day of the year. Anyway, it's Tuesday the
thirteenth that's the unlucky day here – not Friday.
And there are three Friday the thirteenths this year so
we'll have to cancel two more matches as well as this
one. And then we'll never finish the championship.

Extract 2

Right then, ladies and gentlemen, if I could just have
your attention. Thank you for coming along this
evening. I'll get straight to the point. As you know
Tristar Pictures is planning to film a few scenes of our
upcoming feature film *It could happen to you* in your
neighbourhood. We'll be building the set of the coffee
shop on the parking lot at the corner of North Moore
and West Broadway. The reason we've invited you
along tonight is that we want to give you an
opportunity to raise any questions, and to make any
comments, complaints or suggestions you might have.

Extract 3

A: OK, let's see Jackie. Could you give us the answer
to number five?

B: I'm sorry, Mr Rignall. I haven't done that one.

A: Why not? You were asked to do all the exercises
on page 20 for homework. Someone else then.
Tom.

C: Four hundred and sixty-eight thousand two
hundred and twelve.

A: Does everyone agree? What about you, Adela?
How about coming out to the board and showing
us how you worked it out.

D: Do I have to?

A: Come on, Adela.

D: OK.

Extract 4

For how many hours did you say that was? ... I see. So
that's Saturday morning from 8 till 2 and Thursday
evenings from 6 till 9. Umm ... I don't think I
understand. That's nine hours work at £3 an hour,
which comes to £27 – not £20 – by my calculations.
So I would have to pay tax and national insurance
even as a part-timer? That doesn't really seem fair ...

Extract 5

And on tomorrow night's show I've invited someone
whose latest album is really selling like the proverbial
hot cakes. Yes, you guessed it – Mark Williams will be
joining us here in the studio to play some of the tracks
from the album and to tell us a little more about the
dates of his forthcoming world tour. So make sure you
tune in around this time tomorrow evening – 740 on
your dial, Radio Metro.

Extract 6

A: I don't understand. I paid it in on Monday.

B: I'm sorry. It hasn't been cleared yet.

A: But I expected to be able to make a withdrawal
today. I'm going on holiday tomorrow.

B: I'm afraid there's not a lot I can do ... you see I'm
not allowed to authorise payment earlier than four
working days after it was paid in.

A: But it is four working days today.

B: No, today's Wednesday and that's only three
working days.

A: Look, I'd like to speak to the manager if you don't
mind.

Extract 7

It was an amazing thing to say really. I mean imagine
saying that to a judge: 'I just like cash.' Who doesn't,
after all? Anyway the judge wasn't having any of it.
They'd smuggled £600,000 of used bank notes out of
the Bank of England. They kept it under the
floorboards in their house. Anyway, it said that the
judge decided they had to pay it all back plus interest.
Oh, and the bank's suing them as well.

Extract 8

... Yes, a table for thirteen. ... No, not thirty,
thirteen. ... A private room?... No, I don't think we
want that. ... No extra cost? Well, perhaps it wouldn't
be such a bad idea. ... Oh, about 8.30 or 9.00. Oh,
there may be an extra person, but I'll phone and
confirm that tomorrow. ... The set menu?... What
exactly does that involve? ... That sounds a bit

expensive – look, can I get back to you on that as well?

1 1 a)   2 c)   3 c)   4 b)   5 a)   6 a)   7 a)   8 a)

2 1 C   2 B   3 A   4 B   5 B   6 C   7 A   8 C

Vocabulary p.76

1 *Tapescript*

    a) oh one, two four nine, seven four oh, three two five

    b) three quarters

    c) a hundred thousand

    d) six point three seven

    e) one and a half kilos

    f) fourteen degrees centigrade

    g) twenty-five pounds fifty

    h) thirty-five miles per hour

    i) two nil

    a) 01249 740325   b) ¾   c) 100,000   d) 6.37
    e) 1½ kilos   f) 14° C   g) £25.50   h) 35 mph
    i) 2–0

2 1 f)   2 a)   3 i)   4 c)   5 h)   6 e)   7 d)   8 b)   9 g)

3 *Tapescript*

    a) oh one two one, seven three oh, six five four

    b) thirteen

    c) fifty

    d) one and a half

    e) four point seven five

    f) sixteen

    g) three pounds fifty

    h) nineteen dollars ninety-nine cents

    i) six hundred and forty-seven thousand nine hundred and fifty-eight

    j) five million three hundred and forty thousand four hundred and fourteen

Speaking p.76

Tapescript

L=Loukas   J=Julie   O=Olivier   D=Dominique

Interview 1

L: Shall we start? What do you think is the most important?

J: Erm ... I don't know.

L: How about books? I think buying books is never a waste of money. Are you ... do you agree?

J: Yes, I agree.

L: What shall we put next?

J: Err ... private classes.

L: Do you think private classes are important?

J: Yes, I do.

L: Yes, I think they are too, especially if a subject is difficult for you. ... But it's important to get a lot of exercise as well as studying, so perhaps we can put sports next. Do you spend very much money on sports?

J: No. I don't like.

L: I don't like all sports, but I play volleyball so I have to buy good trainers. I don't know what to put after that. What ... what do you think?

J: Erm ... computer games.

L: OK. We could put that next. I suppose computer games help you ... umm ... to ... ummm ... to learn to use a computer.

J: Mmm.

L: Do you think we should put music next?

J: OK.

L: Do you think cassettes and compact discs are too expensive?

J: Err ... yes.

Interview 2

O: Well, I think we should put computer games first because this is the age of technology and everybody needs to know use a computer if he wants to get a good work.

D: Yes, I agree that computers ...;

O: And after that I think clothes and then cosmetics because it is important to have a good presence ... I mean good-lookings.

J: Yes, I think they're important, but for me books and music are more important than make-up and clothes. And spending money on sport is OK, too.

O: I am not agree with you. People spend too much money on buying famous marks. You can get good shoes in the supermarket. My brother, he only wants to wear Nike shoes and I think he is very foolish. The mark doesn't mind. It is the quality. I always buy in the sales because everything is very cheap and good.

D: Yes. That's true, but I mean that it's good to play sport and sometimes you must spend a little money on it. Why don't we put ... err ... private classes next?

O: Yes. Private classes can help you practise your English very much. You can be with your teacher only you practising speaking and this is very good for you, your English. My teacher is very good and she says I speak English very well. Next year I will have private classes in German and err ...

Loukas and Dominique got good marks for interaction.

UNIT *11*

Writing p.77

1 Comments 1, 3 and 4

Reading p.78

1 C   2 B   3 A

Vocabulary p.79

1 C   2 B   3 B   4 B   5 C   6 B   7 A   8 C   9 B

Grammar p.79

1 1 (-)   2 (-)   3 (-)   4 the/(-)   5 the   6 the   7 the
8 a   9 a   10 (-)   11 a   12 (-)   13 the   14 (-)   15 a
16 the   17 (-)   18 the   19 the   20 the

2 line 0: delete first *the*   line 1: delete second *the*
line 4: delete *the*   line 5: delete *the*
line 7: delete *a*   line 10: delete *a*

Vocabulary and grammar p.80

1 where   2 all/other   3 of   4 like   5 mountain
6 from   7 a   8 were   9 down   10 have   11 is
12 the   13 there   14 who   15 their

Grammar pp.80–81

1 1 g)   2 j)   3 i)   4 f)   5 d)   6 a)   7 e)   8 h)   9 b)
10 c)

2 1 Would you mind buying me a coffee? I **must
have left** my money in my other coat.
4 Don't wait for me. I **might be** late.
5 It **can't have been** Mary who stole the money.
She was with me all evening.
8 I **might stay** at home this Saturday night. I've
got a test on Monday.
10 You **should have told** me. I didn't know you
were coming.

Grammar p.81

1 1 PV   2 G   3 G   4 V   5 PV   6 G   7 PV

2 1 put me up   2 can't have been   3 much does
this bag   4 can't stand   5 give up   6 may not
speak   7 taking off

Speaking p.82

Tapescript

I=interlocutor E=Eleni

I: Now I'm going to give you two photographs of
landscapes. I'd like you to talk about your pictures
and say which looks more attractive to you.

E: Erm … well in the first picture I can see a desert. It
could be Africa or perhaps in the USA. There can't
have been any rain for a long time because the
ground is very dry. There might be a drought. I
wouldn't mind visiting this place, but I wouldn't
like to live there. The second photograph is very
different. It might have been taken in Canada or
Alaska. This is a kind of … hut or a cabin … it's
built of wood and I think it looks very attractive. It
must be, must be really … err … cosy inside. There
is a lot of snow on the ground, on the trees and on
the roof of the house, but the sky is blue and there
are no clouds. It must have snowed during the
night. I think this would be a good place to go for
a holiday.

1 1 a) There can't have been any rain for a long time
because the ground is very dry.   b) It might have
been taken in Canada or Alaska.   c) It must have
snowed during the night.
2 a) It could be Africa or perhaps in the USA.
b) There might be a drought   c) It must be really
cosy inside.
3 a) I wouldn't mind visiting this place, but I
wouldn't like to live there.   b) I think this would be
a good place to go for a holiday.

Vocabulary p.83

Listening p.83

Tapescript

P=presenter DG=Dr Goodman

P: And so. Welcome to the studio, Dr Goodman.

DG: It's a pleasure to be here.

P: Now, I know that many of our listeners are already familiar with the biosphere project, but many others are not. Perhaps you could start off by telling us exactly what a biosphere reserve is?

DG: Biosphere reserves are areas that are specially protected by conservationists so that scientists and others can study them. We hope this will make it easier to preserve such areas in other parts of the world.

P: And has this project just started?

DG: No, no. In fact the first biosphere reserves were established over twenty years ago. There are 324 biosphere reserves in 82 countries now,

P: 82 countries! Can you tell us a bit about some of the more recent projects?

DG: Well, we've established a 226,000 hectare biosphere reserve in Brazil, quite near the Brazilian capital Brasilia, and a 2.57 million hectare reserve in the Wadi Allaqui valley near the Nile valley in Egypt. The Brazilian reserve has 44 endangered or threatened animal species and 41 endangered or threatened plant species.

P: And are there only UNESCO scientists working on these reserves?

DG: No. In fact the local community always makes an important contribution to the research and the management of the reserve. In the case of the Brazilian reserve, Brazil has made a big contribution because they already had a lot of experience. You see they already had another reserve – the Atlantic Forest Biosphere. Now that reserve has recently been extended to cover 3,000 kilometres. This is a particularly large reserve.

P: In fact all the reserves you've mentioned so far sound very large. I suppose there are also smaller reserves.

DG: Yes. We have a couple of reserves which are islands. Err, Lanzarote in the Canary Islands is one example, it measures 70,000 hectares, and Menorca in the Balearic islands is another. Menorca is a little smaller.

P: And what about the colder parts of the world? Are there any biosphere reserves in Scandinavia, for example?

DG: Yes, in fact there's the Sea Area Biosphere reserve in Finland. This reserve includes pine forest and small sandy islands so it has quite a lot of variety.

P: And the idea is that scientists working on these projects should share their experiences with others working on reserves in other parts of the world. Now, how do they communicate with each other?

DG: In all sorts of ways. We're about to hold an international conference which will be attended by between 300 and 400 people. This should give everybody an excellent opportunity to compare notes and improve the biosphere project in a number of ways. Apart from the conference, computer technology has made rapid communication very much easier and we also have a news bulletin which provides up to date information for the local community.

P: I imagine that many of the reserves share similar problems.

DG: Yes, indeed they do. We've actually begun to 'twin' reserves with very similar problems so that the people working on them can establish stronger links. For example, a reserve in France and one in Spain have recently been twinned.

P: Well, thank you very much for telling us about the biosphere reserve project, Dr Goodman. I'm sure we all hope that the project is a great success. Now also with me in the studio tonight I have ...

1 No   2 Yes   3 No   4 Yes   5 No   6 Yes   7 No   8 No
9 Yes   10 Yes

UNIT 12

Speaking p.84

Tapescript

I=Interlocutor H=Helmut G=Gloria

I: Tell us, what do you think of television nowadays?

H: Well, in my opinion television is not as good as it used to be. There are a lot more channels, but ... umm ... there is a lot of rubbish on them.

I: Do you agree, Gloria?

G: I agree up to a point, but because there are more channels, there's more choice. There might be a movie on one channel, a quiz programme on another and a documentary on another. So even if you don't like one thing, you can always find something ...

H: Always?

G: OK, often find something you like.

I: So do you think parents should limit the amount of television their children watch?

G: Yes, definitely. I think that unless they limit their children, they will be watching all the time.

H: Yeah, I agree completely. My younger brothers switch the television on as soon as they come home from school and unless my parents made them turn it off, they'd still be watching it at midnight.

I: Is there too much advertising on television?

H/G: Yes!

G: But sometimes ... well ... I enjoy watching the advertisements. I think they can be very original.

H: Yes, I agree with you. Sometimes the advertisements are better than the programmes!

I: Well, thank you both very much for coming.

in my opinion ... ; I agree up to a point, but ... ; Yes, definitely. I think that ... ; I agree completely.; Yes. I agree with you.

Writing p.84

1 B 2 A 3 B 4 A 5 B 6 B 7 A 8 C 9 B 10 A

Writing p.85

1 The writer followed Plan B.   Yes.

Grammar p.86

1 really   2 absolutely   3 really; very   4 really
5 terrific   6 very   7 quite   8 absolutely   9 superb
10 very

Vocabulary p.86

1 I've been trying to **get through to him** ...   2 You really must **get down to** some work.   3 I know how to **get round** our Mum.   4 I don't **get on with Mary** very well.   5 I hope you won't **get up to** anything while we're out.   6 She doesn't earn a lot – just enough to **get by**.   7 I'd never do anything dishonest because I'm sure I'd never **get away with it**.

Grammar p.86

1 1 How many compositions do we have to write?
2 You needn't help with the shopping.   3 You needn't have gone to so much trouble.   4 I've just got to pass.   5 Do you often have to study at the weekend?   6 How many words are we supposed to write?   7 You mustn't use ink.   8 Do we need to write a draft?

2 1 e) 2 b)   3 g)   4 d)   5 f)   6 a)   7 c)   8 h)

3 1 A   2 B   3 B   4 A   5 B   6 B   7 B   8 A

Grammar p.87

line 1: delete *to*   line 2: delete *a*   line 3: delete *the*
line 5: delete *been*   line 6: delete *that*
line 7: delete *of*   line 10: delete *of*
line 12: delete *of*   line 14: delete *of*

Reading pp.88–89

1 A   2 C   3 D   4 A   5 C   6 D   7 C   8 A   9 B   10 C
11 D   12 B   13 B

Vocabulary p.89

1 1 cartoon   2 editorial   3 headline   4 gossip
5 journalist   6 crossword

J	H	E	A	D	L	I	N	E	T
C	O	Y	E	S	L	G	R	G	R
R	F	U	D	M	K	R	F	O	S
O	C	A	R	T	O	O	N	S	L
S	A	K	N	N	X	V	U	S	T
S	P	O	C	H	A	H	E	I	Q
W	G	B	A	W	K	L	Z	P	S
O	E	D	I	T	O	R	I	A	L
R	Q	P	B	I	L	V	W	S	X
D	C	D	X	J	U	X	P	O	T

2 1 frequency   2 batteries   3 headlines   4 soaps
5 aerial   6 remote control

Listening p.90

Tapescript

Speaker 1

We were waiting outside the manager's office when this guy came up to us and asked if we'd mind being filmed for an ad they were making about the bank. I wasn't too sure, but Sharon was quite keen. So when we actually went in to discuss our mortgage repayments, there were hidden cameras filming us having this discussion with the manager. They filmed lots of other people, too. Erm ... it was a bit disappointing really because they didn't use us in the end. They said we seemed as if we were acting.

Speaker 2

Of course I'd sent in lots of others and I'd basically given up hope of ever getting one published. But there it was. I couldn't believe my eyes. I was on the train on my way to work and I opened my copy of *The Times*, turned to the 'Letters to the editor' page and ... well, I just burst out laughing. It really is difficult to get one published in *The Times*, or at least that's what they say. There were a whole lot of replies about two days later. Some of them really made my blood boil, but I suppose that's democracy for you – people expressing their views.

Speaker 3

It was an absolute pack of lies. Not just exaggerated claims, completely false. Not only did the stuff have absolutely no effect whatsoever on the amount of hair on my head, it smelt really disgusting, a bit like turpentine. 'A fine head of thick glossy hair will be yours within weeks.' Haa! So I reported them to one of those consumer protection authorities. I haven't seen it for weeks now, so they must have had other complaints and decided to take it off. Needless to say, I threw the stuff away.

Speaker 4

I was incredibly nervous. I had to get there a couple of hours before though they hadn't actually told me why. I'd never done anything like that before so I didn't know you had to wear make-up. Apparently your face would be too shiny otherwise what with all the very bright lights and you'd look terrible on the screen. So this girl put all this powder and stuff all over my face. She even insisted on that black stuff women use on their eyelashes and lipstick. I was going to nip off to the toilets and wash it all off, but the next thing I knew, I was sitting on a kind of sofa being interviewed. I didn't even see the programme until a couple of days later, because it went out live. You couldn't actually tell I was wearing lipstick – thankfully!

Speaker 5

We'd hardly got out of the plane when this mass of reporters descended on us all shoving microphones and personal stereo recorders in our faces and literally firing questions at us. How did we feel now that we were back home? Could we describe how we felt when Diego kicked the third goal? When were we going to start training again? Lots of people I know heard it on the local station. It was during the nightly sports broadcast. No one managed to record it for us, though. So my one moment of glory is lost for ever. Who knows? Perhaps we'll win again next year.

1 E 2 D 3 A 4 F 5 B

Word formation p.90

1 journalism 2 optional 3 entertainment
4 unavailable 5 enthusiastic 6 advertising
7 creativity 8 production 9 Unfortunately
10 unemployment

UNIT *13*

Vocabulary p.91

1 1 g) 2 e) 3 f) 4 c) 5 d) 6 a) 7 b)
2 1 tail: dog 2 feathers: bird 3 beak: bird
  4 claws: cat 5 wings: bird 6 horn: rhinoceros
  7 mane: lion 8 hump: camel 9 hooves: horse
  10 trunk: elephant 11 fur: tiger

3 1 dog 2 cows 3 lion 4 snake 5 horse 6 cat

Speaking p.92

Tapescript

Here is a map of a zoo. You are at the entrance to the zoo. Unfortunately, you only have half an hour before the zoo closes and you want to see as many animals as possible. I'd like you to talk together to plan which route you will take from the entrance to the exit. You have about three minutes to do this. Would you like to start?

1 1 F 2 T 3 T 4 T

Tapescript

D=Dimitra G=Giorgos

G: What do you want to see first?
D: Well, if we take this path, we could see the koalas and the seals. They're quite close together so we could see both of them and then have a drink at the café which is next to the seals.
G: Yes, that's O.K. What other animals do you want to see?
D: Err, well I really like the giraffes, so perhaps we could go and see them after we've had a drink. See – they're just along this path here. Oh, and then we could have a look at the zebras. They're almost next door to the lions so we could have a look at them as well. What would you like to see?
G: I like to see the lions, too.
D: OK. So after the lions we could go along this path. Are you interested in any of these animals?
G: Yes, I like them.

D: OK, well, err, perhaps we could go and look at the monkeys and the polar bears and after that the butterflies – then we're quite near the exit. I think that's probably all we could do in half an hour.

2 Dimitra

Grammar pp.92–93

1 1 are; works 2 would you buy; won
3 will be; is 4 have; will sew 5 try; won't
convince 6 wouldn't have driven; had known
7 divide; get 8 would have met; had come 9 will
lend; promise 10 were; would tell 11 mix; make
12 will let; finish 13 hadn't stood; wouldn't have
got 14 would you do; were

Vocabulary and grammar p.93

1 than 2 are/reach 3 later 4 and 5 which 6 on
7 them 8 gives 9 without 10 heard 11 but 12 at
13 are 14 to 15 they

Vocabulary p.94

1 1 terraced houses 2 semi-detached houses
3 detached house 4 bungalow 5 block of flats
6 cottage 7 hut 8 caravan

2 1 lawn 2 shed 3 attic 4 drainpipe 5 fence
6 chimney 7 cellar 8 hedge

Writing pp.94–95

1 1 enjoyable 2 glorious 3 unusual 4 delicious
5 spectacular 6 colourful; exotic 7 charming

2 Report 1: Candidate B Report 2: Candidate A

3 Inside I would build a big **fireplace** so that we
could be warm in winter. There would be huge
sofas and comfortable armchairs covered in **leather**.

Grammar p.96

1 promised to lend 2 despite studying/having
studied 3 used to play the piano 4 unless I feel
5 are not supposed to talk 6 put up with 7 in
addition to (having) 8 had worked more carefully

Listening p.96

Tapescript

I=interviewer SM=Simon Marsden

I: Here in the studio tonight we have Simon Marsden, a self-confessed ghost hunter. Simon has devoted his life to photographing ghostly sites all over Europe. He has now visited over 6,000 sites in Britain alone. Simon, do you really believe these places are haunted?

SM: Yes, I do. I think violent events or emotions in the past leave a kind of mark on their surrounding which can then be released in the right circumstances – either atmospheric conditions or by people sensitive enough to pick up on them.

I: And of course one of these places is Dracula's castle. How true is Bram Stoker's story of Dracula?

SM: Well, Dracula was a real person who ruled part of Romania in the fifteenth century. Tirgoviste was his capital city and the palace was an ideal place for the tyrant to watch his victims being tortured and executed in the courtyard below. During his lifetime he is said to have killed over 100,000 men, women and children. There's not much left of the actual buildings now, though.

I: But I understand it was in fact another castle that inspired Bram Stoker.

SM: Yes, that's right. Ecclescrieg House in Aberdeenshire in Scotland is thought to be the model Bram Stoker used for Dracula's castle. And it certainly is a very haunting place. There's a legend attached to the family who lived there until very recently. Earlier this century, Osbert Clare Forsyth-Grant was the commander of a ship with a mixed crew of Scots and Eskimos. He offended the Eskimos in some way and it is claimed they put a curse on him and his family. Soon afterwards his ship went missing and was wrecked in a storm. Forsyth-Grant and the Scots died but all the Eskimos survived. His body was never found.

I: There are quite a lot of haunted castles in Scotland, aren't there?

SM: Yes, indeed. One with a particularly dark history is Dunnottar Castle in Kincardineshire. There was a Royalist rebellion and in 1685 over 160 men, women and children were kept in the dark dungeon and fed on a diet of rotten meat, raw fish and salt water. Many died of starvation and some say their screams and cries can still be heard at night. The cold dark cellar where they were held can still be seen today.

I: Haven't you ever felt scared when you've been photographing one of these places?

SM: Well, yes. I visited one castle in Ireland where the atmosphere was pure evil, the most disturbing I've ever come across. I usually photograph alone, but I got out of there as fast as I could. People say I must be crazy, but I actually prefer this 'other world' to the one everyone else lives in. Now walking down a busy street in a big city like London, to me that's scary.

1 6,000   2 atmospheric conditions   3 fifteenth century   4 capital city   5 100,000   6 Scotland 7 of a ship   8 never found   9 1685   10 160

Reading p.97

2 E   3 A   4 G   5 F   6 B   7 C

UNIT 14

Vocabulary p.98

1 B   2 B   3 B   4 A   5 A   6 B   7 A   8 B   9 B   10 B 11 B   12 A   13 B

Reading pp.98–99

1 B   2 B   3 A   4 C   5 D   6 D   7 A   8 B

Grammar p.100

1 The police **made him stop**.   3 Are you **allowed** to stay out after ten o'clock?   4 Do your parents **make you study** English?   6 They allowed us **to go** to the party.   8 My parents **made** me wear clothes I didn't like.   9 When I was younger, I **wasn't allowed** to go swimming unless my parents were with me.   10 They wouldn't **let me go**.

Vocabulary p.100

1   1 b) and f)   2 a)   3 e)   4 d)   5 c)

2   1 You won't **make up for** lost time by working all night.   2 He just **made it up**. 3 When the police asked him where he had been that night, he **made out** that he had been with me, ...   4 The escaped prisoners tried to **make for** the mountains ...   5 She muttered something under her breath, but I couldn't **make out** exactly what she said.
6 If your friend wants to spend a couple of days here, we could **make up** a bed for her ...
7 ..., but they've **made it up** and are the best of friends again.

Writing p.101

1   1c) mutter   2g) chuckle   3b) consider   4h) nibble 5i) grasp   6f) tiptoe   7d) lob   8a) fidget   9e) order

2   *Possible answer*
He **tiptoed** along the corridor **wondering** what he would do if the gang were still there. When he was about to climb the stairs, he heard someone **chuckling** in one of the rooms on the second floor. He **clutched** the gun and continued to climb the stairs. Suddenly he felt someone hit him very hard from behind and he **staggered** a few steps further and then fell and **writhed** on the ground in pain, telling himself that he had been a fool to try this on his own. The man who had hit him **ordered** him to give him the gun and with what little energy he had left he **tossed** it to him. The man **sniggered** and said, 'Now you're really in trouble, Mason.' He took a bottle from his jacket and drank half the contents in one go. Mason thought he would be lucky to get out of there alive.

Vocabulary p.102

1 B   2 A   3 C   4 D   5 C   6 B   7 A   8 D   9 A 10 C   11 A   12 D   13 C   14 A   15 D

Listening p.103

Tapescript

Extract 1
Excuse me, miss. I'm sorry to bother you, but there doesn't seem to be any space in the overhead locker. I know we're only supposed to have one piece of hand luggage, but my grandson gave me this as a present just before I left. Could you possibly find a space for it further down the plane? You see I've already got my bag under the seat in front of me and if I put anything else there, I won't have any room to put my feet.

Extract 2
A: But you said I could have a go when you'd finished.
B: Well, I haven't finished, have I?
A: But you started to play another one after you finished the first one. It's not fair. I'm going to tell Dad.
B: OK. You can have a go now. But don't break it!

Extract 3

Yes. About two weeks ago. But it's making a very funny noise and it doesn't keep things cold enough. ... My customer service number? Let me see. Would it be this one? 0765872? ... Can't they come any earlier than Wednesday? ... Could you possibly give me some idea of when they'll be here? ... That's fine. I'll be in all morning.

Extract 4

Police were involved in a car chase earlier today after two bank robbers fled from the scene of a hold-up in Malvern Road. The robbers entered the bank at about midday and told the three customers who were waiting to withdraw money, to lie down on the floor. They then forced one of the bank tellers to open the safe and empty the contents into a bag. She was able to give the alarm by pressing a button inside the safe door.

Extract 5

A: Why don't you make it up with her? You're obviously just as unhappy as she is.

B: I just can't. You wouldn't believe the things she said to me. And to think I'd always thought she was such a sweet gentle person.

A: I know she's been under a lot of pressure at work lately. She's really not herself at all.

B: Well, as far as I'm concerned that's no excuse ...

Extract 6

It was fine really. He was so gentle with her that she was even purring for a while. Of course she didn't like it much when he gave her the injection, but then he stroked her and calmed her down so well, she almost rolled over and let him rub her tummy.

Extract 7

Hello ... Hello ... I can hardly ... I can hardly hear you. This is a really bad line. Look, I'm at the station and I just wondered if you wanted anything from the supermarket? ... What was that? You'll have to speak up a bit. ... OK. I'll see you in a minute then, love.

Extract 8

Now we whisk them until they are snowy white and standing up in peaks. And then we pour that in with the melted chocolate and stir ever so gently. And then into the little soufflé dishes and now we'll just pop them in the oven. I'll be back with you to try our soufflés after a short break.

1 C   2 B   3 A   4 A   5 B   6 A   7 C   8 A

Speaking p.103

Tapescript

I=interlocutor N=Nicole D=Diego

I: Do you think young offenders should be sent to prison?

N: No. I am definitely not agree with this. If they go in prison, they will become much worser. Because if a young man he is in prison, he meet other delinquents and he learns new ways to make crime. I think they must to do works in the society like help the old people who is often very alone and need someone take care of them.

I: Do you agree with Nicole, Diego?

D: Yes, I think she's quite right.

I: Why do you think young people commit crimes?

D: Well, there are many reasons for this. Unemployment is an important one.

I: Why do you think unemployment is important?

D: If young people cannot get jobs, they become frustrated.

N: Yes. This is truth. If they cannot to find a work, they cannot get any money and they must to stay in their house all day watching TV. This is very bad. I think another problem is that the young people are not educate. They do not know that crime is a so bad thing.

I: Do you think education is important Diego?

D: Of course, I think it's important ...

1 Nicole P   Diego G
2 Nicole S   Diego G
3 Nicole G   Diego S

Grammar p.104

1 1 is being made.   2 has not been painted for ten years.   3 are provided every year.   4 had been stolen.   5 has to be guarded day and night.
6 might be badly affected by water.   7 were being interviewed (by the police) last night.   8 was finally forced to stop by a police roadblock.

2 1 has been made.   2 are reminded not to put bottles in the overhead lockers.   3 will be refunded in full if you are not satisfied.   4 is being dealt with (by our customer relations office).   5 will be sent a letter inviting them to attend a second interview.
6 were sent on 15th April.   7 has not been delivered by 15th May, please contact us again.
8 will be replaced.   9 is being prepared.
10 was being checked (by technicians).

UNIT *15*

Grammar p.105

1 1 had studied   2 were coming/could come/would come   3 could drive   4 had   5 wouldn't do   6 were   7 would tell   8 knew   9 hadn't done   10 could afford   11 we stayed   12 didn't lend/hadn't lent   13 left   14 recognised   15 arrive

2 1 wish I had phoned   2 suppose we buy/bought   3 only I hadn't said   4 time you went   5 would/'d rather have   6 would/'d rather you didn't tell   7 wish you wouldn't   8 only he were   9 time you started revising

Speaking p.106

Tapescript

I=interlocutor A=Anna F=Francisco

Part 1

I: Good morning.

A/F: Good morning.

I: My name is Sally and this is my colleague Pam.

A/F: Hello.

I: Pam, this is Anna and Francisco. Well, do you two know each other?

A: Yes, we go to the same school.

I: I see. Well, Francisco, let's start with you. Where are you from?

F: I am from here in Madrid. I live very close by.

I: And Anna are you from Madrid, too?

A: No, I come from Alicante, but I live here now.

I: How long have you lived here?

A: Almost three years.

I: Tell us what it's like living here, Francisco.

F: It is great. The weather is good in spring and summer, but it gets quite cold in winter. You can go out to a pub in the evening and listen to jazz or go to a café to meet your friends.

I: Anna, how do you like to spend your free time?

A: I like playing basketball and going to the cinema. But I don't have so much free time because I study a lot.

I: What are you studying?

A: I am studying Economics at the university.

I: And, Francisco, are you studying too?

F: No, I finish my studies last year. I am working in a bank now.

Part 2

I: Now, I'm going to give each of you two pictures and ask you to talk about them. You have one minute to do this so don't worry if I interrupt you. Anna, here are your two pictures. They show people playing games. I'd like you to say how you feel about games like these. Francisco, I'll give you your two pictures in a minute.

A: Well, there are both pictures of people playing games, as you said. In the first picture there are some old men playing cards at a table outside a café I think. They look very concentrated on what they are doing. Some of the men are not playing but just watching what the others are doing. The second picture shows some boys, some teenagers playing games in a ... I think that you call it an amusement arcade. They look as if they are enjoying themselves. I quite like playing this kind of games too, but I don't like playing cards so much. I sometimes play with my grandmother, though.

I: Thank you, Anna. Now, Francisco, here are your two pictures.

F: Well, my two pictures are of chickens ... I mean kitchens. The first kitchen is very modern. It is all in white and it looks a bit like a hospital ... it is very clean. But it doesn't look ... it looks like nobody ever cooked in it. I like the other kitchen more. It looks like my grandmother's house. It have ... I means *has* ... some saucepans hanging up as well as herbs and dry flowers and there is fresh fruit on a plate on the table. I think the second kitchen looks a lot more warm and comfortable than the first one.

I: Thank you, Francisco. So, Anna, which kitchen do you prefer?

A: I like the modern kitchen best.

Part 3

I: Now, Anna and Francisco, I'm going to give you a map of a town in Britain. The local council are trying to decide where to build the new shopping mall. I'd like you to talk together about this and decide which position on the map would be most suitable for the shopping mall. Then I'd like you to say what sorts of shops and facilities the shopping mall should have.

F: I'm sorry. Do we have to decide where each shop should be?

I: No. You need to decide where the shopping mall should be and then decide what kinds of shops should be *in* the shopping mall.

F: OK. Umm ... let's see. We could put it here in the centre near to the post office. What do you think?

A: Yes. But I think it would be a problem for people to park their cars there. There is more space over here near bus station.

F: Mmm ... I don't think there is a very big space there and we don't want it to be only a very small shopping mall.

A: No, that's true. What about outside the, of the town? Here near the motorway.

F: Yes, that's a good idea. I think that would be a perfect place. Then everybody could drive there and there would be no problem for traffic.

A: But what about the people who do not have cars. Can you see any bus stop near there?

F: No, I can't. Perhaps we should build it here, near the bus station.

A: Yes, I think that's better. And what shops and ... shall we have?

F: A sports shop and a shop for animals.

A: A pet shop .... yes, that's a good idea. And boutiques with the last fashions, do you agree?

F: Yes, of course. And a newsagent's. Oh, I think we forgot something.

A: What?

F: Banks. We need banks so that people can get money to spend in the shops.

A: Yes. And a supermarket. We definitely need a supermarket, don't we?

F: Oh, yes. And what else ... a ...?

Part 4

I: Do you enjoy shopping in big shopping malls or do you prefer to go to markets and smaller shops?

A: I like shopping malls because they are very ... umm ... convenient and you don't have to walk too much.

F: Yes, it is much easier to make all your shopping in one place. And you can sometimes meet your friends there, too.

I: In Britain people sometimes think that shopping malls are destroying the small shops in town centres. What do you think about that?

F: My uncle has a shop in the centre of our town and he has lost a lot of customers because of the shopping mall.

A: Yes, not many people want to shop in the centre now and it must be very bad for the shop ... err ... people.

I: Do you think people spend too much time on shopping?

A: Yes, I do. It has become like a hobby. People go shopping instead of playing sport or going for a walk in the country.

F: I am sorry, but I don't agree. I think it is good for the economy of the country if everybody buy a lot of things. And anyway is good fun. Don't you like shopping?

A: Yes, I do. Sometimes, but not with my mother she always wants me to buy really horrible clothes.

F: Yes, my mother is the same way.

I: So who do you prefer to go shopping with?

A: With my best friend. But we don't have much money so we only look at the things in the umm ... in the ...

F: ... the window displays? Yes, I go with my cousin sometimes, but we don't usually buy too much.

I: I don't like shopping at all myself and if I do go shopping I generally go on my own. Well, thank you both for coming. Goodbye.

A/F: Goodbye.

1 1 Anna G   Francisco G
   2 Anna S   Francisco G
   3 Anna E   Francisco E

2 1 saucepans: /ˈsɔːspænz/
   2 fruit: /fruːt/
   3 comfortable: /ˈkʌmftəbəl/
   4 convenient: /kənˈviːniənt/

3 1) bear: /beə/ 2) stir: /stɜː/
   3) weapons: /ˈwepənz/ 4) clothes: /kləʊðz/
   5) money: /ˈmʌni/ 6) scientist: /ˈsaɪəntɪst/
   7) wallet: /ˈwɒlɪt/ 8) occasion: /əˈkeɪʒən/

Grammar p.107

1 had my hair cut last week.   2 are having their house painted.   3 have had my trousers turned up.   4 had her/his wallet stolen.   5 had our photograph taken. 6 had my eyes tested.   7 am having my new jacket cleaned.   8 have had our refrigerator fixed.   9 have their groceries delivered.   10 am going to have my car serviced next week.

Grammar p.108

line 1: delete second *is*   line 3: delete *of*
line 4: delete *as*   line 5: delete *the*
line 6: delete *than*   line 7: delete *it*   line 8: delete *in*
line 9: delete *is*   line 11: delete *do*   line 13: delete *of*
line 14: delete *to*   line 15: delete *a*

Reading p.108–109

1 E 2 B 3 G 4 A 5 F 6 D

153

Vocabulary p.110

```
        ¹M
         E
  ²C O N T ³R A ⁴D I C T
  H     T   O   I
  A     I   W   ⁵S H O U T
  T     O       C
        N       ⁶M U T T E R
                S
        ⁷W H I S P E R
```

Listening p.110

Tapescript

Learning to read is an infinite, continuous, life-long process, not something that takes place at primary school to be quickly and thankfully ticked off the list before you go on to the next thing.

It's like learning to drive. When you pass your test, you've been taught the basics, but you're still a very inexpert beginner who needs to get out on to the road and learn to drive properly. New readers face a similar challenge. They can do it, but it's not yet second nature. And it will only become so through routine daily practice.

Many young people never learn to read other than very slowly. Fourteen and fifteen-year-olds who should have become fluent readers a long time ago, carry the same book around with them in school for weeks.

They read very slowly through a page or two when the teacher tells them to, but their attention is on the mechanics of reading and they never really have the chance to become interested in the content.

Someone who's stuck in this limited position will inevitably turn to television or video because it's faster and easier.

If children are to become 'natural' readers, their reading must be developed and speeded up. No fluent reader, for example, slowly pronounces the words very quietly or reads aloud in his head, mentally articulating every word, apart from when we do this deliberately if we're reading something very complicated like a scientific article.

But many young and adult readers never get beyond the stage of pronouncing every word, which is why they're so slow. When seven or eight-year-olds read 'to themselves' you can sometimes see their lips moving. This should be a brief stage in the process of learning to read, not the end result.

The answer for children lies in giving them lots of accessible books quickly, and plenty of time both at school and at home to read them. It probably means deliberate restriction of television exposure time, too.

It's also crucial that children see reading as an ordinary part of adult behaviour. Children copy adults. I frequently hear teachers and parents complaining that children won't read. In the next breath these same adults are either explaining that they themselves are too busy to read or discussing the previous evening's television programmes at length. Two unmistakable messages are being transmitted to children: Don't read, watch TV.

Learning to read doesn't stop when children leave primary school to go on to secondary school. It doesn't even end when you leave school, but should go on throughout life. Sadly you can lose your ability to read if you don't use it regularly – just like the ability to type, run, swim or play the violin.

Teaching children to read is just the beginning. It's what happens after that that makes the difference.

1 B   2 A   3 C   4 A   5 C   6 A   7 B

Writing p.111

1 a) 8   b) 7   c) 6   d) 8   e) 8   f) 8

2 *statment*: statement; *comunication*: communication; *translattors*: translators; *nattive*: native; *loose*: lose; *sucessful*: successful
people would stop to use: people would **stop using**; *everyone would know a language*: everyone would know **one** language

PRACTICE EXAM

Paper 1 Reading

PART 1	1 B 2 E 3 H 4 C 5 A 6 F 7 G
	Distractor D
PART 2	8 D 9 B 10 B 11 D 12 C 13 D 14 A
PART 3	15 C 16 F 17 D 18 G 19 A 20 E 21 B
	Distractor I
PART 4	22 B 23 B 24 A 25 C 26 B 27 C 28 A
	29 C 30 D 31 A 32 D 33 B 34 D 35 C

Paper 3 Use of English

PART 1   1 C 2 A 3 C 4 A 5 B 6 C 7 D 8 D
             9 A 10 A 11 C 12 B 13 A 14 D 15 D

PART 2   16 their 17 it 18 well 19 by 20 such
             21 with 22 have 23 make 24 how
             25 because 26 of 27 from 28 to 29 up
             30 same

PART 3   31 if it were/was not so
             32 were about to leave
             33 must have been tired
             34 wish people would not talk
             35 is less convenient than
             36 rather I came back
             37 asked if the museum was
             38 have hardly ever
             39 made it impossible for
             40 congratulated her on passing

PART 4   41 he 42 as 43 ✔ 44 than 45 of 46 the
             47 ✔ 48 I 49 of 50 for 51 (second) the
             52 have 53 that 54 it 55 ✔

PART 5   56 safety 57 neighbourhood
             58 unsupervised 59 addition 60 easily
             61 Unfortunately 62 dangerous
             63 creation 64 including 65 ability

Paper 4 Listening

Tapescript

Hello, I'm going to give you the instructions for this test. I'll introduce each part of the test and give you time to look at the questions. At the start of each piece you'll hear this sound (bleep). You will hear each piece twice. Now look at Part 1.

You'll hear people talking in eight different situations. For questions 1–8, choose the best answer A, B or C.

PART 1

Extract 1

A: Yes I can read! But I only bought it … well it can't have been more than a couple of hours ago so I thought you might be willing to …

B: I'm sorry Madam.

A: Look, I know it was very silly of me. I sat down to have a coffee outside and saw it in the daylight. I couldn't possibly wear it. I mean it's just not the right colour at all. I'd be much happier with the pale blue or even the beige if you have it in a size 38, that is.

Extract 2

A: Well, if I were you I'd tell him. You can't go on like this. Look if you like, I'll speak to him for you. If you think it would help.

B: No, I'd rather you didn't. It's really up to me, isn't it?

A: I'm afraid so. Just take a deep breath, dial his number and tell him you don't want the job. That's what I'd do.

Extract 3

Hi. It's me. Look I'm on the train but I'm going to be later than I thought. Yes, I know you've got your meeting. That's why I'm phoning. Do you think you could phone Sam and ask if he'd mind looking after Alex until I get home? Then you can go off to your meeting, can't you. Well, if Sam's not there you'll just have to take Alex with you. I can come via the office and pick her up.

Extract 4

A: Excuse me, but you seem to have dropped something.

B: Oh, have I? No I don't think …

A: This is your glove, isn't it?

B: Yes, of course. How silly of me. Thank you, dear. Is this your stop?

A: Yes, it is.

B: Can you get by?

Extract 5

A: So tell me about the new album. Will it be very different from 'Solar Eclipses and Sunburn'?

B: Yes and no. I hope we'll be able to keep the feel of 'Solar' but I think we've got something new to say as well …

A: Yea, Joe González coming into the line-up must make for a more Latin feel, I would have thought?

B: Let's just say salsa fans should find plenty to make them smile.

A: OK. Now you're also using a new backing group on some of the tracks?

B: Yea. I met these guys on tour in the States and I really liked their stuff …

Extract 6

OK. I hope you've all done the reading for today's session on investment strategies. Right, let's hear from … let me see … What about you, Charlie? I want a summary of the chapter in under five minutes, and I want everyone else listening and picking up anything Charlie misses out on or, horror of horrors, anything he actually gets wrong. You have read the chapter, haven't you Charlie? Great. Over to you then.

Extract 7

A: Look, I realise that this is very short notice, but another member of our party will be flying in this afternoon and I wondered if there was any chance of his staying here as well.

B: Well, it is high season, sir, but I'll just have a look … Mmmm. I'm afraid we're fully booked but … it would be possible to put another bed in your room sir, if, that is, you would be willing to share and then … yes … on the 14th there will be a vacancy.

A: Oh that's wonderful. Thank you so much. Do you need his details?

B: Yes, if you wouldn't mind.

Extract 8

I expected it to be good, but I had no idea it would be like that. I've seen them perform six or seven times before and I've rarely been disappointed but last night's performance was … Well it defies description. The whole auditorium were on their feet at the end applauding for all they were worth. They played six … yes, six encores … and we still wanted more.

That's the end of Part 1. Now look at Part 2.

PART 2

You will hear part of a radio interview about colour-blindness. For questions 9–18, complete the notes which summarise the information in the interview. You will need to write a word, a number or a short phrase in each space. Before you start spend 45 seconds looking through Part 2.

A: So what exactly is colour-blindness?

B: Well, colour-blind people can see perfectly clearly, but they can't distinguish certain colours, mostly red or green (sometimes both).

A: How come? I mean what causes it?

B: Well, we all have colour sensors in our eyes and when these are damaged our ability to see different colours is reduced. There are three types of sensor: some respond to red, some to green and some to blue light. But they work in combination so that we can see all the colours of the rainbow. If one of your sensors is damaged, your colour vision will be disrupted, but if two are damaged you can only see in black and white.

A: I don't think I've ever known a colour-blind person so it must be quite rare.

B: No not at all, unless all your friends and acquaintances are women, that is. Only a tiny proportion of women … about 0.04 per cent … are colour-blind but among men in western Europe as many as 8 per cent are affected.

A: So does it stop them leading normal lives?

B: Yes it can do. There are a number of jobs where distinguishing colours can be very important … electricians for example must be able to tell the difference between blue, brown, yellow and green. But in fact if you drive a car distinguishing red, green and orange is vital.

A: So does that mean if you're colour-blind you can't drive?

B: Fortunately no. We can solve the problem by giving the person tinted contact lenses. The tint tricks the brain into perceiving colour. Usually they only have to wear one so it's not too obvious, but one of our patients, a photographer, couldn't tell orange from green so he had to wear a purple and a yellow lens. I've never had a case like that before. He tells me he does get some funny looks from passers-by.

A: So how did he manage to work as a photographer if he was colour-blind?

B: Oh, he'd learnt to ask people what colour things were without their realising he was asking. None of his friends knew he was colour-blind.

A: It must be fantastic for people once they have the lenses and can see all the colours.

B: Well, yes … though it does have some funny consequences. One woman, who couldn't see red, was horrified when she saw what colour strawberries were. She could never face eating them again after that.

Now you'll hear Part 2 again (Part 2 repeated). That's the end of Part 2. Now look at Part 3.

PART 3

You will hear five different men talking about summer. For questions 19–23, choose from the list A–F how each man spent the summer. Use the letters only once. There is one letter you don't need to use.

Speaker 1

Tim had this friend with an apartment in the Canaries so we were all set to book a charter and get down there. It was on the way to the travel agent's that it happened. I suppose I was lucky to have come out of it with nothing more than a broken leg. I hit that tree pretty hard. So that was the end of my summer. Six weeks on the sofa with my foot on a pillow. The others all went down to Tenerife, I think it was. They had a great time.

Speaker 2

We pack up and go every year. Usually mid- to late July but sometimes earlier if we can manage it. The house has been in the family for generations.

Cynthia's grandparents actually used to live there all year round. It must have been freezing. There's no heating and there's almost always snow at that altitude. It's blissfully cool in summer though and the kids are kept fully occupied by their fifteen cousins.

Speaker 3

I never go away before October. Everything's so crowded in July and August and it's almost too hot. Who wants to be on a beach with several thousand other people when you can wait a bit and have it virtually to yourself? Things are cheaper then too. I don't mind being here when everyone else is out of town. I get more done in one month than I do in the whole of the rest of the year, I always say. And this year was no exception.

Speaker 4

Absolutely nothing … well, apart from eat, sleep and put sunscreen on the kids. That's my idea of the perfect summer holiday … as far as I'm concerned it's the only summer holiday. We always get full catering so we don't have to think about shopping or cooking or boring things like that. I like to go somewhere where I don't understand enough of the language to read the newspaper headlines. That's what we did this year and I really recharged the batteries, I can tell you.

Speaker 5

It's the only chance I have so I'm always determined to really make the most of it. I never go back to the same place because I've usually covered every inch of it by the time my two weeks are up. No, it's somewhere different every year. Obviously I prefer somewhere a bit cooler with plenty to see in terms of museums and architecture, that kind of thing. This year I went a bit further than usual. To Sydney. I loved it. I might even move there.

Now you'll hear Part 3 again (Part 3 repeated). That's the end of Part 3. Now look at Part 4.

PART 4

*You will hear a conversation about university accommodation in Britain between a teacher, a student, called Paul Lucas, and his mother, Mrs Lucas. Answer questions **24–30** by writing **T** (for teacher), **P** (for Paul Lucas) or **M** (for Mrs Lucas) in the spaces provided. Before you start, spend one minute looking through Part 4.*

T: Right, I believe you and Paul were wanting to talk to me.

M: Yes, that's right. Thank you ever so much for sparing us your time. Well, as you may know Paul is going off to Reading to study Law in September.

T: Yes, that's great news. Well done Paul!

P: Thanks.

M: We've had this booklet from the University Accommodation Office and we're really not sure what to do about it.

T: Let me have a look … PAUSE Well, it looks to me as if you have to choose between the various halls of residence … and fill in your preferences on this form.

P: I know which one I want to go to. It's this one here. Wetherleigh Hall.

T: So you need to fill it in as your first preference and then choose a couple of others just in case you don't get in to Wetherleigh.

M: Well it's not really that simple. You see I did my degree at Reading too and when I was a student I lived with a family and I think …

P: Oh Mum, we've already been through this millions of times.

M: Just let me finish Paul. Well, I think that Paul would be much better off with a family rather than in one of these halls where they get up to all sorts of things. In fact the family I stayed with are still in the area and I know they'd be delighted to have him. Anyway, we wanted to know what you thought.

T: Paul, how do you feel about all of this?

P: I already said. I know what I want to do. Live in Wetherleigh Hall.

T: Why Wetherleigh particularly?

P: Well, it says here that it's the most modern of the halls; all the rooms have their own bathrooms, there are cooking facilities …

M: (interrupting) Oh for heaven's sake Paul, you don't even know how to boil an egg.

P: … with microwave ovens as well as a dining room if you want your meals cooked for you. And if you look on the map of the campus here you can see that Wetherleigh is closest to the Law Faculty.

T: Have you got any friends there?

P: My cousin is doing third year engineering and he's in Wetherleigh. He says it's really good.

M: Paul, you know very well that he had to repeat his second year. That's what I'm worried about, Mr Eliott … there are so many distractions in these halls … it's very hard to study with other people playing their stereos and going off to the bar for a drink and so on.

P: But if I stay with a family I'll never meet anyone. I'll have to be back there for dinner every night at 6 o'clock or something and I'll just have no social life at all.

M: Of course you will. The Wilkinsons will introduce you to lots of people.

P: Mum. The Wilkinsons are in their seventies and all their kids have grown up and left home.

T: Mrs Lucas, Paul does have a point. Moving away from home to study can be a miserable experience if you don't make friends and being in a hall is an excellent way of getting to know people. It's also often a help with your work if you've got friends doing the same course and if Wetherleigh is closest to the Law Faculty then it's bound to attract a lot of their students.

M: So you think Paul would be all right in a hall.

T: Yes, I do. Things have changed quite a bit since our day, though I was in hall myself back in the 70s. It certainly didn't do me any harm.

M: Well, if you think it's the best decision, I suppose …

Now you'll hear Part 4 again (Part 4 repeated). That's the end of Part 4.

Paper 4 Answer Key

PART 1   1 A   2 A   3 B   4 A   5 C   6 A   7 C
              8 B
PART 2   9 red and green   10 three   11 in black and white   12 8 per cent   13 electricians 14 drive a car   15 perceiving colour 16 obvious   17 orange and green 18 strawberries
PART 3   19 C 20 B 21 A 22 F 23 D
PART 4   24 M 25 P 26 M 27 P 28 T 29 T 30 M

Paper 5 Speaking

Tapescript

PART 1

Interlocutor: First of all we'd like to know something about you so I'm going to ask you some questions about yourselves.

Where are you from? *(bleep)*

What's it like to live there? Have you ever lived anywhere else? *(bleep)*

What are the people like where you live? *(bleep)*

What about your family? Could you tell us something about them? *(bleep)*

How long have you been learning English? *(bleep)*

How do you think you will use English in the future? *(bleep)*

What kind of music do you like to listen to? *(bleep)*

What is your favourite instrument … and why? *(bleep)*

What do you not like to read? *(bleep)*

How good are the magazines in your country? *(bleep)*

PART 2

Now I'd like each of you to talk on your own for about a minute. I'm going to ask each of you to talk about two photographs. Candidate A, these are your two photographs. Please let Candidate B see them. They show people exercising. I'd like you to compare and contrast these photographs and say what would be pleasant or unpleasant about exercising in places likes these. Remember you only have about a minute for this so don't worry if I interrupt you. All right? *(two bleeps)* Thank you. Candidate B, which place would you prefer to exercise in? *(bleep)* Thank you.

Candidate B, these are your two photographs. Please let candidate A see them. They show mothers spending time with their children. I'd like you to compare and contrast the photographs and say how interested they are in what they are doing. Remember you only have about a minute for this so don't worry if I interrupt you. All right? *(two bleeps)* Thank you. Candidate A, do you like shopping? *(bleep)* Thank you.

PART 3

Now I'd like you to talk about something together for about three minutes. I'm just going to listen. I'd like you to imagine that you have just arrived to spend two weeks studying English in London, but your luggage has been lost in transit. The airline expects your luggage to be found within three days but they have given you £100 to spend on essential items. First decide which of the items you would be carrying with you or wearing. Then say how you will spend the £100.

You have only about three minutes for this, so, once again, don't worry if I stop you.

Please speak so we can hear you. All right?

(bleep)

Thank you.

PART 4

What are the advantages of travelling by plane?

What are the disadvantages?

What about other kinds of transport?

How do you prefer to travel?

Have you ever had an unpleasant or amusing experience when travelling?

What precautions do you take when travelling?